THE POINTBLANK DIRECTIVE

OSPREY
PUBLISHING

THE POINTBLANK DIRECTIVE

The Untold Story of the Daring Plan that Saved D-Day

L. Douglas Keeney

"Everyone knew that the ensuing days would determine whether or not all the months of steady hammering had been in vain, whether or not a buddy in some parachute battalion or a brother in some tank corps or a cousin in some artillery unit would live or die as a result of the air protection we would provide. If we had been extremely important before D-Day we were certainly indispensable now."[1]

Corporal Melvin Applebaum,
Within the Parenthesis

First published in Great Britain in 2012 by Osprey Publishing,
PO Box 883, Oxford, OX1 9PL, UK
PO Box 3985, New York, NY 10185-3985, USA
E-mail: info@ospreypublishing.com

Osprey Publishing is part of the Osprey Group

A CIP catalogue record for this book is available from the British Library

L. Douglas Keeney has asserted his right under the Copyright, Designs and Patents Act,
1988, to be identified as the Author of this Work.

ISBN: 978 1 4728 0750 2
e-book ISBN: 978 1 78200 895 8
PDF ISBN: 978 1 78200 896 5

Index by Sharon Redmayne
Typeset in Trade Gothic Lt & Adobe Garamond Pro
Originated by PDQ Digital Media Solutions Ltd, Suffolk
Printed in China through Worldprint Ltd.

14 15 16 17 18   10 9 8 7 6 5 4 3 2 1

Osprey Publishing is supporting the Woodland Trust, the UK's leading woodland
conservation charity, by funding the dedication of trees.

Front cover: B-17s of the US Eighth Air Force and P-47s of the US Fifteenth Air Force.
(NARA via Douglas Sheley)

www.ospreypublishing.com

CONTENTS

LIST OF IMAGES

5.   Point 4 of Spaatz's report to Arnold noted the achievement of air superiority as a successful prerequisite to D-Day. "L. of C." is Army jargon for roads and rail, as in "lines of communication."

6.   Hap Arnold talks with Doolittle.

7.   The B-17, seen here, and the B-24 were the workhorses of the airwar.

8.   The B-24. Both this and the B-17 typically carried a 6,000-pound bomb load and bristled with .50-caliber machine guns.

9.   The bulk of a bomber is used to cradle the stack of bombs. The bomb racks were in the center of the plane. The ball turret is retracted in this view of the B-24.

10. Representatives from Boeing were in England and helped visualize the chin turret later added to defend the B-17 against frontal attacks.

11. An aerial view of an American airbase in England. Some twenty bombers are lined up for takeoff. Hardstands dot the perimeter track. Most of the men used bicycles to get around the base.

12. The control tower on an American airbase in England is seen to the right of the runway.

13. Ground view of a lineup of B-17s pre-takeoff.

14. Hap Arnold watches a takeoff from the control tower.

15. These three fighter pilots have been briefed and are on the way to their planes. Notice their parachutes and life vests.

16. The bulky flight gear worn on a bomber is clear to see in this image.

17. A navigator looks back from inside the Plexiglas nose of a B-17.

18. Two ground maintainers crowd in at the waist gunner positions.

19. These tired P-51 fighter pilots walk through their just-completed D-Day mission as part of a debrief.

20. A ten-man crew huddles over a map and completes their own briefing. Every mission began with a briefing: target, route in and out, time hacks, bomb load, rally points, and so on.

36. A Messerschmitt Me-410 is hit by the .50s.

37. An Me-109 comes in for the kill. Notice the engine feathered on the left side. (John England, from collection of M. C. Olmstead, Paradise, California)

38. A German twin attacks a formation of B-17s.

39. German flak batteries poured shells into the sky at the rate of several thousand per downed bomber. Photographs simply fail to capture the intensity of flak. Notice the ammunition bunkers surrounding the gun.

40. A bomber takes a direct hit, leaving four flaming engines and a potpourri of smoke and vaporized steel as the only indication that it was ever in the sky.

41. A shell explodes off the port side of this B-17. A shell this close could do serious damage depending on how the fragments erupted. The inside of a shell was grooved to direct the shards of steel.

42. Flak explosions pock the sky with their greasy, black bursts. While only the airmen knew precisely what type of fire they were caught in, this simultaneous explosion of so many shells was typical of barrage fire. The open bomb bay doors indicate that this Fort was holding straight and level on the bomb run.

43. A heavy bomber was little more than a dozen sticks of high explosives wrapped in thousands of pounds of flammable gas and sprinkled with volatile cylinders of pressurized oxygen. Here a B-17 pitch-poles forward out of control as it dies in the air.

44. Flames engulf the wing of this stricken B-17. Notice the rail yard across the ground below. Eisenhower directed increased attacks against transportation targets to cut off the D-Day beaches from the interior.

45. The wing folds up on this burning Fort.

46. An airman looks through the hole blasted in the side of this B-17. (From the collection of Carmine J. Auricchio.)

47. This sequence of images display aerial combat seen through gun camera footage aboard American fighters. German pilots served until they were either killed or unable to fly. Any German fighter pilot who served several years almost certainly bailed out at least once and, if merely injured, nearly always returned to flying status. Here a P-47 flies into the line of sight of another fighter as they both pursue a German twin-engine fighter.

48. A German pilot bails out from an Me-109.

49. A FW-190 takes hits across the engine cowling. Both planes were claimed as kills.

50. One of the most important decisions made by Spaatz was to bomb the German airfields within a 130-mile radius of the Normandy beaches. Not only did this level the playing field, because American fighters launched from England, but it denied the Germans access to the forward bases from which they could launch fresh attacks. Post-holed runways and destroyed hangars can be seen in these battle damage photos, and here the bombed-out hangars of the German Luftwaffe complex at Villacoublay, France, outside of Paris.

51. Bombs rain down on the German airbase in Memmingen, Germany, in Bavaria. Fragmentation bombs such as these were extremely good at destroying airplanes outside on an airfield.

52. The Luftwaffe fighter complex at Chartres, France, 60 miles outside of Paris.

53. Strafing an airfield or a train exposed a fighter to ground fire from every direction, but was often successful. Here a machine gun fire hits these fighters parked on the ramp.

54. Planes parked along the edge of the woods. Note the bullets streaking across the grass toward the parked planes.

55. A P-38 with invasion stripes strafes a train.

56. Some airbases were little more than open fields. These aircraft are lined in opposite directions so as to be able to scramble the most planes in the air as quickly as possible.

57. Reconnaissance photography was invaluable, and the invasion beaches were photographed just days before D-Day. Notice the Germans scrambling for cover amid this forest of stakes and timbers topped with Teller mines.

58. Two derricks used to dig post holes are visible, as are antitank traps.

59. These are likely the British invasion beaches or the Pas-de-Calais area. The contrast between the tools of death and sunbathing is jarring.

60. A P-38 sits on the Emergency Landing Strip just behind Omaha Beach days after D-Day.

61. As the soldiers moved inland, the engineering battalions built several hundred Advanced Landings Grounds (ALGs) such as these. ALGs were numbered 1 to 99 and were preceded by the prefix of A-, Y-, or R-. "A" signified USAAF. After 99 fields were opened, the suffixed switched to "Y" and started again. With few exceptions all "R" suffixes designated a field in Germany. British ALGs started with a "B."

62. Actual D-Day mission orders for the bombers: "Shorts likely to fall on landing craft …" caution the planners.

63. D-Day orders specifying six-ship formations.

64. Invasion stripes clearly identify this C-47 as a friendly aircraft. Ships can be seen offloading in the background near the top, and beach obstacles are visible just behind the wing to the left.

65. Two war-weary generals walk Omaha Beach: Hap Arnold and General Omar N. Bradley. Bradley commanded the landing forces, while Arnold commanded the air forces. This sand was their sand and the sand of all the men who sacrificed to get the boys ashore. The success of D-Day was the crowning achievement of Pointblank. (Courtesy the Robert and Kathleen Arnold Collection.)

66. Every time a B-17 or B-24 spiraled out of the sky, the Great
     Stonecutter started chiseling another set of names into a slab of
     marble, several hundred of which are in a military cemetery
     near the author's home. This one memorializes one of the crews
     that went down during Big Week. We owe them all so very
     much.

FOREWORD

"The thundering ships took off one behind the other. At 5,000 feet they made their formation. The men sat quietly at their stations, their eyes fixed. And the deep growl of the engines shook the air, shook the world and shook the future."

— John Steinbeck, 1942

The airwar over Nazi Europe was the "grimmest fight to the death" airmen have encountered in human history, as well as the war's longest and most deadly battle for the Americans and the British. Author L. Douglas Keeney has examined the role of Allied airpower in the run up to D-day in his new work, *The Pointblank Directive*.

Before the Second World War, no one had seen—and only a few had imagined—the horrors attendant to hundred-mile-long armadas of two thousand bombers and fighters regularly and methodically razing the cradle of Western Civilization.

In his 1942 book, *Bombs Away*, John Steinbeck neatly summed up the challenge facing bomber crews and their commanders: "Of all branches ... the Air Force must act with the least precedent, the least tradition. Nearly all tactics and formations of infantry have been tested over ten thousand years ... But the Air Force has no centuries of trial and error to study; it must feel its way, making its errors and correcting them."

For the Allies, part of "feeling its way" in occupied Belgian and French airspace involved the use of the rural resistance—the Maquis— to man secret airstrips lit in many cases with hand-held torches, and above all, the use of clandestine air-to-ground "drop" networks. These nets and safehouses allowed spies, ammunition, gold, explosives, radios, custom single-use silenced pistols made to resemble bicycle pumps, and assassins to infiltrate and distract Nazi commanders along the English Channel. The Secret Operations Executive was told to "set the continent aflame" by Churchill.

The "errors and corrections" were recorded in blood, as L. Douglas Keeney shows in *The Pointblank Directive*, his well-researched and dramatic account of the USAAF's all-important contribution to Operation Overlord.

That the equipment needed to launch sea and air assets for Overlord even existed is in itself a testament to the industrial sword America had forged in the late 1930s. America's air and sea assets would never be larger, nor would she ever again assemble 10 million in arms. This was the peak, and Overlord was the tip of the spear; the thin, fragile edge of a wide wedge that the Allies used to wrench Europe from the Nazis, first by airpower, then with boots.

The U.S. Army's Air Corps' budget had nearly doubled from 1935 to 1938, but Franklin Delano Roosevelt knew it still wasn't enough. On October 16, 1938, the president approved a secret plan, in a politically risky move, that called for the production of fifteen thousand warplanes annually. FDR ordered Army Chief of Staff General Malin Craig to prepare personnel and facilities for the first of many increases in annual bomber production, the weapon Roosevelt knew would be critical in deterring or fighting the war he saw looming between the Great Powers.

A flabbergasted Craig, who desired traditional munitions expenditure increases instead, demanded, "What are we going to do with fifteen thousand planes? Who [are] you going to fight, what are you going to do with three thousand miles of ocean?" The world as we know it was likely saved by the president's response.

On November 14, 1938, Roosevelt again called in his military advisors and demanded a "huge air force so we do not need to have a huge army to follow that air force." Deputy Army Chief of Staff George C. Marshall simply nodded, while Air Force Chief General Henry "Hap" Arnold, the only aviator in the room, began figuring production numbers in his head.

A month later, Roosevelt ordered the U.S. ambassador to Germany home "for consultations." It would be more than a decade before another U.S. ambassador returned.

Until D-Day, June 6, 1944, the Allied strategic bombing campaign was the only way in which Britain, and after 1942, the United States, could hit Nazi Germany, then the overlords of continental Europe. The bombers and fighters, as we now know, gave Supreme Allied Commander General Dwight D. Eisenhower the air superiority he needed over the D-Day beaches and began the march to Berlin that brought Hitler down.

In lives, the bombing campaign was bloody beyond belief; "among every hundred RAF Bomber Command aircrew in the course of the war, fifty-one died on operations, nine were lost in crashes in England, three seriously injured, twelve taken prisoner, one was shot down and escaped capture, and just twenty-four completed a tour of operations." The same could be said of the young men of the United States Army Air Forces.

The Allied bombing campaign was ordered by Churchill and Roosevelt at the Casablanca Conference of January 1943. There, the two leaders announced that the combined Allied offensive war in Western Europe would begin in the air, with round-the-clock bombing of Germany's military, oil, industrial, and transportation infrastructure. RAF's Bomber Command would take the night shift, and America's Eighth, Ninth, and Fifteenth Air Forces would bomb by day. The communiqué issued at Casablanca included the following unambiguous goal for the Allied air forces: "The progressive destruction and dislocation of the morale of the German military, industrial and economic system and the undermining of the morale of the German people, to the point where their capacity for armed resistance is fatally weakened."

In February 1944, as the Allies were preparing to unleash the full fury of The Pointblank Directive through a week of continuous bombing that would rank as the most violent aerial combat yet, Churchill took a moment to address the issue of terror bombing in the House of Commons, reminding the world and Hitler of both the Blitz and the hangman. "I shall not moralize further than to say that there is a strange, stern justice in the long swing of events."

Bombers were the only way to strike Germany until the Allies could mount D-Day. Said one military historian: "Without the bombing campaign, German industry would have been able to increase war production capacity many times over if required. Bombing disrupted production and held the full potential of the German industrial machine in check."

Historian Richard Overy was more to the point: "The critical question is not so much 'What did bombing do to Germany?' but 'What could Germany have achieved if there had been no bombing?'"

As an historian with the RAF Bomber Command noted, "Albert Speer, Hitler's Armaments Minister, knew more than anyone else in Europe about the true effect of the bombing campaign. He summed it up thusly: 'It made every square metre of Germany a front. For us, it was the greatest lost battle of the war,'" and clearly paved the way for D-Day, the land assault of Europe; history's greatest and most critical battle by far.

The airwar victory justly stands as one of the most important accomplishments of the Allied air forces. Had the Luftwaffe freely roamed the skies, the invasion, already one of the bloodiest days of World War II, might very well have been a stunning setback. We have a noble group of airmen to thank. Air superiority paved the way to the end of the Third Reich.

Stephen Frater,
author of *Hell Above Earth*
www.stephenfrater.com
June 2012

INTRODUCTION

One of the most remarkable stories of World War II is, of course, D-Day—not only the overwhelming triumph of the soldiers who battled their way ashore, but also the story of the largely unseen battles in the sky that prevented the German Air Force from attacking on that fateful day. Hardly a single Luftwaffe aircraft challenged the landings on June 6, 1944, but why? Where were they? What happened to one of the most powerful military air forces in the world?

On January 21, 1943, the American Joint Chiefs of Staff and their British counterparts signed a formal agreement that called on their combined bomber forces to target the elaborate and sprawling German industrial complex. Foremost on the extensive target list were the aircraft factories that supplied the Luftwaffe with combat airplanes and the airbases in Western Europe from which the German Air Force would oppose the D-Day landings. The Americans would bomb by day, the British by night. Through this day-and-night bombing, German fighter production would be halted, German frontline air forces would be decimated, and the German Air Force could be defeated by D-Day.

It was an utter failure.

By October 1943, American B-17s and B-24s were being shot down so frequently that it was statistically impossible to complete a twenty-five-mission tour of duty. The British, far from bombing airframe factories, were bombing German cities. Equally, the American bombing accuracy was so poor that one U.S. airman joked that the safest place to be in Germany was on a German airbase.

Not that anyone was amused—least of all Henry A. "Hap" Arnold, commanding general of the U.S. Army Air Forces. Arnold could see that the bombing campaign was scarcely leading to the defeat of the Luftwaffe. He acted decisively to change that, and what emerged was a far more realistic objective that called for air superiority over the D-Day beaches—The Pointblank Directive—and for sweeping changes to his own command in England. Showing his brilliance and his determination, Arnold swept his house clean and put General Carl A. "Tooey" Spaatz and Spaatz's right-hand man, Jimmy Doolittle, in charge of the air war against Germany. Along with the fiery Pete Quesada, these three airwar generals set out to do in five months what their predecessors had failed to do in the preceding fifteen months. Eisenhower wanted air superiority on D-Day; these men were going to give it to him.

For many historians, the defeat of Germany in 1945 represented the triumph of the bombing campaign. But for Eisenhower—indeed for the free world—it was D-Day. Had D-Day failed—and it almost did—everything else would have failed or fallen dreadfully far behind. But it didn't. Spaatz so utterly defeated the Luftwaffe that on the most important day to the survival of the Third Reich, they were incapable of mounting a significant defensive attack.

But it was close.

So what happened? How could the Luftwaffe, the largest, most aggressive combat military airpower in the world, with a nearly endless supply of fast and deadly fighters armed with cannons, rockets, bombs, and machine guns, not to mention experienced, unemotional pilots, go from nearly complete control of the skies over occupied Europe in

November 1943 to near invisibility on June 6, 1944? How could the ever-so-meticulous Germans, with their vast array of coastal radars, battle-tested commanders, and countless spies in England, have failed to stop the invasion?

The answer is complicated, but the story is inspiring. For one, most histories are largely wrong about the airwar. Long-held theories that the Germans bungled their way through D-Day or that Hitler's near lunacy caused them to be slow to react to the invasion and paved the way to the success of the D-Day airwar are clearly wrong. D-Day was no accident of a crazy man.

The fact is that an all-in aerial swarming of occupied Europe and Nazi Germany by tens of thousands of American fighter pilots, reconnaissance pilots, B-26 Marauders, A-20 Havocs, Forts, and Liberators; the bombing of targets that served only to mask the American intentions; the 130-mile no man's land around the beaches; the rail cutting and bridge dropping—that's what did it, and it was far from easy.

True, a lucky miscalculation that saw the most competent German fighter wing with more than 120 combat hardened pilots and their fighters inadvertently moved away from Omaha Beach the night before D-Day helped. But it was through a series of brilliant decisions, smart tactical moves, gutsy determination, and a modicum of luck that the Luftwaffe was outplayed, outgunned, and outsmarted on D-Day. A day earlier and the outcome would have been different. A day later, same story. But on June 6, 1944, the American Air Forces gave Eisenhower air superiority—on the only day that truly mattered.

D-Day must surely be the most important airpower achievement in the history of military aviation. Not a single significant air attack was mounted by the Germans while the invasion forces battled to get ashore, and that may very well be why the infantry finally pushed over the bluffs on Omaha Beach when, by the slimmest of margins, they were very nearly thrown back.

In writing this book, I had to make some choices. Some of them were easy; others were not. For example, the Me-109 was also called the Bf-109, but I choose to call it the Me-109 for several reasons, one of which is that the German pilots called it a Messerschmitt or an "Me" but never a "Bf." I could reedit their quotes or just use the nomenclature they used, which is what I did.

In a similar fashion, I tried not to bog down the reader with too much nomenclature. I don't often identify an Me-410, for instance, or differentiate it from the He-111; rather, I typically say a particular twin-engine fighter was "a twin-engine fighter." Equally, I don't distinguish between a German day fighter or a night fighter; whether a B-17 was a B-17E or B-17F; or whether a P-47 was a razorback or a bubble canopy, which many authors choose to do. Nor did I detail every bomber mission or include the names of both American bombers when describing a raid. If B-17s went with the B-24s, I may just say "the B-17s." I won't win any game shows, I admit, but too many books become too much inside baseball and dilute the triumph of a strategy or the determination of the men on a mission.

One of my biggest challenges had to do with the execution of the airwar on D-Day. In truth, the airmen didn't do nearly as well as they had hoped to, notwithstanding the glowing reports of other serious historians. As many as half of all of the German fighter pilots who attempted to attack the invasion beaches actually got through—a puzzling outcome considering the overwhelming advantage the Allies had with thousands of airplanes acting as top cover. Indeed, some Luftwaffe pilots strafed the beaches, got home, and spent the rest of D-Day by the pool sunning themselves. Worse, our own heavy bombers missed their targets entirely and failed to soften the German defenses, resulting, most tragically, in the near retreat on Omaha Beach. The airmen who flew the bombers that day said it straight up, and thus I do, too. Against Omaha Beach, the predawn raid to soften the beaches sent bombs so far off target that many landed as much as 3 miles inland. Most histories rationalize this by saying that the misses "rattled the cages of the Germans behind the lines." Well, that's not how the airmen felt about it back then, and they said so: "We didn't do so well" was more or less the common sentiment. It was bad planning, bad execution, and of no help to the men coming ashore on Omaha. The Ninth Air Force did a brilliant job on Utah, but the Eighth botched it on Omaha.

The happy circumstance of finishing a book is occasioned by the opportunity to thank those who helped along the way. No one deserves it more than Doug Grad of Doug Grad Literary Agency. Doug is both a well-respected literary agent in the publishing industry and a World War II historian himself. When we discussed this book, he saw the story in an instant. My thanks.

I spent many days at the Mighty Eighth Air Force Heritage Museum in Savannah, Georgia, and poured through their extensive collection of oral histories. This is truly a unique source of primary documents that cast light on years of extraordinary valor in service to this nation. I worked under the guidance of Dr. Vivian Rogers-Price, and for her time and advice I owe my deepest gratitude.

Jeff Ethell passed away in a warbird crash and today flies on the wings of angels, but in the years before his accident, we worked together on several World War II projects and spent hours talking about the airwar. As I wrote this book, I pulled up many of his old photos and histories and found gems that are part of this book. Sadly, his magnificent collection of oral histories is gone, but his wonderful books remain.

I read many memoirs written by former Luftwaffe pilots, including Wolfgang Fischer's powerful *Luftwaffe Fighter Pilot* and Hermann Buchner's new book, *Stormbird*. These two authors seemed to sum up the sentiments of so many other former pilots that I found it impossible not to use their stories in this book. Both books are well written and engaging, and I recommend them to you.

Equally, I recommend to you a lost history of the airwar that I served as editor on, now restored and republished under its original title, *The War Against the Luftwaffe*, plus many of the documents on World War II held at the Air Force Historical Research Agency at Maxwell Air Force Base. Both resources were essential to this book.

Virtually every World War II bomber and fighter group has its own website. I used many of them to one extent or another, and I thank all of the veterans who have gone to the trouble to capture valuable histories from this great generation of airmen. I am particularly indebted to the Wisconsin Veterans Museum Research Center oral history project, the Experimental Aircraft Association's oral history project, and the late Stephen Ambrose for their histories. One also should always mention the National Archives and the Library of Congress, both of which yielded treasures.

My thanks to Kelli Christiansen, who edited this book. We went through three drafts, and each round made the manuscript just a little bit better than the last. My son, Alex Keeney, also read this manuscript and made helpful comments that are reflected herein. I also thank my wife, Jill Johnson Keeney, who trumps any literary achievement of my own with her brilliant touch as editorialist, a book reviewer, and former magazine editor.

Perhaps one day we'll pay tribute to the airwar victory with a monument in Washington, D.C., or a statue, but until then, I wish to dedicate this book to the magnificent airmen who cleared the way for the boys coming ashore on D-Day. A tip of the hat to you all.

PREFACE: 1943

They fell through the sky cocooned in feelings of indescribable bliss. The clouds were welcoming, the sky was vast and blue, the ground so distant yet so sure. They were free.

"The feeling I got when I opened the chute is impossible to describe," said Jim Skinner, a navigator. "After the roar of the engines, the racket of the guns, the chatter on the interphone, the fear and anguish of the fire and the bail out into God only knew what—then suddenly, dead silence and a peace I had never before experienced. I wanted to float on forever ..."[2]

"When I jumped the chaos and Hell turned into Heavenly peace," remembered a B-17 copilot. "I thought I had died and gone to Heaven."[3]

Lt. Howard Snyder bailed out from a burning B-17. The Nebraska pilot's cockpit had exploded in flames when a tracer round found the oxygen tank. "A most wonderful and peaceful quiet settled over me. It seemed as if I had come out of hell above into a heaven of peace and rest. Up above I could now hear the heavy deep sound of the Flying Fortresses mingled with the angry rasps of the fighters. But with the peaceful country coming up to meet me, baked in sunshine, the war and all that happened only a few seconds before seemed like a bad dream long ago."[4]

CHAPTER 1

AIRMEN

They were free spirits drawn to the air, young and optimistic, warriors animated by a quest to be airmen, aggressive with quick reflexes, pilots who knew airplanes only as tools of war. They entered the greatest aviation training program in history, molded and burnished like polished steel until they became pilots of enormous four-engine bombers and commanders of fast and agile single-seat fighters. They came from farms and cities and would travel halfway around the world to dogfight Germans over Amsterdam, Paris, and Berlin, but they were hardly worldly and had scarcely seen the country they'd been born in.

With boundless optimism they boarded great ships and sailed the Atlantic Ocean to join the war, breathing the saltwater air as they became familiar with their fellow passengers, all of them airmen and soldiers, too. They were off to England, to enter the skies of Germany, where they would sip oxygen through a mask held fast against their faces as their fighters and bombers slipped through the thin air at 25,000 feet. They would be wrapped in electrically heated suits to ward off temperatures that would plunge to minus 40 degrees, and they would crease the upper limits of the atmosphere where one could see the curvature of the Earth. As the bow of their ships split apart the surface of the Atlantic Ocean, they huddled over their cards playing poker with their friends; in every game and in every hold, where the cigarette smoke hung thickest in the air and when the talk was at its loudest, there was always one who would slap down a pair of aces and well up his chest and vow that he would be the one who would kill Adolf Hitler.

Such were the Disraeli gears of war in 1943. "We were in a new dimension where nothing seemed normal and much worse, it wasn't going to get normal," said Homer King, an airman from Natchez, Mississippi, who arrived in England aboard the *Queen Elizabeth*. "We fought the enemy, weather, boredom, no mail, off-brand cigarettes, no heat, cold showers, lousy grub, irregular sleep and every day was bringing more of the same or worse."[5]

The graveyard has no voice except to those consigned to hear it, and no sooner had the airmen steamed into port and landed on British soil than were their romantic notions of aerial combat shattered by reality, and in that reality they began to hear the whispers of the dead. "We reached England from New York in March of 1943," said airman Robert O'Brien. "We landed in northern England. What an experience that was. There were sunken ships all over the place. We had to march through the city, and the buildings were all bombed."[6]

The airmen arrived day and night by ship and plane. When they landed, they were funneled into a well-oiled transportation network that moved them around this foreign land with near-clockwork precision from docks to trains that took them to London where they transferred to the buses and trucks that trundled them out to the 122 American airbases scattered like seed around the East Anglia countryside. With each step forward, the realities of war held them tighter in its grip. They passed a cathedral that rose out of a sea of charred rubble silhouetted by a landscape that was painted by the devil himself. "Nothing was left standing," remembered a newly arriving airman. "Just a huge desert of broken bricks, caved in walls and steel girders twisted by the heat … high up on a jagged wall a toilet bowl was held in pace by its pipework … no floor … no ceiling."[7]

They motored out of the city into the countryside and found a place redolent with history and culture and brimming with farms and vegetation, but they saw things they couldn't yet comprehend. At sunset, certain objects seemed to clutch the ground as if embedded in the soil by dark spirits, silhouettes that at dusk had an odd familiarity that made them uneasy. R. E. "Lefty" Narrin was a twenty-three-year-old lieutenant. He was on a train traveling across the countryside to his airbase when he looked out the window. "All those wrecked B-17s and B-24s laying scattered and haphazardly and grotesquely along the snow-covered countryside of southern and western England that I saw shocked me into an awareness and stark realization that here was the real war."[8]

And that war changed everything. When he was a teenager, one airman liked to take out his .22 rifle and plink cans off a tree stump. After the war, it would never be the same. During an early mission, a 20-mm cannon shell from a German fighter hit one of his friends. His head exploded like an apple on a sawhorse, and his body slumped to the floor of their B-24. Another airman had been so afraid of heights that he had never climbed a tree, but during one mission he kicked a jammed bomb through the open bomb bay doors of a B-17 at 25,000 feet with absolutely nothing below his boot but cold air. On the bases back home, they loaded their bombers with 6,000 pounds of dead weight so they could feel what it was like when a heavily loaded plane mushed into the air, but here the bombs were real.

The typical B-17 was like a stick of dynamite wrapped in gasoline. So long as the thrust of the engines and the lift of the wings combined to exceed the 65,000-pound weight of the bomber, the miracle of flight occurred and the bomber lifted into the air. But if an engine stuttered or if the morning heat thinned the air density just enough, the propellers would lose their grip and the bomber would wobble, the worst of them simply exhausting the laws of physics and pancaking into the ground in a fireball fed by the bomber's own fuel.

A young navigator in the nose of a B-17 bomber was facing the center of the runway as his own plane began its takeoff roll. At the far end of the runway, a bomber lifted up into the air. It seemed to hesitate. Then it winged over and crashed into the ground. A fireball blossomed into the sky, and plumes of black smoke rose like a curtain over the departure end of the runway. Nothing could be done. "We were sickened and shakened at the sight of the flaming wreckage, but well aware that once committed, 'the show must go on.'"[9]

Such was 1943.

At another airbase, a line of bombers waited their turn to take off as other planes roared down the runway and quickly disappeared into a wall of fog. This went on with regularity, one bomber taking off every thirty seconds until an engine froze or a wing dropped or something else happened up front and then, behind the fog, there was a brief, bright flash and flames that suffused the mist in an orange glow. "Nothing was said over the radio but everyone knew what had happened," remembered one of the airmen waiting to take off. "The big sweat was that bombs might detonate as we passed over the crash site."[10]

They trained in aerial gunnery and flew mock combat missions and did exceedingly well—back home. But here the combat was swift, and the margin between life and death was razor thin. A copilot on a bomber glanced to his right just as a German FW-190 fighter rammed into the B-17 next to his. It was a terrifying sight: "For a moment it looked just like a whale trying to swallow a shark. They hit head on and disintegrated instantly in a ball of fire!"[11] During a particularly vicious fight, a formation of American B-24 bombers was set upon by German FW-190s and Me-109s. Bullets and cannon fire laced the bombers, punching through their aluminum skin as if it were rice paper. A fire broke out inside one of the planes and grew steadily larger until the riddled bowels of the ship were seared black and the control cables were melted through and the bomber gasped one last gasp and simply reared up to die. The volatile fluids that snaked through the metal ribs of the plane were feeding the flames with the ship's own blood: "The leading Liberator, on fire from nose to tail, came swinging towards us like a severely wounded animal, then peeled away as if to pick a spot to die," remembered a crewman on the bomber next to it. "The next bomber moved up in its place. One Liberator with two engines on fire on the left wing came up from us to explode when it reached our altitude. A human form fell out of the orange-colored ball of flame. As he fell through space without parachute or harness he reached up as if to grasp at something." A second crewman was on board and saw it all: "Our ship, *Bonnie Vee*, had been hit several times—two engines were on fire and the interior of the plane was in a shambles. The gunners kept firing but finally they were all wounded or dead. At this time I knew we were in serious trouble with no hope of flying any longer. I finally gave the bail-out order because at this moment only one engine was running, and not too well. I asked my co-pilot to unbuckle my seat belt before he bailed out. Just as he stood to do so a 30-mm cannon shell cut him in half."[12]

Oftentimes, the planes operated beyond anything poured into the calculus of flight by the aeronautical engineers at Boeing or Consolidated. Because flying in a tight formation provided the most defensive firepower, the B-17s were bunched up close to one another, but with consequences that added to the carnage. In one B-17, there was a sudden, sharp sound. Recounted one of the survivors who remembered the chaos, "A man bails out of a ship in front of us and comes down into our ship breaking our Plexiglas nose, injuring our bombardier and navigator and throwing them into the catwalk of the ship. I look down at the ground and see many small fires and large ones burning. These are enemy fighters and our Forts. Another man bails out of a Fort in front of us. His chute hits our propellers. They cut the top of his chute. I see him falling, looking back at his flapping chute lines. He falls to the ground still alive until he struck the earth."[13]

The tight formations gave men who scarcely had a beard to shave images they'd see again and again in their nightmares. "We were flying in the number six position and I was busy looking for the group leader to drop his bombs when the plane in front of us took a direct hit in the wing at the tanks," recalled a twenty-four-year-old pilot from Massachusetts. "The plane, which was no more than 20 feet in front of us, burst into flames. The explosion threw him up and right back over the top of us. I remember the searing heat for an instant as it disappeared behind our plane."[14] On another mission, a tail gunner was overwhelmed by the sight of tracers streaming through the air, bombers arcing up and over into near-vertical death dives, bullets pounding into his own Fort. Then he saw the agonizing end of another bomber prolonged only by the physics of flight. "As we were fighting our way through this hell I glanced down and saw a B-17 breaking in half having taken a direct hit from flak," he remembered. "The front half—radio room, wings, engines, cockpit and nose—went straight down intact but I didn't see any chutes because my attention was riveted on the incredible sight of the B-17's tail section. It was gliding steadily down as if in normal flight. Behind the bomber was a German fighter and in the tail the gunner was still firing at the enemy plane apparently unaware that the complete front half of the B-17 was gone."[15]

The airmen of World War II would be awarded medals, including the Medal of Honor, but everyday heroics happened so often and so quickly they could scarcely be recognized except as footnotes in long-forgotten histories. During one mission, a radio operator on a B-17 dashed to the waist gun to return fire against attacking German fighters, but the bomber was fatally stricken. It was time to bail out. He turned to retrieve his parachute, but his radio room was by then in flames. Facing certain death if he stayed aboard and certain death if he jumped, he froze. The ball turret gunner, the second to last to leave the dying plane, calculated the possible outcomes and took it into his own hands: "Seeing the radio operator's dilemma, and thinking quickly, he embraced his fellow crewman in a bear hug and they both bailed out on one chute. They reached the ground safely."[16]

In the end, the reality they came to know was written in the empty bunks of the countless crewmen who never came home and the battle-scarred ground beneath them as they flew home. An American fighter pilot was returning to his airbase after a terribly bloody air-to-air battle. He looked out of his cockpit and saw a surreal portrait of war. "The sky was now void of the Reich defenders. Only white-streaked contrails left by the angry hornets seeking their adversaries fluttered in the brilliant blue," he said. "Down below, a few broken machines jabbed back and forth amid the rising acrid smoke, soon to take their place in the graveyard of broken dreams."[17]

To the locals, the wreckage of an American bomber became something of a novelty. German soldiers posed to have their pictures taken as they stood beside the back half of a B-17 that had crashed near Villacoublay, France. The cockpit and front section of another B-17 came to the ground near a German village. Children climbed over it, and mothers had their picture taken standing next to the shredded metal where the fuselage had torn apart. Another B-17 came down on the edge of a canal in Holland. Souvenir hunters stripped it bare. A P-51 slammed into the ground near Rotterdam. The tail section looked as if it had been fed into a mechanical tree shredder. A section of a B-17 landed in the courtyard of a home in Hoorn, Holland. German soldiers were seen inspecting the twisted wreckage. A B-24 plummeted into a farm field near Rottweil, Germany. More photos. The undercarriage of a B-17 or a B-24—no one was certain which it was—washed ashore from the North Sea.[18] As one American airman summed it all up, "This is one school where 'A' is the only passing grade."[19]

The Germans were quick to create a network of locals to capture the surviving airmen and take them prisoner. Civilians, older people mainly, were trained to get to a crash site quickly, check for survivors, and then conduct an area search inside a one-mile radius. They had no pity on the Americans they found. The Germans sometimes made the ones who could walk go back to a crumpled bomber and clean out the bits and pieces of human flesh inside, often the bodies of the same men they'd had breakfast with that morning. Those lucky enough to bail out and get a clean chute might survive in freedom only long enough to see their cards fold when they landed in a farmer's backyard or near a German village.

Villagers didn't take too kindly to having their homes decimated from the skies. Strategic bombing was offensive to German civilians. War had always been remote, undertaken by armies in trenches far from their cities, never as close as it was now. They had no human experience to deal with either the bombers or the bombing and so they were outraged, furious. As it continued, and as they heard that a relative had been killed in Hamburg or Munich or Berlin, they came to hate the Americans. Van Pinner, a crewmember on a bomber, celebrated his twenty-third birthday by gathering up his parachute in a German field after bailing out. Pinner was immediately surrounded by an angry crowd that was out for blood. He pulled out his pistol. "One old man had a long scythe, he looked like Father Time—I'm sure he would have sliced me up for washers if he hadn't seen the pistol. Some of the others started throwing rocks at me but the pistol stopped them."

The civilians had a name for the American fliers: *Terrorflieger*. Others called them *Gangsterfliegers* or *Amerikanische Gangsters*. Adolf Hitler reached inside his oratorical bag of tricks and did them all one better. He called the Allied bomber crews "pirate-pilots."[20]

American airmen unlucky enough to land in German territory were all too often lynched from trees, brutally pitch-forked to death, shot point blank, or simply beaten until there was nothing left but bloody flesh. In a strange turn of events, German soldiers were often called in to save them. Larry Pifer, a ball turret gunner on a B-17 that went down during a raid on Berlin, saw the intensity of the German anger and survived. "I was taken by train to the Hermann Goering Hospital in Berlin. We arrived the afternoon of March 5, racked with pain and bloodstained from our wounds. The following day, March 6, the Eighth Air Force bombed Berlin with a force of over 600 bombers, and it was simply awesome. They hit Berlin again on 8 and 9 March and the hospital began filling up rapidly with more injured flyers, theirs and ours. During the night of 12 March, with much of the hospital and surrounding district heavily damaged, the German guards sneaked us out to prevent the panic-stricken and frenzied Berlin civilians from lynching us."[21]

Major Clarence Evans was from Epps, Alabama. In Epps, almost everyone knew each other. Grandparents were respected. A day's work ended with a family meal. That all seemed a world away when Evans was shot down over Germany. He got a clean parachute, but he was shot at by a German fighter pilot while he floated down through the sky. When he finally landed, he was too injured to walk. Some Germans found him and put him on a makeshift sled and, with some other airmen, took him away. They came to a small town, one not much different from Epps. "The whole village turned out to see the American *Luftegangster*, as they called us captured airmen," remembered Evans. "There was an old grey-haired woman standing there with a little boy and the little boy spat on me as I went by on the sled."[22] The old lady didn't twitch the tiniest muscle.

A combat mission wasn't over until a bomber taxied around the perimeter track to its hardstand and the crew lowered themselves to the ground. There was one geographic obstacle to that moment. The English Channel is 350 miles long and as much as 150 miles wide at its widest. It was a finish line of sorts, but the trick was getting across and making it back home. Although a crippled bomber would often fly longer and further than any slide rule could have predicted, the last drop of fuel often drained there, over the sea, too far from land to make it. On a calm day with the surface of the sea as flat as a millpond, it was possible to survive a ditching. But for the most part, the Channel was cold, and the face of the sea was swept by with one- and two-foot rollers. A crash landing was just as likely to be fatal on the water as it was on the ground. If a plane sunk too quickly, it would take the entire crew beneath the waves and disappear into dark waters that dropped 800 feet to the bottom. If the crew got out, they had life vests and small rafts, but for others, the water was just a grave.

One German fighter pilot was badly shot up during an attack on his B-17, and he bailed out over the North Sea. Against improbable odds, he survived and climbed into his inflatable raft. He slipped in and out of consciousness as he floated on the water. "It was just after midnight when I woke up. Clouds had moved in and waves began tossing my tiny boat to and fro. An object I couldn't identify was floating beside me." The pilot was too tired to do much of anything, and he continued to flit back and forth in and out of consciousness when he was jolted awake yet again. "The dark object was now drifting close beside me and I realized to my horror that it was the body of an American. His green parachute was drifting just beneath the water's surface." Out of the corner of his eye, the German saw more shadows and only then did he understand where he was: an entire bomber crew was in the water with him. "I now realized that there were other bodies floating around me. I counted twelve in all. It was probably the entire crew of a Flying Fortress … I began to paddle like mad with both hands but they appeared to be following me."[23]

Even as the airmen had the first glimpse of their home airfields in England and began to think about a cup of whiskey and the reassuring strength of the earth beneath their feet, the Germans attacked. German night fighters would use the cloak of darkness to sneak up behind a bomber and without warning pour out fire in streams of deadly lead. One bomber was in the landing pattern waiting to land when to its right there was a sudden flash in the night sky and flames began to drop toward the ground. "We noticed streams of tracers appearing over the nearby B-24 base at Middlesham," remembered the pilot. "B-24s in the landing pattern were suddenly catching on fire, exploding in mid-air, and going down. Then the dreaded news came over the radio—German intruder aircraft, Me-410s, had followed the bombers back to East Anglia and were having a field day shooting down unsuspecting Allied aircraft as they attempted to land."[24] Three bombers went down.

The United States Army Air Forces entered the war in Europe in 1942 with all-new bombers and fighters and well-trained aviators who, to a man, knew nothing of the violence of war in the air but who arrived ready to fight the Nazis. Lieutenant Bill Rickman was driven by a sense of duty that animated his every move. "I enlisted in the army air force in December 1942, ready to serve my country and start a new life," he said. Rickman saw his first airplane as a youngster in Nashville and dreamed of flying. When war broke out, he was ready to go. "We were all hyped up about the dirty Japs and the terrible Nazis. Everybody wanted to go get them."[25]

Getting over there to go get them was a slow, muddled road, though. The newly established American Eighth Air Force arrived in England in early 1942, took up operations, and received its first B-17s and B-24 bombers and put them to use. They flew their first combat mission on August 17, 1942, against the rail yards in Rouen, in occupied France. They attacked with just eighteen bombers in all, a miniscule force. There were no losses, but equally, they did very little damage. One year later, on the anniversary of that first mission, the Eighth had grown immensely. On that day, 3,760 men were assigned

376 bombers to attack and destroy the Messerschmitt factory in Regensburg, Germany, and the ball-bearing factories in Schweinfurt with the full power of more than 3,000 bombs, a far cry from a year before.

Although by 1943 the Eighth was a larger and much more powerful airforce, it was still finding its way. The anniversary mission, as it was called, was a near disaster. A total of 552 young men were lost during the attack that day, with 60 bombers shot down and another 168 so badly shot up that most of them would be grounded for repairs. Aboard the bombers that made it back were six more dead and twenty-one who were seriously injured. Indeed, even a year since the bombing of Rouen, things were going so poorly and airmen were being shot down so quickly that it seemed unlikely that anyone would get out of the war alive. New bombers rushed in almost daily and replacement pilots were brought in so fast that one sometimes forgot which group one was with. "The turnover was so great that it was not uncommon to be among strangers even in your own squadron," remembered Robert Copp, a B-17 pilot. Making twenty-five missions seemed utterly unreachable.[26]

Little by little, though, the crews became a fighting force, and little by little, they gained confidence in themselves and their mission. They became the Mighty Eighth, the largest strategic bombing force in the world at the time, with more than a thousand bombers and a like number of fighters to escort them. Their mission tempos increased, the size of the formations grew, and they became better organized with fighters and combat boxes and generals who burned with a passion to pursue and kill the Luftwaffe wherever they could be found. "We became part of this awesome fighting machine where men and machines covered the skies as far as you could see," remembered airman Homer King from Natchez, Mississippi. "How incredible it is for a man today to look back and say he could load a plane up with gasoline, bombs and nine other men and then go out and fly a mission, get shot at, come back, and do it again and again and again and again."[27]

And they did do it again and again, with determination and conviction and a reason for doing so that made it intensely personal. Remembered Captain Ellis B. Scripture, a navigator on a B-17, "All of us are well aware of the countless atrocities committed by the Nazis in the name of the German people." In case someone didn't get it, his commanding officer spelled it out: they were at war. The Germans had been killing innocent people all over Europe for years, and it was their job to get rid of the Nazis, no ifs, ands, or buts. There were no soldiers to help them, no army, no navy to do the job for them; just the airmen and their bombers. Fighter ace Tommy Hayes remembered how it felt: "I had no feelings of guilt or remorse," he said. "After General Doolittle assumed command, our job was to destroy the Luftwaffe."[28]

B-17 pilot B. J. Kiersted didn't hesitate to let his crew know the substance of his will. Radio operator Larry Goldstein remembered the moment: "On the first day that we were assigned to our B-17 in England, our pilot asked the crew chief how many crews had he had. When he answered 'You're my third in three months,' that might have shaken a weak man, but B. J. merely said, 'We will be the crew that completes our 25 missions.'"[29]

From June 14, 1943, to June 6, 1944, every mission, every bomb load, every bullet in every P-51 Mustang and B-17 Flying Fortress had one reason for being: The Pointblank Directive. According to Pointblank, the highest priority for every combat mission flown into Occupied Europe by every Allied bomber and fighter was to defeat the Luftwaffe in order to pave the way for all the soldiers who would inevitably land on D-Day. The airmen could bomb German aircraft factories, crater their airfields, or shoot their fighters down in twisting dogfights that laced the skies with deadly steel, but on the defeat of the German Air Force, everything hung in the balance. "It was intended to prepare the way for Overlord," wrote an Air Force historian of the Pointblank Directive. "In order to assure the success of Overlord it was first necessary to eliminate the threat offered by the GAF."[30]

And therein lay a military objective unlike any of World War II. The men of the airwar would not seize a single island, as did the Marines in the Pacific. Nor would they liberate as much as one country, as would the Allies as they crossed Europe. They would have no parades through the Arc de Triumph, nor would there be as much as a single battle named after the ground they took. In this peculiar war of theirs, success would be measured by the number of German airmen killed, by the number of German fighters destroyed, by the number of German airfields rendered unusable, and by the number of German aircraft factories bombed to rubble. Air-to-air combat, strafing, dive-bombing, strategic bombing, and reconnaissance flights—all of it had to come together for just one day, and if it did, it would be their Yorktown. "Hitler himself coined the term Fortress Europe," remembered Luftwaffe commander Adolf Galland. "This fortress was to be defended to the last breath."[31] But as President Franklin D. Roosevelt said to a hushed Congress, "Hitler forgot to put a roof over his fortress."[32]

And thus Pointblank. While the D-Day landings would be the first combat mission in France for the United States Army, it would be the 394th combat mission for the airmen of the airwar. Before the first soldier died on Omaha Beach, the Army Air Forces already would have suffered more than 42,000 casualties to prepare the way.[33]

And yet so little is known about this great airwar that led to D-Day victory. Corporal Melvin Applebaum saw the irony in this in the way the finality of combat gives certain facts the stark clarity they sometimes require. "During the month," he wrote, "Tom Dewey became the Republican candidate for President, the G. I. Bill became law, Babe Didrikson won a golf championship, the St. Louis Browns stayed up on top, the Russians opened their summer offensive, and everywhere you looked were pictures of Betty Grable's baby. Over here, June was a big month, too."[34]

Allied Supreme Commander General Dwight D. Eisenhower summed up what Pointblank meant as he and his son John walked on

Omaha Beach one week after D-Day. Armored trucks and tanks crawled bumper-to-bumper in a traffic jam as thick as rush hour traffic in Manhattan. Said the young Eisenhower to his father, "You'd never get away with this if you didn't have air supremacy."

His father didn't miss a beat. "If I didn't have air superiority, I wouldn't be here."[35]

In October 1943, Pointblank teetered on the brink of failure—and with it, D-Day. After a year in England, the Eighth Air Force was far from achieving any of its goals, and it was most certainly far from securing the skies over the D-Day beaches. How the tables were turned is the untold story of great military minds, the unilateral application of blunt force, and the matching of wits as two air armies fought each other to the very last for control of the skies over Germany. This is that story.

CHAPTER 2

AUTUMN 1943

The morning light shot across the airfield at the Luftwaffe complex at Rheine, Germany, revealing the dull gray shapes of four Focke-Wulf aircraft parked on the ramp. From inside a cavernous hangar on the corner of the field, a handful of ground maintainers in gray coveralls walked out and headed toward the planes. They looked sideways at the building that housed the ready room where the pilots were assembled. The grass was thick and green with a slight sheen of morning dew, the sky a striking blue.

It was autumn in the fourth year of the German conquest of Europe, a day that dawned with a canopy of clear skies stretching as far as the eye could see and providing nearly unlimited visibility over France and Germany. Gerd Wiegand, a handsome German fighter pilot not yet twenty-five years old, was in a group of a half dozen other pilots, each going through their morning routines. To a man, their hair was combed straight back, and each wore flight suits with their life jackets strapped around their legs. They tied white scarves around their necks, and had arranged them so they conspicuously showed under their open-collared shirts. Wiegand was noticeably taller than the rest. He had Gary Cooper-good looks with jet-black hair and a lantern jaw that belied a smile that could freeze a bar maid in her tracks. He had posed for a photograph at the Luftwaffe airbase in Wevelgem, Belgium. In it he looked entirely at ease. He had one shoulder cocked down and his hands in his pockets in a way that gave him an air of confidence unmatched by the other pilots next to him as they stood in front of a Focke-Wulf and squinted against the sunlight.

Wiegand had been shot up once already. His plane had taken punishing hits in an air battle with a B-17 Flying Fortress. Fifty-caliber shells ripped off chunks of steel as if his fighter had been so much balsa wood. He was hit and had been wounded. He was forced to bail out, catching air in his parachute only after free falling straight down a few thousand feet. He beat death, and you could see it: Wiegand had the look of a guy who dared anyone to have the temerity to kill him—not an American, and certainly not in his FW-190.

It was Sunday, October 10, 1943, in Hitler's Germany. A stale mixture of sweat, coffee, and cigarette smoke suffused the air as a radio crackled to life somewhere in the back of the pilots' ready room. The news was more or less the same as it had been all summer: rationing. Night raids. More Americans arriving in England. The war had not yet come as far as this Luftwaffe airbase in Rheine, and so there was a sense of sanctuary here, although the raids against Germany were becoming both more frequent and more deadly. The Americans had been in England for more than a year, and most of the pilots on the base were acquainted with them, although few to the extent of their friend Wiegand.

A few of the German pilots drifted outside to take their coffee in the sun, sitting in the sling chairs beside the door positioned there for just such things. Good weather was often a prelude to a stream of B-17s, and this Sunday morning had the makings of all that, but who knew? The glorious sun beckoned, so they sat and smoked. The pilots no doubt nodded approvingly as they watched the ballet of ground maintainers pulling engine covers off their crates and stuffing belts of ammunition into their wings. They most certainly glanced skyward as if measuring the heavens for their planes, reading the messages written especially for airmen in the curves of a cirrus cloud, the anvil of a cumuliform, the counterclockwise gust of wind that came from a system to the west. Perhaps they could feel the miniscule but rhythmic changes in the air pressure caused by the concussive shock of some nine hundred three-bladed propellers that at that moment had begun to slap the air at a dozen airbases in Britain some 170 miles away. Perhaps they sensed such things but, if they did, they knew better than to let it show.

Deep inside a darkened concrete bunker in Holland, Walter Grabmann, a German fighter controller, watched a bank of radar displays and listened to the intercepted radio communications coming from the airbases in England. He had noticed a spike in American radio traffic, and from experience in such matters, he concluded that an American bomber attack was in the works. He checked the clock and mentally calculated the possibilities. It was too late in the morning for the Americans to launch a mission deep into Germany, so he presumed the target would be along the coast or within 50 miles of the English Channel. It would take two hours for the lumbering giants to spiral up into their formations and another hour to get over the Channel. He had time to sort things out.

As a precaution, Grabmann ordered a squadron of fighters at the Luftwaffe base in Lille, France, to shuttle over to the airbase in Deelen, Netherlands. He then ordered a second group of fighters to reposition themselves forward to Rheine, both groups thus nearer to the coast and, if Grabmann had played this correctly, under the likely path of the attackers. "Here we were held at readiness until the enemy's intentions were clear, awaiting orders to scramble if the bomber stream was reported to be headed towards our region," said Wolfgang Fischer, a German fighter pilot who knew the routine. If they were scrambled, they would attack using their machine guns and their devastatingly powerful 20-mm cannons. A few hits by a 20-mm cannon could flick a B-17 into the hereafter as if it were a mere insect.

Satisfied, Grabmann put the rest of his fighters on alert and paced back and forth in front of an enormous glass wall dotted with pinpoints of light that moved about the face of the glass like water fleas. The situation display told him that planes were already on the move.[36]

Across the Channel, the whine of starter motors pierced the morning quiet as large piston engines spinning three-bladed propellers began to cough to life. One by one a plume of black smoke spat from their exhaust pipes as the Wright Cyclones kicked to life in an explosion of energy that was a bomber coming to life. It was East Anglia, England, a farming district north and east of London plowed under for the war and over which now spread the most concentrated collection of airbases ever in history: some 700 airfields on which were based Allied fighters and bombers, including 122 of them in use exclusively by United States Army Air Forces.

On October 10, 1943, the Eighth Air Force was about to mount its 114th raid against Nazi Germany. It had been exactly thirty missions since the disastrous August 17, 1943, raid when nearly 40 percent of the B-17s and B-24s had been shot down or badly damaged during the dual raid on Schweinfurt and Regensburg. Today's mission would be flown as all had been to date, which meant the bombers would attack in bunched up defensive formations that optimized their mutual fire support, called combat boxes. Fighter escorts would wing alongside them to the limits of their fuel tanks, and then they would turn back. From that point on, the aircrews would use their firepower to take the battle to the target.

A total of 2,740 men had been assembled for this mission, the target being a major rail center located in the city of Münster, Germany.

The airmen would fly 274 B-17 bombers, each armed with twelve .50-caliber machine guns and loaded with a stack of 500-pound bombs. They would fly a direct route across the English Channel inland about 120 miles into Germany. They would blast their target and then turn around.

Based on past experiences, the mission would be anything but a milk run. The Münster raiders faced an imposing array of German ground and air defenses that together barricaded the Third Reich behind a wall of electromagnetic radiation and a sky that would be laced with bullets and flak. Around the western perimeter of Occupied Europe was a complex, interconnected web of German early-warning radar stations connected to a series of hardened control bunkers inside of which were Luftwaffe radar controllers that would monitor their every turn and would alert the ground flak batteries and fighter units ahead of them so they could mount their attacks. They would fly over expansive belts of no-man's lands 20 miles wide bristling with German 88-mm antiaircraft guns. They would be attacked by the fighter planes piloted by experienced airmen like Wiegand, who would take off from any of the more than one hundred German fighter bases in Western Europe, each packed with Messerschmitts, Focke-Wulfs, Heinkels, and Junkers. They would be shot up, and some would be shot down. That was almost a certainty. The only question was whose name was on which bullet.

In October 1943, the Luftwaffe was an imposing 1.7 million men strong, and, as combat aviators, they were terribly good at what they did. The overwhelming majority of their frontline fighter pilots had come through flight school in 1942 and were now hardened combat pilots who had fought on both fronts, Russia and the West. Some of the pilots had more than twenty aerial kills; most of them had experienced the B-17s and had engaged the American Thunderbolts and Lightnings that escorted them in and out.[37] They were good pilots, aggressive fighters and well trained. But, more to the point, they were fierce protectors of their homeland, and they had no intention of letting some American farm boys bomb their homes.

Among the Germans were pilots like Adolf Dickfeld. Dickfeld was born in Berlin and had claimed his first kills on the Eastern Front against Russia before coming to fight in the West. The steady attacks by the Americans and the destruction caused by the bombs falling on his homeland made the war intensely personal for him. "I was fighting for my home, to defend the fatherland, to bring an end to the terror against our civilian population," he wrote in his memoirs.[38] Field Marshal Erhard Milch, the Luftwaffe's second in command, said as much as he spoke about the combat: "Germany is the real front line. The bulk of our fighters must go for the defense of the homeland."[39]

The passion that animated the German fighter pilots was nothing compared to the resolve of the American bomber crews. The men of the Eighth Air Force came from every state in the union and brought with them a mixed bag of political beliefs, family values, and ambitions. They had enlisted in the Army Air Forces when their most urgent reason to fight was to avenge the attack on Pearl Harbor, yet they ended up in Europe to kill Adolf Hitler. Despite the contradiction, they were fine with that. Their worldview was pure and clean, unmuddied by statesmanship or rhetoric or the sort of spin-doctoring found in politics. "We knew [Hitler] was doing terrible things to millions of people," said an airman from Wisconsin. "We knew that he was after the world and we knew that he was killing people, and killing civilians … we wanted to beat Hitler and beat the German army."[40]

The B-17s and B-24s they flew did remarkable things with wings and engines and bombs. The propellers clawed at the thin air and pulled their planes forward mysteriously and magically using no more than the ever-so-slight curvature of their wings to give them the lift they needed to roam the atmosphere miles above Earth. The planes were sturdy and trustworthy and tough, but they were just steel and gasoline until they were animated by the fighting spirit of their crews. Captain Bush Cole was from Livingston, Texas. At the age of sixteen, Cole went to work in the oil fields around Corpus Christi and was making good money at it when along came Pearl Harbor. His father sat him down, and from the look in his eyes, Cole knew it was serious. "I grew up in a patriotic family," he remembered. "My daddy always used to tell me and my brothers that he would rather bury his sons on the prairie than see them not serve their country." What Cole's father meant was that if that's what it took, America was worth dying for. Cole enlisted in the Army Air Forces, where he served his country well. He became a bombardier on a B-24.[41]

Bomber pilot Edward Tracy learned to fly at the Army Air Forces Base in Roswell, New Mexico. When he won his wings, he was nineteen, and when he received his command, he was the youngest man on his bomber. Tracy was hopelessly in love with his Boeing bomber. "The B-17 was the most forgiving airplane ever made and therefore one of the easiest to learn to fly," he said many years later.

Tracy's name appeared on the top of a list that was pinned to a bulletin board where replacement crews were given their assignments overseas. "I could not help being proud because, in the listing of my crew assignment, I was named pilot, and my name was at the top of the crew list. It was *Tracy's* crew from now on, in spite of the fact that I was among the youngest on board. My copilot was twenty-six, as was my bombardier, and my navigator was twenty-seven."[42] Tracy had just turned twenty.

Part of what made a crew effective was discipline in the air. Erwin Koppel, also twenty, was from Wisconsin. The ten-man crew that manned a B-17 had clear divisions of labor and a code that ran deep, he said. "We believed in discipline. We respected officers. We followed commands."[43] B-24 bomber pilot Lieutenant Jim Kirkland was one such officer, and his drive focused his crew. When he arrived in theater, he spoke to his men to reveal the substance of his will. He intended to take them to war. "My philosophy of flying missions as a B-24 pilot [in combat] was simple: stay busy. I didn't like to sit around and think about missions. I told my crew my goal was to fly every mission possible. That meant often flying deeper and deeper into enemy territory to bomb, but, so be it."[44]

John Watson, a pilot in a medium bomber, echoed that sentiment. He made a quiet but profound promise to himself, and he put his reputation as a man behind it: "I had vowed to myself that if I were leading, we would attack any target which seemed at all reachable."[45]

For the balance of the war, it was a promise he kept.

The Münster raiders were stirred from their sleep at 0300 hours and ate a hot breakfast of farm-fresh eggs. They attended a briefing during which the mission was laid out in exacting detail, and then they gathered their flight gear and made their way out to the hardstands where their planes were fueled and loaded with bombs. After a blessing from the preacher, they climbed up into their B-17s, almost three thousand men in all, each ready, trained, and afraid.[46] John Hibbard, a radio operator and waist gunner on a B-17, recalled how a fellow waist gunner, Myron Sanchez, nicknamed "Snatch" by his buddies, had handled his fear. "That was Snatch; he was scared silly until he started to shoot, and then he was all business on the friendly end of his .50-cal machine gun. It is the same with everyone. When you can fight back, to feel the gun bucking in your fists, you aren't afraid."[47] Pilot Bill Kamemitsa liked to say that one part of fear came about from what you didn't know but that the other part was what you did know, and that was the tough part: "You have these moments when you remember how intensely scared you were, how frightened you were when you saw the first aircraft go down and the first time you got shot at. It's something you can never tell anybody about until you've been there yourself. Somebody's trying to kill you and mother isn't there!"[48]

The aircrews manned their bombers and began to spin up their engines. For the next two hours, the airbases reverberated with the sound of propellers beating the air in a symphony of noise that was the unmistakable sound of war. In villages 5 miles away, the locals lifted a head and nodded: another mission was underway.

One by one the bombers shuddered from nose to tail with a particular sense of urgency as the pilots coaxed their lumbering giants off their hardstands with a burst of engine power. With the airframe shaking, they inched around the perimeter track like cats low on their haunches until they eased into a line for takeoff that stretched back a dozen planes. It was a ballet of well-orchestrated motions, timed to smoothly put several hundred heavily armed airplanes in the sky, one after the other. "The missions were so precisely planned, that you had a time to be in your plane, a time to start engines, a time to taxi out which was designed to put you in the proper place in the formation," recalled Eighth Air Force bomber pilot Lee Toothman. "When your turn came, you rolled into the center of the runway, pushed the engines to full power with the brakes on, and waited for the green light, released brakes, and prayed that once again you could break the bonds of earth."[49] In an operational cycle that would surely cause a modern air traffic controller to faint, a bomber took off every thirty seconds.

When their turn came, the pilots swung the noses of their bombers down the centerline of the runways and pushed up their throttles until their engines were at full power and their Forts were straining against their brakes. All ten crewmen felt the shaking down to the very marrow of their bones, and more than a few cast a quick prayer to God. With one hard jerk, the pilot released the brakes and the bombers lurched down the runway, cradling 6,000 pounds of high explosives, gaining precious airspeed as the runway grew ever shorter until to the relief of all on board the nose lifted up and they climbed into the air in a banking left-hand turn, swirling up ever higher like a swarm of hornets rising from the ground.

Out of the windows of the cockpit, to the left or right, the pilots could see other B-17s rising above their airbases as far as the eye could see.

Inside, the gunners held their fifties in their fists and began their watchful vigil. Little did anyone know that they were flying into a trap.

German radar stations along the coastal area of Pas-de-Calais, France, pointed their beams toward the marshaling areas above East Anglia, where they picked up the first hint of the incoming B-17s. The German fighter and flak units in western France, Belgium, Holland, and northwestern Germany were notified and immediately put on fifteen-minute alert. Grabmann continued to cipher the radar echoes, playing an exquisite game of chess with his counterpart in England using measured, calculated moves. Where were the bombers headed? How many were there?

To order his fighters into the air too soon would waste precious fuel, but to wait too long would mean missing the bombers altogether. Grabmann believed the Americans would be flying a shallow penetration mission, which meant that the target had to be somewhere in France or western Germany. Playing out his hand, he held his fighters on the ground, a cruel delay for the Luftwaffe pilots who were ready to go. "For me the minutes between being ordered to Cockpit Readiness and receiving the order to take-off were the most terrible of all," said Luftwaffe fighter pilot Lieutenant Hans Iffland. "After the order came to get airborne one was too busy to think about one's possible fate, but waiting to go, with nothing to do but think about what might happen, that was the worst time."[50]

Inside the ready rooms, the clock ticked. German pilots crumped down their cigarettes only to light another. At 1138 hours, the first wave of B-17s turned toward the English Channel. The second wave followed at 1153. The clock soon ticked passed 1200 hours.

The Münster raiders were following a method of attack that had been largely unchanged since the introduction of the combat box formation by General Curtis LeMay in the spring of 1943, but the Germans were doing anything but playing by the old script. For a country that had been on the offensive for almost four years, the fact that American bombers were getting through to targets inside their own borders was viewed as a serious military shortcoming that needed to be quickly remedied. Such was the situation in October 1943.

Several months earlier, in July 1943, British bombers had flown through the German air defensive in such strength and with such ease that they were able to burn down most of Hamburg in a night of bombing so thoroughly devastating that smoke lingered over the northern city for days. Hamburg was added to "the growing list of those which are now liabilities and not assets to the enemy," said the British in their dry assessment of the results. In fact, Hamburg had been nearly burned to the ground. Hundreds of civilians had been caught in a firestorm of unheard lethality, killing women and children as well as men. When news of Hamburg crossed Hitler's desk, he exploded with such venom that the Luftwaffe's chief of staff committed suicide rather than face him another day.[51]

The rest of the Luftwaffe, however, looked for a solution, and the focus was on shooting down the Americans. The first B-17 arrived in England in the summer of 1942, an impressive war machine from front to back. Nearly three times the size of a German fighter, and larger still than any British bomber, the American B-17s, and the B-24s like them, dwarfed anything yet in the sky. It was 74 feet long with a 103-foot wingspan. It was powered by four Wright Cyclone engines, each rated at 1,200 horsepower. It flew as fast as 295 miles per hour, but carried some 9,000 pounds of bombs. In a time when a large aircraft had a crew of four or five airmen, the Flying Fortress was enormous: it carried a crew of ten.[52]

At first, the German fighter pilots were intimidated by its size and how it filled their windshields when they attacked. "When the American Viermots came we really had to get used to their size and numbers," said one German fighter pilot. "The things grew bigger and bigger and all of our attacks were commenced and broken off much too early as we were afraid of flying into the 'barn doors.'"[53] The volume of fire a single B-17 could unleash was staggering. Guns on the bombers bristled like the quills on a porcupine. There were two .50-caliber machine guns in the Plexiglas nose, a chin turret below that with two more .50-cal guns, twin fifties in the ball turret, twin fifties in the top turret, machine guns on either side at the waist of the bomber, and two more fifties in the tail. More than seven hundred rounds of bullets were stacked in boxes beside each gunner, each round capable of blowing a hole in the engine of a Me-109 or a FW-190. For the unwary German, the B-17s were killing machines. And they only grew in potency.

With every passing month, the size of the American bomber force grew. More pilots and more aircrews arrived. Missions of eighteen bombers soon became missions of thirty bombers, then fifty bombers, and then ninety bombers per mission. By July 1943, more than a hundred bombers would assemble for the raids against Nazi Germany, and by September the number was up to three hundred. Moreover, those missions were now reaching into the Fatherland, not just the Western European rail yards and airfields under German control. Bombs were hitting their homeland.

By October 1943, American manufacturers were producing airplanes at such prodigious rates that bombers and fighters could now forest a farm in England with aluminum wings so tightly packed that scarcely a ray of light would reach the ground. Already some one thousand P-47 Thunderbolts, P-38 Lightnings, and the new P-51 Mustangs were in England with an equal number of B-24 Liberators and B-17 Fortresses. Although the American forces had yet to land a blow as devastating as Hamburg, it was increasingly evident that it was only a matter of time. The German Armed Forces Command Intelligence Service that month issued an estimate that the American armament programs would continue to produce some five thousand airplanes a month and that fresh aircrews would be arriving in England in numbers that would nearly match that pace. With the certainty that the size and frequency of the American bombing attacks would only grow, the German air defense commanders took radical action. Stopping the B-17s was now an imperative.[54]

In the aftermath of the Schweinfurt–Regensburg victory, the Luftwaffe began a series of experiments to find better ways of avoiding the guns on the bombers while also taking out more of them in a single attack. The successful Schweinfurt–Regensburg defense, which was a disaster for the Americans, had really been an anomaly for the Germans. It was a long mission involving many hours over enemy territory and thus exposed the American bombers to lengthy and repetitive German fighter attacks along the entire route of flight. Not all raids would give the Luftwaffe that same margin of time. A solution was needed to shoot down the American bombers faster, and with fewer losses of their own fighters.

The Germans first tried coming in from the behind, as they had done so successfully against the Russian bombers on the Eastern Front, but the Forts were too well armed in the tail and German losses were high. Attacks in the midsection were even worse. But there was one weakness: the Forts were poorly armed from the front. "This was our only chance of surviving," said Luftwaffe fighter pilot Adolf Dickfeld. "The huge, four-engine bombers had scarcely any defenses to the front, just one puny machine gun. Behind, beneath and to the sides they fired at us poor swine with twelve heavy weapons. It was easy to figure out how quickly we'd be shot down."[55]

"We were scared to fly in from almost any direction but the front," agreed another German fighter pilot. "They could release such a volume of fire at us."[56] Yet a third fighter pilot compared the cone of firepower around a B-17 to a shower: "Just imagine standing under a shower with 160 jets of water pouring out and not getting wet!! That of course is quite impossible. Even when we attacked with four planes line abreast in an effort to split up the defensive fire statistically there were still 40 guns firing at each one of us."[57]

The frontal attack had the makings of a brilliant solution, save for the blinding speeds at which the planes would converge while guns were blazing. Said a German pilot, "The new method did have one disadvantage however; attacker and target raced towards one another at almost 1,000 kph. Firing time had shrunk to fractions of a second and if one's reactions weren't lightning fast then you were into the American bomber and you can imagine what took place then."[58]

But the frontal attack was a solution, and in various German experiments, it had worked spectacularly well against the American bombers. To teach this new tactic to their fighter squadrons, the Germans made models of the B-17s, complete with small sticks radiating out from the gun ports. The models circulated and they held meetings with the pilots until their frontline forces were retrained, and frontal attacks were added to the mix of strategies.

More importantly, the German fighter pilots came to understand that their job was not to fight American pilots, but rather to destroy American bombers. Unexpectedly, American airwar doctrine helped achieve that end. The Germans were quick to notice that American escort planes invariably ran low on fuel and had to turn back, which left the bombers open to attack. More puzzling, they also noticed that American fighter pilots rarely continued a dogfight if that dogfight took them too far away from their bombers. German fighter pilot Hermann Buchner experienced that during his first encounter with a bomber stream when his opponents suddenly stopped and went back to the bombers. "Almost immediately a wild turning fight began," wrote Buchner of the first stage of his attack. "I circled and shot at the enemy. Luckily, the majority of the U.S. fighters had quit the turning battle and had continued on their course." Incredibly, rather than staying in the fight until one plane or the other was shot down, the Americans were simply breaking off the engagement, allowing Buchner to regroup.[59]

Combining the frontal attack, and with a focus on the bombers rather than the fighter escorts, resulted in a deadly new German attack profile. "It was our aim to break up the bomber formation and destroy it," wrote Luftwaffe Commander Adolf Galland. "Thus we tried if possible to attack the same formation over and over again in order to weaken its defensive power."[60]

Attacking a formation was one thing; choosing the right weapon for maximum effect was another. This, then, became the next step in the German reorganization. During the summer of 1943, the Germans also experimented with new ways of taking down B-17s. Adolf Galland ran off a list that sounded like a menu of death written by the Devil himself. Said Galland, we tried "rockets, increase in aircraft armament, aerial bombs on bomber formations, the trailing rope with or without bomb attached, rocket batteries and cluster bombs with automatic photocells. The men and the fighter force were experimenting and constructing all the time."[61] The Germans flew up and dropped bombs on the B-17s from above and fired mortars into them from the side. They tried dragging chains through the sky with explosive bundles snapping at the ends. They launched surface-to-air missiles and experimented with large, 30-mm cannon shells. But time and again, they came back to the rockets. Of all the ways to take down a bomber, the air-to-air rockets worked surprisingly well.[62]

Changes were now afoot. The results of the summer experiments were combined with the new frontal attacks, and a new German attack strategy was adopted on October 1, 1943. The German fighters would form up as a group with the heavier, twin-engine fighters armed with air-to-air rockets under their wings in the front with single-seat fighters behind them. The twins would blow holes in the escorts and create gaps into which would come the more maneuverable German fighters with their machine guns and 20-mm cannons. The German twins would continue to use their rockets to break apart the bomber boxes while the single-engine fighters would follow with their bullets and shells. Frontal attacks were preferred, but any attack was ultimately acceptable.

The first opportunity to test the new tactics occurred on October 2 when the Eighth Air Force launched a raid against Emden, Germany. Unfortunately, most of the American bombers had to abort due to bad weather, and nothing came of it. The next opportunity came on October 4, but once again weather wreaked havoc and the 250 American bombers never found their targets—nor did the German fighter pilots find the bombers. Poor weather kept the B-17s grounded until October 8, when the Americans attacked again, but the weather remained bad, forcing nearly half of the Forts to divert to a secondary target and leaving the rest of the formations poorly organized and barely escorted. The Germans were able to shoot down more than thirty of the bombers, but it wasn't a fair test. The Americans were too disorganized, and the hunting had been too easy.

Restless to see their new tactics tested in action, it was the Münster raid on October 10 that provided the first full combat experience. The weather was clear, the fighter controllers were tracking the bombers, the German airbases were alerted. Barring any unforeseen circumstances, the Germans would have a real test of the new doctrine.

It had all the makings of a massacre.

As a major rail yard within the elaborate route structure of the German national rail system, the city of Münster was almost entirely given over to a giant erector set-like assembly of tracks and switches that ultimately and importantly served as a gateway to the industrial Ruhr Valley. In the Ruhr, enormous factories with towering smokestacks carpeted a region along the Rhine River, a region that was well known for excellent natural resources and ample electricity. Coal, iron ore, steel, and petrochemicals came from the Ruhr, as did materiel manufactured from them, such as tanks and guns. Cutting the rail lines at Münster would significantly disrupt the Ruhr, and as went the Ruhr, so went the German war machine.

By 1300 hours on October 10, 1943, the entire force of 236 B-17s was in the air, a virtual sky full of aluminum fuselages and wings made even denser by 216 P-47s flying top cover. The formation was 15 miles long and took five minutes to pass over a fixed point on the ground. Groups of eighteen bombers were clustered in self-defending boxes with three boxes each flying as a single group. Grabmann watched them on his radar screens and elevated the alert. He now had 350 German fighters poised to jump, with the antiaircraft gun crews crawling over their 88s like ants.

"The scenes in Germany's skies are indescribable," remembered Major Günther Rall, a top Luftwaffe ace. "Nobody who has sat in a fighter aircraft and seen the thousands of condensation trails stretching from east to west like a huge ruler being drawn across the heavens will ever be able to forget the sight."[63] By 1400 hours, Grabmann was certain that the lines now pointed toward Münster. He ordered his fighters into the sky.[64]

The launch of a German fighter group is a kinetic event unlike any in military aviation. It was uniquely Luftwaffe, where wide fields rather than concrete runways were the norm and fighters could take off with scarcely a moment's separation. In an explosion of noise that sent a burst of adrenaline down the flight line, Gerd Wiegand's airbase erupted in a cloud of black smoke as engines roared to life. In a prearranged order, four planes took off shoulder to shoulder in a line abreast formation, rooster tails of dust and dirt rising behind them as they raced across the grass and roared into the sky. "The fighter scramble takeoff was normal for German fighter unit," said a German pilot. An entire squadron could be airborne in barely a moment.[65]

The leading elements of the Luftwaffe defense winged their way toward their prebriefed assembly area marked by colored smoke shells fired by 88-mm flak crews. They arrived promptly and organized themselves for the attack, forming into their combat groups as they listened to updates on the progress of the B-17s that were being broadcast over their military frequencies. As the bombers made their last turn, the German controllers ordered transports and training flights to get down immediately. The Battle of Münster was on.[66]

If the measure of a good airplane was how it handled in the sky, the measure of a good bomber crew was how it comported itself in battle. A sure indication of that was silence. The best crews scarcely breathed a word on the ship's intercoms until they had something important to say, such as reporting an enemy plane coming at them. Even then the call outs were short and crisp: "Enemy! Nine o'clock!"—and that was all it took. Remembered one navigator on an American bomber, "On every raid I was on, the stickier the situation got, the more intercom discipline. Mostly silence interrupted by terse calling out of fighter locations and other germane information."[67] On some occasions, a crewman from one bomber crew was forced to substitute on another bomber, and the differences in discipline were often telling. One seasoned B-17 tail gunner had to fly with a greenhorn crew. When he heard the newbies jabbering on the intercom, he could scarcely hide his contempt—and he let them know it: "The crew was inexperienced and they really showed it. They kept tying up the intercom with a lot of nonsense till I lost patience and told them to stay off the wire unless they had something important to say. It worked for a while."[68]

As important as intercom discipline was, it was even more important to have a good set of eyes and a swiveling neck sweeping the airspace for the first tiny spec in the distance that signaled the approach of a Me-109. At the speeds of fighters and bombers, battles started and ended in seconds, and the Germans used every trick in the book to get the jump on the bombers. There was nothing worse than letting a Messerschmitt hide in the sun or climb up a thick contrail behind a bomber with no one the wiser until the first shotgun blast of a cannon shell exploded against the fuselage. "I saw the approaching fighter up ahead in the distance," remembered a ball turret gunner of the approach of a German fighter. "It quickly passed from my view and I gave the word to the top turret gunner. He must have lost it in the sun because a few minutes later the entire plane shook as the control wheels flew out of the hands of the pilot and copilot. A burst of cannon fire had cut the control cables. The airplane flipped upside down showering me in shell casings. The navigator struggled forward without his parachute and opened my turret door saving my life. Just as I emerged from the turret the airplane exploded. The next thing I knew I was hanging in space from my parachute."[69]

That's how quickly a good day turned bad. As the Münster raiders penetrated the airspace over Germany, the gunners on the B-17s had their heads on a swivel and were sweeping the barrels of their fifties across the skies.

The intercoms were absolutely silent.

The coastal flak batteries opened up first, barking fire skyward at the murderous rate of between 3,000 and 16,000 shells per downed bomber. In the event of a pointblank hit, the only evidence that a B-17 had ever been in the sky was usually little more than a cloud of smoke and four engines falling away. Near misses were just as sudden and unforgiving. A nearby burst might send pieces of shrapnel punching through the skin of the bomber as if it were made of rice paper. One man's arm was neatly cleaved off at his elbow by a fragment of flak; another survived a near miss but it was so close that he felt the heat of the shrapnel as it passed through the navigator's station. Flak was unpredictable; it killed suddenly and without warning—and there was little an airman could do but take it. It was the unnerving feeling of being hunted that made flak fields so terrifying. Remembered one airman, "Whenever I left a heavy flak area, I cooled down as if after some violent and heavy exertion."[70]

The batteries fired their deadly shells skyward, but the first round of German flak was ineffective. Puffs of black bracketed the formations, but most of it was off the mark and of little consequence. The bombers pressed on.

In the sweep of the phosphorous arm over the face of the radar scope, Grabmann scanned the boxes for gaps and holes, and he saw that one group of B-17s was flying without its fighter escort, a nice opening for his men. Grabmann calmly turned two hundred of his fighters toward the unescorted boxes and using precise commands, steered his pilots alongside the bombers, just out of range of their guns. He then rolled another force of aircraft forward and prepared them to turn in for the head-on attack.

It was masterful. Minute by minute the Germans inched into position. From abeam the formation of B-17s, with their propellers clawing at the thin air at 20,000 feet and their mouths covered by oxygen masks, the Luftwaffe pilots slowly turned their heads and looked. The American airmen could nearly see the whites of their eyes. "It was shaky waiting for them to attack," wrote a tail gunner in his diary. "They flew alongside our formation on both sides, but just out of range. All I could do, besides being scared, was to spray each as they came in and call for evasive action."[71]

John Hibbard was at his waist gun as he watched the German fighters in the distance. They seemed to be exceedingly confident, he thought, getting organized before they picked their moment, but not in any hurry whatsoever. "There were between sixty and seventy

AUTUMN 1943

Me-109s and FW-190s out there in a jumbled mass milling around like a swarm of mad bees that someone had just stirred up." As one fighter group shadowed, the other group flew forward to get ready. "They flew ahead of our formation just out of range of our guns and formed a long line three or four deep to attack," said Hibbard.[72]

When they were ready, those lines would come in guns blazing. And so they did.

American bomber formations were designed to cocoon the B-17s in a sheath of defensive firepower created by clustering the bomber together in a three-dimensional grid that layered them in the sky so that in total the group had the most guns possible pointed out toward the enemy. The basic building block of a formation was the combat box. A combat box was built in increments of three bombers that flew together and joined up with three other bombers and so on until eighteen bombers were assembled. This combat box of eighteen bombers would them form up with two more combat boxes until a combat element of fifty-four planes had been assembled.

In a combat element, there was the high box, the low box, and a lead box. The lead box directed all of the bombers in the element. When the lead pilot in the lead box turned, they all turned. When he climbed, they all climbed. And when he toggled his bombs, they all toggled theirs. The trick was to stay close together. The slightest gap in a formation gave the enemy an opportunity to pry open a box and gang up on the weakest bombers. If the enemy gained that toehold, one by one the German fighters would persist until the bombers were gone and they had extinguished an entire element.[73] "Close, tight formation was the secret of survival from fighter attacks because of the concentrated fire," said Robert Copp, a B-17 pilot. "Circumstances also played a big part in whether you can survive. Your chances were a hell of a lot better the further up the box you could get. The fellows in the back of the formation were the most vulnerable. Somebody gets shot down from the middle of the pack and your protection begins to break down."[74]

The massing German fighters were about to execute their new strategy against the Münster bombers. The attack would be predicated on breaking up one box at a time and then systematically picking off the strays until all fifty-four B-17s were gone. The three boxes in the lead element of the Münster formation were made up of the 95th Bomb Group, the 100th Bomb Group, and the 390th Bomb Group. The attack began against the low box, the 100th Bomb Group, which flew under strength with thirteen bombers. On command, the German fighters turned into the bombers and came in with their rockets firing and guns chattering. In an explosion of rockets, cannon shells, and bullets, steel poured out of the fighters and into the formation. Bullets punched through the cockpits, shredding windshields, cutting cables, blowing apart instruments panels, and slamming into the bodies of the pilots. The B-17s shuddered under the impact as German pilots streaked through the formations, pouring out everything they had. Bullets pierced the aluminum skin of the Boeings; some hit oxygen tanks, hydraulic systems, fuel tanks, and bombs. In one bomber, a fire flared up and grew in intensity as it fed off the bomber's hydraulics. The cabin became a chaotic blast furnace of flames as crewmen scrambled to get out, but the heat was so intense and the fire burned so fast that most of the men were incinerated in seconds. The dying B-17 arced away from the formation trailing fingers of flames.

With guns rattling on both sides, the sky became a blizzard of debris. The blast overpressures from the German 20-mm cannon shells were blowing off pieces of the B-17's engines, rudders, ailerons, and wings, and each piece was becoming a deadly missile of its own. American airmen bailed out, and they themselves became the hazards. Bodies fell through the sky, some dead, some alive, some without parachutes. "The Luftwaffe must have put up every fighter they had," remembered one airman. "Fighters hit us from every angle. I saw Forts blowing up, Forts and fighters going down smoking and burning, wings coming off, tails coming off, the sky full of parachutes. One guy floated into a low Fort—he was churned up by the propellers and took the Fort with him. It just rolled over into a dive. The sky was so full of tracers, 20-mm cannon shells exploding, and even rockets. Steel was ripping into our ship with sickening sounds. There were times when I was afraid to shoot for fear of hitting one of our own planes or some poor guy in a parachute."[75]

Within seven minutes, twelve of thirteen bombers in the low box had been fatally wounded or shot down. Of the 140 air officers in the 100th who had arrived in England in the weeks leading up to Münster, only three were left on flying status the week after.[76]

With the low box all but wiped out, a second group of German fighters unleashed their rockets on the high box. *Whoosh! Whoosh!* The rockets raced through the sky and blasted away. "The fighters laid back about 1,000 yards out of range of our 50-caliber machine guns and began firing air-to-air rockets and 37-mm cannon fire into our formation," recounted James Goff, a navigator.[77] Thirty-five Me-110s bounced the Forts and shot some seventy rockets into them. Two bombers took direct hits, one disappearing in a grisly burst of steel, vaporized fuel, black smoke, and human flesh with streaks radiating outward marking the final flight of the four engines. The attacks were vicious and unrelenting. "We were leading the high squadron of nine planes—only two of us got back," said a crewman. "They attacked the tail four abreast and four deep—sixteen at a time. Their wing guns lit up like Luna Park (in Coney Island). These guys were not fooling."[78] Eight of the eighteen B-17s were shot down or fatally wounded. The rest were hammered by shells and bullets.[79]

The second box was now all but gone.

Mercifully, the fighters pulled back and held their fire as the bombers came over the city of Münster. Here, though, was a new problem: they encountered antiaircraft batteries. Roy Kennett, a radio operator, remembered the flak: "The target run, when you hit the initial point, the plane locks in and the bombardier takes over. When he's on the run, we just stay in formation. That's where the flak is heaviest—protecting the target. We've got five or six minutes just going down the line of death with those greasy black puffs going off all around you … all you can do is sit there and take it. You can't go left, you can't go right—you just go down the gauntlet."[80]

An 88-mm antiaircraft gun had a 23-foot-long barrel that could fire a 25-pound shell 12 miles in any direction. Each shell was manually set to explode after a certain number of seconds. Once it did, a fiery blast of some 1,400 shards of jagged metal was violently blown in every direction, capable of killing a B-17 even 20 yards away. "Although the fighter was the deadlier of the two you could do something back at him and that relieved the tension," said a gunner. "But whenever there was a heavy concentration of flak all you could do was squeeze yourself into a ball and hope they won't kill you."[81]

"Flak was worse than fighters," agreed William B. McGuire, a ball turret gunner. "Flak hitting the plane sounded like someone was flogging the fuselage with a length of chain. Sometimes it would explode so near you could feel the concussion."[82] Black puffs dotted the sky like mushrooms. Some of the flak was grouped in barrage fire, and some of it tracked the planes. The shells that missed were terrifying in their own right and triggered nervous thoughts of what might have been.

Lieutenant "Doc" Thayer watched the shells coming up at his plane. "I could see the vivid red flashes of flames from the gun barrels, and then, for the first time ever, I saw the 88-mm flak shells themselves, distinct against the snowy background, coming all the way up as if in slow motion, then rapidly accelerating the closer they got." Most of the shells burst above his formation, but one went through Thayer's airplane, cutting a clean path all the way through bottom to top. Miraculously, it was a dud.[83]

Looking down, one pilot saw that the ground was covered by the muzzle flashes from the 15,000-pound guns. The shells could reach up and kill as high as 35,000 feet. Some pilots used the winking points of light on the ground to steer clear of the shells. "By looking over the side of the cockpit, at the gun emplacement, we could see every time the battery fired in unison," remembered one pilot. "A slight turn in either direction of a few degrees and the 88-mm shells would burst off to the side of our formation, an exciting spectacle to behold. When the battery stopped firing the gunners were adjusting to allow for our change in course. The next time they started firing a salvo, we would begin a slight turn in the opposite direction."[84]

In the frenzy of the Münster battle, Luftwaffe pilot Gerd Wiegand forgot where he was until he looked up and saw one of the bombers open its bay doors and the first stick of bombs falling away. Pulling up sharply, he streaked to the top and rolled over onto the tail of a B-17. His machine guns stitched a line across an engine on the left wing before hitting a fuel tank on the right. Wiegand kept meticulous notes on all his missions; he and his wingman followed the smoking B-17 to the ground, where it exploded 12 miles outside of the city.[85]

After bombs away, the Münster bombers bobbed and weaved, but then, like a breath once exhaled, the flak was gone and it was suddenly quiet. "We all knew what that meant," said a B-17 pilot.[86]

The fighters were back.

With the low box gone and the high box bloodied, the fighters wheeled around and bore down on the lead box. Once again, the attack started with rockets. "They would stay out of range and then their wings would light up with a large orange flame and out came two rockets like a large ball of flame," remembered a waist gunner.[87] The rockets blew gaps into the formations into which the single-engine fighters streaked in and laced the Boeings with their machine gun fire. Like the blades of a saber flashing through the sky, the fighters darted in and around the bombers, firing with everything they had. The bombers poured out lead in defense, and they did a fine job. Wrapped in their electrical suits and draped in aprons lined with steel plates, the gunners looked like butchers in a meat shop. With their fifties bucking in their fists, they followed the Focke-Wulfs around the sky. Smoke wrapped around them and shell casings covered their feet as the burnt cordite cocooned their facemasks in gray. Their tracers arced toward the Focke-Wulfs and Messerschmitts, the aim always just ahead of the planes. One gunner laid fire across the back of a German pilot's canopy and then cut off a wing like a hot knife through butter. The Focke-Wulf spiraled out of the sky. Another put out a field of fire and held it while a German pilot flew right into it. Another German was gone.

Despite the incredible volume of return fire, the Boeings were nonetheless taking a beating no structural engineer ever thought possible. Webb Pruitt Lee was a pilot from Oklahoma. He would earn almost every medal the Air Forces had, but Münster was his most difficult mission. He survived the flight into the target, he survived the flak over the target, and he even made it off the target—but it came at a price that neither he nor his crew would have willingly paid. Struggling to stay airborne on his last working engine, and with FW-190s circling above, ready to come in and finish off his plane, he called for help. Out of nowhere, a lone American fighter found him and tucked in just off his wing. It was an answered prayer. The Germans scattered. "He stayed with us a long time, talking to us on the radio until his fuel started running low," said Lee. "I asked him to stay with us a little while longer. He said, 'No, I have got to go. I'm not going to have enough fuel to make it back as it is now. I've got to go.' We told him goodbye and as he started to pull up, he got a direct hit. All we saw was a puff of smoke and he was gone. You can imagine how all our crew felt."[88]

Of the 274 American bombers that took off, 38 aborted because of mechanical reasons, leaving 236 in the attack, of which 182 made it to the target and released their bombs. The bombing was effective: the rail yard was reduced to twisted steel and burnt-out buildings.

Luftwaffe records show that more than 530 German fighter sorties were flown against the Münster bombers. Pilots on both sides remember that the fighting was as intense as any in the war.

The new tactics worked better than anyone in the German high command could have possibly imagined. Of the 236 American bombers that flew the mission, 30 were shot down and 105 were badly damaged by flak and gun fire; 306 airmen were missing and presumed to be dead or taken as prisoners of war. Inside the returning bombers, two more airmen were dead and eighteen were injured.

Against those devastating numbers, the Luftwaffe had lost just twelve men. Celebrations welled up at the Luftwaffe airbases as pilots zoomed in over their airfields and waggled their wings, a sure sign of an aerial victory. The talk was energetic and animated and not entirely the exaggerated boasts of adrenalized fighter pilots. If thirty bombers could be blown out of the sky in a matter of forty minutes, one could only imagine the possibilities with more fighters and more time to pick apart the Forts.[89] One could imagine the bombers being stopped once and for all.

Exhausted, tired, and in shock, the battered survivors of the Eighth Air Force limped home. It was a resounding defeat, no matter how accurate the bombing had been. Years later, one crewman remembered it as if it were yesterday. "This old Fort really took a beating—I don't know how it stayed in the air. The damage   half the nose blown out; six feet of the vertical stabilizer blown off; cables severed; all of my windows blown out; one 20-mm went through the left side of the tail above my hands and blew up just outside of my windows. All in all, the ground crew counted 136 holes."[90]

A weary radio operator lowered himself to the ground and watched his tail gunner being lifted out of the cabin. The gunner had taken eleven hits, including one round squarely between his eyes. "The Lord was showing no favorites that day," summed up a pilot who suffered a similar mission. None of the Münster crews could have said it better.[91]

During the debriefs that followed with the bomber crews, the battle was reconstructed, but the fog of war shrouded any real insights. The rockets, the shells, the machine gun fire, the twin-engine fighters—the sheer intensity of it all was the story the intelligence officers heard from the beat-up airmen. They were given a glass of whiskey and sent back to their huts.

What hadn't come out was a truth far more troubling than the combat losses, and that truth was that the Germans had been completely and thoroughly coordinated. What hadn't come out was that the Germans were evolving into more sophisticated life form, and like all evolved life forms, their instincts for self-preservation were finely—and dangerously—honed. For the first time ever in the airwar, an entire combat box had been functionally destroyed, a second nearly so, and an entire combat element mere minutes from being wiped out. The insight the Americans were missing was chilling. If the Germans could do this once, they could do it again. Strategic bombing could very well grind to a halt.

The Eighth Air Force needed to change. No military organization could suffer the loss of 10 percent of its forces in a single day of combat and still function as a serious fighting force—and yet that was exactly what was happening to the Eighth. Repeatedly.

But no documents suggest that any particular message was deciphered from the ruins of Münster. Rather, next to nothing was being done by anyone to change anything as the next raid against German was being planned.

Indeed, before the month came to an end, the Münster losses would soon seem trivial.

Only then would things finally change.

CHAPTER 3

POINTBLANK

President Franklin D. Roosevelt gave no quarter to those who held fast to the idea that the average German had no accountability for the actions of Hitler, and thus he demanded that there be no negotiated peace with Germany. In Roosevelt's view, Hitler mirrored the will of the nation, and vice versa. "Too many people here and in England hold to the view that the German people as a whole are not responsible for what has taken place—that only a few Nazi leaders are responsible," said the President. "That unfortunately is not based on fact. The German people as a whole must have it driven home to them that the whole nation has been engaged in a lawless conspiracy against the decencies of modern civilization."[92]

The job to drive that home was started by the airmen. The formal statement of operations that aligned the operations of the British Royal Air Force with those of the United States Army Air Forces into a cohesive battle plan for an air attack against Germany was called the Combined Bomber Offensive. The CBO distilled Roosevelt's position into language as stark as any written during the war. The mission of the heavy bomber was to cause "the progressive destruction and dislocation of the German military, industrial and economic system, and the undermining of the morale of the German people to a point where their capacity for armed resistance is fatally weakened."

As definitive as that sounded, it was in fact, surprisingly vague.[93] Through the early summer of 1943, the calm weather that canopied England and Western Europe was ruffled by a heated debate that raged between the Americans and the British over how to best pull that off. Because not a single Allied soldier was as yet doing battle on the continent of Europe, the debate centered entirely on how to best use the bombers. On that point, the Allies were split by positions that were scarcely nuanced. The British believed in area attacks, a term that generally meant indiscriminate bombing of German cities. The British argued that by destroying population centers, the Allies could eventually bring about the collapse of German society and with it the will to fight, thereby meeting the objective to fatally weaken the German war machine, leading to unconditional surrender. With most of the women and children evacuated to the suburbs, the argument held, a German city was now in fact little more than "labour camps employed almost solely by the war effort," or so said the British. And if a factory that manufactured war materials was destroyed in the process, all the better. Furthermore, they argued, civilians' homes should be viewed as military barracks. As if actions could prove their point, the British began their bombing campaign by launching nighttime raids. Cities were so large that at night, you didn't have to aim.

The Americans believed in a different approach. American targeting committees had painstakingly dissected the industrial and economic veins through which the lifeblood of the German military pulsed and identified essential factories and transportation synapses that, if destroyed, would create shortages and bottlenecks sufficient to catastrophically weaken the German war machine and thus open the continent to the land invasion codenamed Operation Overlord.

Overlord would begin the invasion that would end in the final assault on the German capital and trigger, by land forces and heavy artillery, the total surrender of Hitler's Third Reich. A successful land invasion, not bombing cities, was thus the precursor to the collapse of Germany, and the defeat of the Luftwaffe was a precursor to Overlord. The American position was that D-Day required air superiority, which in turn required the elimination of the Luftwaffe, which in turn required precision bombing of military targets. Area attacks would do nothing to reduce the fighting capability of the German war machine.

In the end, the British accepted a vaguely worded agreement that allowed each side to interpret their orders more or less as they wanted. The British could go on bombing cities while the Americans bombed factories. Although in many British quarters there was the faint hope that their own favored strategy would pay off before the invasion, in the end the British knew the truth. "The final blow," wrote British planners, "can only be struck across the Channel."[94] A targeting compromise was crafted as a codicil to the Combined Bomber Offensive and was issued on June 10, 1943. It was called The Pointblank Directive.

The Pointblank Directive prioritized the Luftwaffe for destruction over all other German targets as the immediate objective leading to the D-Day invasion. The focus for the British and American air forces would be "(1) the destruction of the German Air Force, its factories and supporting installations and its ball-bearing plants; and (2) the destruction of transportation facilities."[95] The Luftwaffe would be attacked behind the lines, cutting off the flow of new planes forward and on their front lines to destroy their airfields.[96] As it happened, it would be executed almost entirely by the Americans.

Henry A. "Hap" Arnold, commanding general of the United States Army Air Forces, was as near a cradle aviator as any could be. A West

Point graduate of modest accomplishment, Arnold had watched the development of the airplane with eyes that saw the magic of Bernoulli's Principle (a phenomenon that applies to the lift of an airplane) as the future of warfare. In 1911, at a time when the most dashing and daring in the army sought out the artillery, Arnold instead sought out the Air Corps, which sent him to train under the Wright Brothers, who taught him to fly and certified him as a military pilot. Tall, energetic, and with eyes that could sear a subordinate as easily as they could charm a diplomat, Arnold's determination caught the attention of fellow U.S. Army officer George Marshall, who would later become Army chief of staff. Stationed together in the Philippines during the early years of their career, Marshall, who outranked Arnold, jotted down Arnold's name in a black book he carried in which he listed people he believed would be important to the future of the Army. Marshall watched the young lieutenant rise through the ranks over the next several decades.

Despite the potential Marshall saw in him, Arnold did as much as anyone could to derail his own career. Hap Arnold was a principled person—and not always in ways that advanced his own cause. He believed from the start in the very devilish possibilities of raining down war on the enemy from the heavens. While others vacillated and debated the potential of military aviation, Arnold saw the future. It was aerial bombing, and he was all in. When the exceedingly powerful 1920s Navy fought the Army over the practicality of aerial bombardment, Arnold rallied to the side of Billy Mitchell, the undisputed pioneer in the field. It was Mitchell who had sunk a test battleship in 1921 by aerial bombardment, and it was Mitchell who would become the outspoken critic of the Navy's continued—and outdated, in his mind—investments in battleships. Although regarded as a hero in World War I, Mitchell soon became known as an agitator who rankled both the Army and the Navy.

As a midcareer officer, at a time when the slightest step outside of the rigid lines of conventional doctrine would doom any career, Arnold testified on behalf of Mitchell when he was court martialed for comments related to a ballooning accident. Arnold continued to support Mitchell even after his conviction in the case, and for that was promptly exiled to an airbase in Kansas. But Arnold's career was far from over.

Through the years, senior officers in the Air Corps kept taking note of his abilities, and as the Mitchell drama wound down, Arnold's responsibilities grew. He commanded one of the most important airbases in the Army Air Corps and proved to be a master in the difficult art of procurement. He advocated research and development in the field of aeronautics, and as a pilot he won the prestigious Mackay Trophy for the most meritorious flight of the year for a round-trip flight to Alaska that began in Washington, D.C. In doing so, he proved the long arm of bombers. His belief in airpower led to his appointment to the Department of War's Air Board, which in 1939 issued a blueprint for the future of military aviation that underscored the importance of airpower to world defense and of the bomber to that power. As it happened, Arnold's report arrived on the very day that Hitler invaded Poland. The recipient was George Marshall, the chief of staff of the Army at the time.

While Arnold strongly believed in airpower, he had enough sense to realize that airmen had a lot to prove, even more so than ordinary soldiers. That meant handling the administrative side of the Air Corps' bureaucracy with absolute accuracy while taking pains to demonstrate the near limitless possibilities of powered flight without embarrassing mistakes. Arnold excelled at both.

As World War II approached, President Roosevelt viewed bombers as one of the vital weapons to defeat Hitler, too. Someone with a deep belief in airpower was just what Roosevelt needed to modernize and expand the Air Corps' capabilities. Marshall turned to Arnold to build for the nation an air force that could defeat Germany. Roosevelt, who would come to have complete faith in Marshall, agreed with his selection. Arnold was named commander of the United States Army Air Corps.

Air combat operations against the Germans up to and through 1943 had been uneven at best. While B-17s and B-24s had streamed into the airbases in England, the number of missions that the Eighth Air Force had flown had been surprisingly few. Between January and June 1943, just thirty-one bombing raids of any sort had been flown, most of them dealing with the U-boat crisis in the Atlantic. Arnold's bombers were attacking submarine pens and shipyards along coastal France and Germany to destroy the U-boats that were sinking the convoys that carried war materials to England. As far as aerial bombardment was concerned, the German Luftwaffe did not yet have much to fear from the arrival of the heavy bombers. The missions of 1942 and 1943 were generally shallow penetrations over Occupied France, hitting only a few strategic Luftwaffe factories.

The basic Allied bombing doctrine was to assemble as many bombers as possible, bunch them in a tight formation, and fly them to their targets with a shield of fighter escorts alongside. The escorts would stay as long as they could before departing. That was acceptable because the bombers literally bristled with machine guns and there was little question that they could take care of themselves.

But could they really? Time and again, missions beyond the range of the fighters suffered losses well in excess of what could be sustained. When the fighters turned back, the Luftwaffe savaged the bombers. The first attempt at solving the problem was a self-defending formation large enough to survive the German fighters. On April 17, 1943, a small but ambitious force of 106 B-17s made a direct attack against the German Focke-Wulf fighter factory in Bremen, Germany. The bombers flew the entire mission without the benefit of a fighter escort, but they used the LeMay combat boxes. Reflecting the importance of the airplane factories to their war effort, German fighters rose to meet the bombers and shot sixteen of them down while heavily damaging another thirty-eight. The losses were terrible, but they could have been worse—at least that was the thinking of the operations staff. Perhaps with even more bombers in the formations, the combined firepower would show the concept would work.

Between April 17 and June 11, 1943, the Eighth flew ten more missions, most of them small formations totaling fewer than a hundred bombers per raid, almost all of them against the coastal U-boat pens, with a few striking German airfields in Western Europe.

On June 11, things got serious. The test of large formations was at hand. On that day, a force of 252 American bombers hit the shipyards at Wilhelmshaven, while on June 13, another 221 bombers took off with 151 of them hitting Bremen and a separate force of 76 B-17s bombing the submarine yards in Kiel, Germany. As was policy, none of the attacks was escorted but again, despite the number of bombers, the losses were overwhelming. At Kiel, twenty-two of the seventy-six American bombers were shot down.[97]

The fighter forces of the Eighth consisted of the agile P-47 Thunderbolts and the fast P-38 Lightnings. The basic fighter doctrine was to keep the escorts close to the bombers to fend off the enemy without straying far from the wings of the Forts and Liberators. This largely ran against the grain of independent-minded fighter pilots who wanted to roam the skies untethered. So, as an experiment, the P-47s were allowed to fly what were called "fighter sweeps." The idea behind a fighter sweep was that of trespassing. In theory, by "trespassing" into German airspace, the Germans would feel compelled to defend their territory and come up to fight. Unfortunately, nothing could have been further from the truth. The Germans had a lot of interest in shooting down bombers but almost no interest in engaging the trespassers, save for a gaggle of German pilots who happened to be up that day and wanted to see what the Thunderbolts were up to. Three P-47s were shot down.

The question of how to most effectively employ fighter escorts remained a thorny one and a point on which there was much disagreement. The commanders within the Eighth Air Force saw the heavy combat losses suffered by the B-17s as a problem with the bomber formations and not as a problem of escorts. The escorts were providing protection during the critical initial penetration of enemy airspace, where it was believed Luftwaffe opposition would be the heaviest. Once the escorts got the bombers through the initial shield of German fighters, it was believed, the bombers were equipped with guns enough to fly the rest of the way to their targets by themselves. The problem, some still contended, was that the bomber formations were simply too small—so far.

The first indication of just how wrong this was came about in the aftermath of the bloody August 17 dual raid against Regensburg and Schweinfurt. Both targets were well out of range for the P-38s and P-47s, and both were heavily defended. Rather than attack the bombers during the initial penetration of their own airspace, as American theory more or less held, the German fighter pilots simply waited until the Thunderbolts reached the limits of the fuel reserves and were forced to turn around. Once the escorts were gone, the Germans moved in. Sixty American bombers were shot down. Some two hundred more were so shot up that they could barely make it home. "They threw everything at us," remembered a Wisconsin airman. "The flak was fierce. The 88s were just blowing away at us. They knock you out of formation and the fighters would finish you off. My airplane got all shot to heck. I had a hole in the right side of my airplane that you could almost drive a jeep through. We were really badly shot up. Everybody was. I mean we didn't have a flyable airplane the next day. They asked how many we would get together, we called in and we said we didn't have any that were flyable right now."[98]

There was, however, a positive side note. The P-47s flying escort had just enough gas to engage the Germans before they had to turn for home. In a brief but telling battle, eighteen Germans were shot down against three American losses. And a new storyline was beginning to emerge. The American fighter pilots were remarkably good at air-to-air dogfighting, even against Germans, many of whom had more than forty kills under their belts.

In deciphering the message from the uneven record of the first eight months of 1943, Hap Arnold sensed failure. German targets, including aircraft factories, had been attacked with some success, but far too few of them with far too few bombers and with far too many losses. Thousands of heavy guns in concrete-and-steel emplacements dotted the coastal regions of France. Behind the coastal defenses lay the full strength of an entire German-occupied continent laboring in a war economy that produced guns and ammunition for crack Panzer divisions, elite ground forces, and the deadliest airpower on the planet, the Luftwaffe. Airplanes and engines poured out of aircraft factories not only in Germany, but also from factories in Italy, Hungary, Austria, and France. Antiaircraft batteries totaled more than ten thousand guns and protected key targets. German airfields in France, Holland, and Belgium were operating with near impunity.

A pensive Arnold penned a message to his Royal Air Force counterpart and good friend RAF Air Marshal Sir Charles Portal. Arnold was never one to complain, nor did he burden someone with his own problems, but he could be introspective. When he and President Roosevelt were both in Egypt for a fall 1943 conference, they ended up in a car together going on a small excursion to see the Sphinx. They talked as they drove, discussing the allocation of American bombers to Britain and China and the nearly unbearable pressures to produce more materiel, but then they both lapsed into a silence that lasted several minutes. "Hap," the President finally said, "here we are, three of the world's most silent people, the Sphinx, you and I." Hap's letter to Portal was equally introspective. "The planned invasion hangs directly on the success of our combined aerial offensive," wrote Arnold. "I am sure that our failure to decisively cripple both the sources of German air power and the GAF itself is causing you and me real concern."[99]

It wasn't the only reason to be concerned. During a three-day pause that followed the October 10, 1943, Münster mission, statistics that painted a disheartening picture were presented in London to the commanders of the Eighth Air Force. Despite the bombing of their factories and combat engagements with their pilots in the sky, German factories were manufacturing more aircraft than the Germans were losing in the war. Since the issuance of The Pointblank Directive in June 1943, a net increase of more than four hundred new fighters had been added to the frontline strength of the Luftwaffe, with fighter production expected to increase by more than 30 percent to more than eight hundred new fighters per month. The German goal, according to new intelligence reports, was to produce two thousand fighters a month by January 1944.[100]

As if Arnold or Portal needed further explanation, the Combined Joint Chiefs of Staff for the Americans and the British expressed the obvious: "If the growth of German fighter strength is not arrested quickly, it may become literally impossible to carry out the destruction planned and thus create the conditions necessary for ultimate decisive action by our combined forces on the Continent."[101]

On October 14, 1944, the Eighth Air Force put together yet another maximum-effort mission, this one once again against Schweinfurt. More than three thousand men were briefed on the attack, which would use 291 bombers and 150 fighters as escorts. The plan was to hit the three ball bearing plants with a concentrated spread of bombs and shut them down for good. Just as important, the size of the bomber stream would prove once and for all that with proper planning and proper execution, unescorted bombers could blast their way into a target.

It was a disaster.

Once again the German air traffic controllers spotted the bombers as they assembled over England. It took the formation almost an hour to gather and another hour to cross the English Channel. As the first B-17s swept in over Holland, the German controllers alerted their fighters along the length of the expected raid. Hundreds of Messerschmitts, Focke-Wulfs, and Junkers were readied to take off as gun layers scrambled into position on their 88-mm flak batteries.

Over the farms and the cities of Occupied Europe, wispy contrails traced lines across the sky, marking the arrival of the first wave of the inbound bombers. Inside, the gunners swept their .50s as freezing air seeped into their flight suits. "The planes were drafty and cold," remembered Erwin Koppel, a Wisconsin airman. "The side [windows] were always open. I flew in the front turret which was very drafty on many of my missions. The wind was coming through at 300 miles per hour, forty below zero."[102]

The pilots tightened their combat formations as the Germans rolled out their deadly welcoming mat. The first of the German fighters arrived and floated alongside the formation, shadowing the combat boxes just out of range of their guns. On board the Forts, it was easy to see what lay ahead: rockets were slung under their wings.

Unlike Münster, this time the Germans didn't wait for the P-47s to turn back. The first round of attacks was directed at the escorts. The German fighters unexpectedly turned into the American P-47s, as much to draw them away from the bombers as to shoot them down. Behind them came a second flight of Me-109s that streaked into the American bombers head-on with guns and cannons firing. They quickly shot down thirteen bombers out of a box of sixteen. Immediately behind them came another gaggle of twin-engine German fighters that unleashed a heavy volley of rockets.

Some 830 sorties would be flown against the second Schweinfurt raid in an air battle that would go on for more than two hours. German pilots would exhaust their ammunition, land, rearm, and go back up for more attacks. It was relentless, savage. The pounding went on with machine gun fire, cannons, and the most intense use yet of air-to-air rockets. It was the new German attack strategy writ large. "It was the most daring attack I had witnessed to date, and it was apparent the Hun knew where we were going," said George Roberts, a radio operator from Mississippi who flew that day. "They were prepared to stop our formations at any cost. In the ensuing hours we noted 200 to 300 fighters attacking us from all directions and planes from our other two squadrons of B-17 began to go down. Twin-engine fighters flew above and in front of us and fired their rockets into the bombers while the single-engine fighters lined up on the tails section from six o'clock high to fire their 20-mm cannons." A 20-mm shell exploded in the radio room and sent pieces of the transmitter flying in all directions. One man was badly wounded and was bleeding profusely. One by one the gunners around Roberts' ship ran out of ammunition. "As I looked out the left window to see how many planes were flying with us, I noted several feathered props, smoking engines and holes in the fuselages and counted only five 306th panes in the sky." They had left with eighteen. Three aborted, leaving fifteen to fly the mission. Only five bullet-riddled B-17s from that box returned.[103]

The Germans drilled into the heart of the American formations using their rockets to open up creases through which came the fighters to mop up the cripples. From above, a flight of Stukas dropped bombs on them as if they were ground targets.[104]

Over the target, the flak was intense and deadly accurate. It, too, found the bombers. "We were up there, we were working our bombsights, we were vectoring in the altitude, the speed of the plane, we were all factoring that in," said a B-17 crewman. "[But] the Germans were down there with their flak guns, their 88s. They were factoring in the same factors for the shells going up."[105] The bomber pilots banked left and right to shake the fighters off their tails. The gunners swung their barrels through the sky tracking the Messerschmitts and Focke-Wulfs, but they were overwhelmed. Withering streams of .50-caliber machine gun fire crossed the smoke trails of 20-mm cannon shells as bullets ripped apart flesh and steel on both sides. The sky rained men, metal, and pieces of planes, all mixed with parachutes, American and German alike. Planes spiraled out of the sky like dying comets. Smoke rose up from the ground marking the graves of bombers, fighters, and airmen. One by one the gunners ran out of ammunition. They faked it anyway, swinging their barrels as if they were fully loaded. It did the trick.

In the end, it was one of the longest air battles of the war. "They called that the Schweinfurt mission because that was the target," said Jack Miller, one of the pilots on the B-17s that were attacked that day. "But there was a lot of fighting going on before you even got to the target … and after you're leaving the target."[106]

"It occurred to me," said a young navigator, "that there was a marked difference in watching the demise of a B-24 Liberator as compared to a B-17 Fortress. The end of a Liberator appeared to come suddenly, ugly and rather clumsily. In marked contrast, the death of a Fortress seemed to happen slowly, gracefully, and with great dignity. It was like watching a large beautiful eagle, mortally wounded but still proud and gallant to the end."[107]

Despite the brutal aerial combat, the American bombing was remarkably accurate. Damage to the ball bearing factories was considerable. Factory floors collapsed on top of each other, crushing German workers inside. The side of one major manufacturing plant pancaked down five floors. Smoke billowed skyward from another building. Dazed workers and rescue teams stumbled aimlessly among the rubble. Glass from blown-out windows littered the streets. A line of workers made their way back through the devastation to search for their friends and colleagues. Sirens wailed. Corpses were removed.[108]

When the dust cleared, thirty-two bombers had been shot down on the way to Schweinfurt and another twenty-eight had been lost on the way out. A total of 594 airmen were missing and presumed dead or captured, plus five more dead on the returning bombers and forty-three wounded. Of the 291 bombers sent up, sixty had been shot down, one bomber ditched and sank in the English Channel, six more were destroyed when they crash landed, seven were so badly shot up that they were written off entirely, and a total of 131 more were damaged. Instead, of the 291 planes that left that day, 203 were missing, destroyed, or damaged on what was to be known as Black Thursday. The Luftwaffe had triumphed.[109]

The bloody month of October 1943 finally came to an end. The losses had been so bad that the reorganized Luftwaffe so devastating that the Eighth Air Force was all but grounded for the rest of the year. Missions would be flown, but none that went deep over Germany. A total of 186 bombers had been shot down during the month, with half again as many badly damaged up or written off as junk. Worse, nearly 1,860 of the highly trained airmen who had arrived in England just months before were now dead or in German POW camps. Letters began arriving at American homes notifying loved ones of their losses.[110]

What was the darkest day for the Eighth was the finest month ever for the Luftwaffe. The new attack strategy had been a stunning success. Of the 186 bombers shot down in October, no less than 139 had been destroyed by their fighters, the highest total of any month since the beginning of the airwar by a factor of nearly two fold. The revised Luftwaffe strategy had worked better than any could have hoped for: the frontal attacks, the rockets, and the focus on the combat boxes seemed to be the winning formula for stopping the B-17s.

Arnold scarcely acknowledged the losses of October and said nothing to the public. Rather, the military spun the story as best as they could. Privately, however, Arnold saw much more in this than the loss of men and planes. There was a pattern in England that if left unchecked boded poorly for the future, and Arnold could no longer deny the feelings he had inside. Something was wrong with the Eighth Air Force, and while that meant many things to him, above all else it meant he needed a new man, and something called drop tanks. Only then would he prevail.

CHAPTER 4

LIFE ON BASE

American airbases in the United Kingdom were home for the tens of thousands of men who flew the combat missions and maintained the planes. This was where they slept, this was where their missions began and ended, this was the place they so urgently wanted to leave and never see again.

The airbases themselves were little more than land-based aircraft carriers, and they served the same narrow purpose as their sea-based cousins: war. Beyond the briefing huts and mess halls and the always-busy operations center, there was little by the way of human comforts. The crews lived in Quonset huts set off from the base in small compounds that surrounded the runways. Inside the huts, life was sparse. Each man had a narrow bed and a small area for clothes and personal items. A stove heated the hut during the winter.

The bases were somewhat pastoral, and the men could go for walks or ride their bikes. Even so, boredom set in quickly, interrupted only by the missions. A favorite time of day was mail call, but unless there was a mission, the rest of the day would be spent in some form of training or by fighting boredom with a deck of cards.

Small villages were close to the airbases and thus the local pubs. London was nearby, too, and many of the airmen came to know it better than their own state capitals back home. Some loved the British; some did not.

One young bomber pilot wrote a letter to his parents just two days after D-Day. He remembered something that he had wanted to say but had forgotten to include in one of his earlier letters. He had no particular fondness for the British, he said, and the dirty streets and bustling crowds did all they could to keep it that way. But he did understand something, and the young twenty-year-old wanted to say it before he flew on D-Day. He was grateful. "I went to London a couple weeks ago," he wrote his parents. "These people sure took a beating and they are plenty glad we are over here. I'm just glad all of this is not taking place in the States—people over there don't know a war is going on but they sure do here."[111]

The bases stretched across rural East Anglia, an area of England dotted by farmland and small villages that had scarcely been interrupted by time. The average airbase had between forty and sixty planes and, with more than a hundred airbases cut from the ground, congestion in the air was a constant problem. A map showing the location of the American airfields looked like a diagram drawn by an electrical engineer. Everything seemed to overlap. Large runway icons were placed in the center of broad circles with gridded departure and arrival tracks indicating one field's airspace and the beginning of another's. Because East Anglia was relatively flat, there were few geographic references to separate one base from another, save for a church steeple or a line of hedges easily seen from the air.[112] "It was not about finding the field," remembered an amused reconnaissance pilot, "it was finding the right one. They were all over the place."[113]

The standard architectural plan for an American airbase was called a Class A Airfield. Each airfield was an enormous construction project that involved the removal of some 400,000 cubic yards of soil, 8 miles of hedges, and some 1,000 trees, all to be replaced with 200,000 cubic yards of cement, 10 miles of roads, and 4 miles of septic systems. By 1943, the basic configuration was a single main runway 50 feet wide and 6,000 feet long with a box-like controller tower on the departure end in what was called the technical area. The technical area held the machine shops and engineering spaces that serviced the planes.

Around the runway ran a perimeter track that looked something like a dented bicycle wheel. This track connected smallish loops of concrete pads called hardstands on which the bombers and fighters were parked. It was about 3 miles around the perimeter, and just off the track, a few hundred yards off the main airfield, were the living quarters and the briefing rooms as well as storage areas and maintenance shops where preparations were made for the missions. Parachute riggers packed the chutes; avionics crews fixed radios and direction finders. Weaponeers, ordinance men, and armorers checked the belts of ammunition, bombed up the bombers, and sighted the guns. Well away from the active areas of the base were the bomb and fuel storage areas.

Most missions were launched in the hours before dawn so the bombers could get back before dark. Standing beside the runway during the late afternoon and waiting for the planes to return was a ritual. Men crowded the balcony around the control tower, searching the horizon for the pinpoint dots that heralded returning planes. Along the runways and taxiways, others lay on the ground or stood next to their bikes, looking, listening. "Ground crews worked their cans off in the night in freezing cold, rainy weather and got no recognition. We owed our lives to them," said pilot John Truluck, a South Carolinian some twenty-five years old. "They probably sweated out my missions more than I did. When we came in to land they were sitting there waiting for us."[114]

During one mission, ground crew chief Bill Frizell's men had fifteen bombers in the air. They learned that two had crash-landed near other bases in England, but they waited beyond any reasonable hope for the other thirteen to arrive. "Toward dusk that afternoon, all ground personnel waited—and continued to wait in the darkness—for the sound of engines," said Frizell. "None were heard."[115]

Colonel Leon W. Johnson was a commander of the 44th Bomb Group. His group flew missions for two months, but his replacement crews were stalled. For almost eight weeks, no new men arrived. During those two months, he saw his forces whittled down—a fact made all the more evident by the empty bunks around him. Each bomber carried ten men and when one was lost, so too were ten men. "Every time we went out, while we might lose none, we might lose one or two. At dinner that night over at the club, there would be vacant seats. It was awfully hard. You didn't have to be very smart to figure out that if your force was going down all the time and you were doing the same number of missions and you were losing one and two and getting no replacements, your chances of surviving didn't look so good."[116]

Empty bunks were cleaned out quickly. More than once a late-arriving crew would come back only to find their gear being removed. That's the way it was. There were no funerals, no time given to honor the dead. Replacement crews took up empty bunks as fast as airplanes were shot down. Remembered airman Erwin Koppel: "The next day they flew in new planes and new crews. And life went on."[117]

Though some liked it over there, most American airmen had no particular fondness for England, and the weather seemed to conspire to do all it could to keep it that way. The winter of 1943–44 was one of the worst yet for Britain. Located north of the latitudes of most American cities, the airmen suffered from a steady diet of fog, rain, and a persistent chill that never seemed to go away. On particularly bad days, rain turned footpaths into rivers of mud and grounded planes. Airmen had no choice but to bundle up, hunch a shoulder against the wind, and slop from one hut to another. "England was cold and wet," said B-24 pilot Bill Kamemitsa, speaking for almost all of the American airmen in Britain those years. "I was never warm a minute of the time I was there."[118] Some pilots encountered walls of fog that started at the surface of the English Channel and rose tens of thousands of feet. In the thickest of the fogs, an airman could walk up to a building and not see it until he could touch it. "We were flying blind from the time our wheels started to roll," said Kamemitsa.[119]

The weather over Europe was scarcely better. Clouds rolled in and sat over targets as if the Germans had ordered blankets to cover their cities. "I flew my first five missions over Europe without seeing any of it," said Lieutenant Arlen Baldridge. "My sixth [mission] gave me a glimpse, and little more."[120] Weather delays and cancelations plagued the mission tempo. Raids would get started only to be recalled. Go/no-go decisions had to be made at the last minute. Clear skies over Europe might very well necessitate a hair-raising takeoff in terrible weather over England. Said Robert Copp, a B-17 pilot, "Day after day you just took off in the soup, and when the wheels came up, you were on instruments." Copp was hurried out of bed one morning to blow the fog off the runway at his airbase. He was told to use the prop wash from his bomber. "You would take off in front of everyone and circle the field in a steep bank, then drop down in front of the other guys as close to the ground as you could get. That would blow the fog away so the others didn't have to come up through it."[121]

One of the most dreaded consequences of flying blind was a midair collision, and with the density of airplanes coming and going, they were all too common. In one midair collision, three bombers went down in the blink of an eye. It began when the first bomber hit the turbulence of the prop wash from a bomber in front of him. Like a giant tornado on its side, the counter-rotating gusts of the prop wash spun him over and into the side of the plane to his left. His propellers neatly cut that bomber in half before he himself broke apart. The severed tail section from the second bomber then tumbled back through the air and slammed into the wing of yet a third bomber, cutting it in two. By the time it was all over, twenty-six men were dead.

Near misses weren't fatal, but they seared into one's imagination the frightening image of what might have happened. One group of bombers was flying home through a heavy cloud deck when another group of bombers flew directly through them. At combined speeds of some 500 miles per hour, it was a near-death moment of sheer terror as wings and propellers streaked across windshields, missing each other only by scant inches. Some airmen nervously smiled as they talked about these moments, called "shuffling the deck." The thought of shuffling the deck haunted some of the airmen for decades.

Even the ground was no assurance of safety. Instead of taxiing off the runway and on to the perimeter track, one pilot lost his way and in the confusion taxied down the mist-shrouded runway. He promptly slammed head-on into another bomber as it roared down the runway to take off, killing ten men.[122]

By day the bases buzzed with noise and hummed with activity, but at night they were nearly silent and completely still. Because of the threat of airstrikes, lights were doused, doors were sealed, and the few windows in the huts were blacked out. From above, the airfield blended in with the darkened landscape. "My plane was located in a dispersal on the far side of the field, across from the control tower, with only a few feet separating it from the farmer's field to the north," wrote Will Lundy, a ground crewman on a bomber base. "It was completely separated from all other sections of the base, and separated from east Dereham by a few miles of farmland, leaving one with a feeling that he was completely alone. With the rapid approach of darkness, the nearby planes dotting the area adjacent to the taxiway quickly melted into the void as well." Lundy's base at Dereham was directly west of occupied Holland, just across the North Sea from where the Germans were based. In the dark of night, it was impossible to shake off the creeping fear that a team of Germans might infiltrate the base and loom out of the dark with throat-slitting knives or that from above a lone German bomber might see a light and attack with his bombs. Lundy recalled that, "During the daylight hours, it seemed that there was activities all around the perimeter of the airfield. But with the sudden fall of darkness, not only did the hustle and bustle stop, so did all sound. One has to have lived in the country to appreciate just how quiet silence really is. There was just not a sound to be heard—not even insects, nothing."[123]

The airfields were indeed an attractive target, yet they were rarely attacked by the Germans with any real effort. More common were what the airmen called "red alerts," which was the brief appearance of a "scaredy cat" strike by one or two German fighters zooming in to quickly release a bomb and then streaking home to safety at the lowest possible altitude.

Far more dangerous were the attacks by the German night fighters that crept up behind the bombers and followed them home. These Luftwaffe pilots had a special radar array attached to the noses of their twin-engine fighters. They used the radar to find a bomber in the dark. Because they themselves ran completely dark, they could sneak in behind a plane and stay there without being detected. When they were ready, they would fire their rockets. "Two weeks ago when the bombers came home some came in just after dark, a few Me-410s followed them over and shot 13 down," remembered Captain Harry Ankeny, a bomber pilot. "We stood outside the barracks and saw three go down. Really was a mess." To counter the problem, fighter pilots were eventually sent up to escort late-arriving bombers, but the attacks persisted.[124]

The problems of war aside, the bases were home, and home was a far cry from a cold foxhole or a crowded bunk in the bowels of a ship rolling in the ocean swells at sea. There were the villages to visit during days off, open spaces with shade trees to walk in, and meals—however bad— served in a mess hall where the floors were steady and incoming shells few and far between. There were long, boring hours interrupted by missions of sheer terror, yes, but the sooner the airmen could bomb Hitler out of existence, the sooner it would all be over.

CHAPTER 5

SPAATZ

The October disasters underscored a fundamental weakness in the compromise that governed Pointblank. As the end of 1943 approached, Germany was hardly reeling from the air attacks by the British or the Americans. In fact, her factories were making more war planes than ever before, including the first of a new generation of airplanes, a jet fighter that was superior in speed and maneuverability to the P-38 Lightnings and the P-47 Thunderbolts. To allow the Germans to surge ahead in the air was to doom any hope of an invasion. Arnold had two problems: one about which he could do something and one about which he could do nothing.

Air Marshal Arthur Travers Harris of the Royal Air Force was a staunch advocate of area bombing. Prime Minister Winston Churchill frequently yielded to his powerful rhetoric on the matter. The RAF was almost entirely engaged in night attacks over German cities, and Harris offered a convincing reason why this was so. "The Nazis entered this war under the rather childish delusion that they were going to bomb everyone else, and nobody was going to bomb them," said Harris. "At

Rotterdam, London, Warsaw, and half a hundred other places, they put their rather naïve theory into operation. They sowed the wind, and now they are going to reap the whirlwind."[125] It was impossible not to feel stirrings of patriotism at the sight of German cities burning to the ground, and the feelings against Germany being so strong.

Arnold had no such feelings, however. In his eyes, as well as in the eyes of most Americans, city bombing was little more than terror bombing. Arnold argued that daylight bombing of fighter factories and Luftwaffe airfields was the only way to destroy the Luftwaffe, but about this there was nothing he could do about the British.

But he could do something about the Eighth Air Force.

Ira Eaker was born the son of a Texas tenant farmer. He worked his way into an Oklahoma teachers college and joined the Army as a reservist. He advanced in the military and chose aviation as his specialty. Eaker became an excellent pilot, and he was equally as good as a speaker and a writer. He would ultimately coauthor a book about aerial tactics with his friend Hap Arnold.

In 1929, Eaker and Army pilot Elwood R. "Pete" Quesada flew a record-setting endurance flight that involved the novel concept aerial refueling. In a flight that lasted a lengthy six days in the air, Eaker's plane was refueled numerous times, and food was brought up and passed from one plane to another, all conducted as the two planes circled the city of Los Angeles. He was the darling of the media.

During the early years of the war, Eaker was called on to use his considerable powers of logic and persuasion to convince Churchill that the American policy of daylight bombing made sense. Churchill had been against the daytime attacks and was determined to force the Americans into night raids against cities, but Eaker presented his case and finally gained Churchill's blessing, which would mean around-the-clock bombing of Germany: the British against cities at night; the Americans against factories by day.

Eaker was a firm believer in the strength of the bomber. His vision for how bombers should be employed was bold and convincing, but it was wrong. In Eaker's mind, bombers would be nested inside a protective shell of fighter escorts that as a group would penetrate German airspace. The fighters would engage the enemy fighters around the perimeter of the formation until the Germans were beaten, and then the bombers would burst through with their own guns blazing while the escorts turned around. The bombers could take it from there largely because of their powerful weaponry and the number of .50-caliber machine guns that pointed in every direction. They would bomb their targets, turn around, blast their way back, and then pick up fighter escorts to take them home.

Eaker believed in this attack profile and insisted that his fighters stick with the bombers during the escort phase. If they got out of range during a dogfight, they were to break off and come back. They were required to stay above 18,000 feet and to never roam the ground for targets of opportunity.[126] Moreover, the escorts were instructed to stay in front. The rear of a bomber formation would defend itself with the twin tail guns in each bomber, while the front of the formation was weaker and should be shielded by the fighters.[127]

On paper, the approach was sensible. But in practice, it was a disaster. Eaker's concepts presupposed that the Germans would engage the package of fighters and bombers as they entered German airspace. But they did not. Worse, although the bombers did have impressive firepower, they rarely flew in formations tight enough to fully shield themselves. Nor did they have the precision of gunnery to prevent the fighters from cleaving a wedge and breaking them apart. Once their boxes were loosed by rockets, or by the sheer force of attack, the Germans picked apart the weakest ones and worked their way through the stream.

But there was even more to it than that. A fighter aircraft was a powerful aerial weapon with three-dimensional mobility flown by a pilot who earned his wings largely because of his natural competitiveness. Pinned to the side of the bombers, these innate advantages were entirely neutralized. Eaker failed to see this. Instead of mapping strategies that played into the aggressiveness of a fighter pilot's instinct and letting his men hunt down the Germans when they were most vulnerable—during takeoffs and as they formed into groups—Eaker's policy turned the advantage back to the Germans. Pinned to the side of their bombers, it was up to the Germans to pick the time and place of the attack, not the other way around. Militarily, that ran against everything army strategists knew.

In the end, Eaker seemed to complicate the problem rather than solve it. In addition to his belief in the current attack profile, he was known for coddling his bombers in the hangar, seeing to it that repairs were nearly meticulous. He also refused to challenge the weather; indeed, he seemed stymied by England's bad weather. During one month in which he launched just three missions because of bad weather, for example, the British launched almost a dozen. Eaker truly believed in the self-defending bomber. With calculations known only to himself, Eaker made it known that he needed a minimum of three hundred bombers per mission to fully exploit the self-defending capability of the B-17s. Anything less and the advantage was gone.[128]

About all of this, Arnold had his doubts.

Thus was marked the beginning of the end for Eaker, closing the door on his command of the Eighth. Nearing the end of his rope, Arnold ordered Eaker to turn his fighters into offensive weapons, without spelling out exactly what he meant. But rather than freeing his escorts to fight on their own, which seemed like the obvious response, Eaker repeated the fighter sweeps of June. He sent gangs of pilots across the face of Germany in a freewheeling hunt for airplanes to shoot down, but, as had happened before, not a single Luftwaffe plane was to be found. In August 1943, the Eighth Air Force intensified the sweeps. On one day they launched 347 P-47s across western France, but they all came back empty handed. They did it again a week later with ninety-five fighters, but again the fighter pilots saw absolutely nothing. The Germans scarcely moved.[129] Wrote a frustrated Arnold, "I cannot comprehend what value is derived from the frequently reported so-called offensive fighter sweeps in which the enemy is rarely sighted. Except as a means of consuming gasoline, I can see no purpose in this practice."[130]

Nor did Arnold see any purpose in delaying the change that needed to come to the Eighth if Pointblank was to succeed. None of Eaker's concepts of fighting an airwar could stop an idea whose time had come. The Eighth Air Force needed new blood, and this new blood would change everything.

Carl Andrew "Tooey" Spaatz was a remarkably uncomplicated person with a casual demeanor that masked a warrior's clear focus. A West Point graduate, Spaatz saw aerial action during World War I. He was sent to Europe to overhaul a complicated training program that fed pilots to the front. Itching for action himself, he received a brief assignment to a pursuit squadron and shot down three Germans. A modest man with a quick wit, Spaatz explained two of his victories in an unattributed quote in a *New York Times* article that referred to an airman who had shot down "two planes, and my own." On reading this quote, Spaatz's wife recognized her husband's sense of self-effacing humor and knew in an instant that it was Tooey. He had shot down two Germans, true, but he also ran out of gas on the way back to his airbase and crashed his own airplane.[131]

In the airwar against Nazi Germany, the Eighth Air Force was the first military air force established by the Americans to bring the war to

Germany. Later, the Fifteenth Air Force would be established in Italy, and the Ninth Air Force would arrive in England with their fighters and medium bombers. But the first and most dominant airpower in the war against Germany was the Eighth. Its original commander was, ironically, Tooey Spaatz.

Spaatz was ordered to assemble the bombers and fighters and command structure that he needed to run a campaign against Germany. In June 1942, he felt he was well enough organized to move his headquarters to England. By August of that year, he had enough bombers on British soil to launch his first raid against Occupied Europe at Rouen, France. From that date forward, the Eighth was at war with Germany. Between August and November 1942, Spaatz built his command to some 850 heavy bombers and 450 fighter aircraft, and he launched sixteen missions against German targets with about fifty to ninety bombers in the largest attacks.[132]

The November 1942 invasion of North Africa brought the airwar against Occupied Europe to a near halt and shifted the focus from England to the Mediterranean. General Dwight D. Eisenhower commanded the North African campaign. Eisenhower asked Hap Arnold to send him his most experienced, combat-ready air assets to support the campaign. Arnold scarcely missed a beat. He selected Tooey Spaatz.

Arnold asked Spaatz to set up the air forces Eisenhower needed. Spaatz immediately pulled out of the Eighth Air Force in England his best squadrons of fighters and heavy bombers and sent them to North Africa. He also tagged one of his most trusted generals in England to go down with them: the well-known aviator General James Harold "Jimmy" Doolittle. Doolittle assumed command of Mediterranean-based forces of some 1,200 B-17s and other aircraft.

Spaatz stayed behind in England, but not for long. So intent was Eisenhower on completely dominating the Germans in the Mediterranean that at one point he asked Arnold to shut down the

Eighth Air Force entirely. But Spaatz mounted a convincing argument to keep both air forces in action against the Germans. Eisenhower persisted. The combat in North Africa involved both American and British air forces, and coordination issues were a problem. Eisenhower decided he wanted an overall military commander for his combined air forces, one who had extensive experience in the air, who could get into battle immediately, but also one who could deal with the personalities of the senior British air commanders. Spaatz, who was well liked by both the Americans and the British, was the answer.

In 1942, Spaatz left England and moved down to North Africa, where he assumed his command not only as Eisenhower's senior air officer, but as the overall commander of American air forces in England and in North Africa. Hap Arnold then reached out to Ira Eaker, whom he admired and had worked with stateside, to take over the Eighth in England.

The decks now reshuffled, Doolittle and Spaatz got to work against the Germans in North Africa while Eaker took over the bombing of Occupied Europe from England. One worked out well. One did not.

Spaatz was exactly what Arnold thought he could be: a spectacular commander in combat. Allied aircraft were in the thick of battles and were flying almost every type of airpower mission possible. Pilots were dogfighting against the Germans in aerial combat, intercepting German resupply flights and troop movements crossing the Mediterranean, taking their planes down to the ground in high-speed, rib-pounding close-air support strikes for the ground soldiers, and even mounting logistically improbable bombing missions into Europe, most notably against the oil refineries in Ploesti, Romania, which was launched from Morocco. Spaatz's planes poured deadly steel into anything German, choked on dust, and engaged the enemy in adrenalin-charged missions that put the deadly Panzer tanks of German Field Marshal Erwin Rommel squarely in their bombsights. They did all this operating from tents and dusty airstrips that made the English airbases look like luxury hotels. Moreover, their all-in, roaming style of combat had a certain intensity that decimated the Germans. "Our pilots were exhausted to a terrifying degree," said Luftwaffe commander Adolf Galland. "The superiority of the Anglo-Americans was overwhelming."[133]

The airwar in North Africa and the Mediterranean served as a precursor to the airwar in Europe. In one of the more brilliant campaigns of the Mediterranean, Spaatz's close friend and Ira Eaker's old partner in the refueling stunt, General Elwood Richard "Pete" Quesada, led the combat air attacks that hit the reinforced German garrisons on the island of Pantelleria. So thorough were Quesada's forces from the air that the garrison forces surrendered without an invasion, leading Spaatz to cable Arnold that air bombardment was now a bona fide military tactic to win wars. "The application of the air available to us," wrote Spaatz, "can reduce to the point of surrender any first-class nation now in existence."[134]

By May 1943, a tired, worn down, dirty, and exhausted Spaatz was able to tell Arnold that he had air domination of the Mediterranean and that nothing could dislodge him. Spaatz had executed a campaign in North Africa that all but cut the Luftwaffe off at its knees, giving Eisenhower the freedom to engage the Germans on the ground without tipping a chin skyward to worry about an attack. Out of the gauzy haze that rose over the battlefields of North Africa emerged airmen who had a firm grasp on the art of airwar and in whom Eisenhower and Arnold had complete confidence. Tested, bloodied, but victorious, they were uniquely prepared for whatever role came next.[135]

Said Galland of Spaatz's command: "Here in Africa could already be seen what in a year was going to happen on a larger scale on the European battlefield."[136]

Though it boded ill for the Germans, it was welcome news for Spaatz. You are "my most trusted air advisor," Ike wrote in a letter to him. It was time for the next war.[137]

On December 6, 1943, Roosevelt named Eisenhower the Supreme Allied Commander for the D-Day invasion of Europe and the battle to defeat Germany. Two days later, Hap Arnold met with Roosevelt and Eisenhower in a joint meeting to outline a change of his air command for Europe. Arnold relieved Eaker of his command the Eighth and put Doolittle in his place. Tooey Spaatz was elevated to the position of the overall commanding general for all of the American air forces in Europe and would be responsible for the Fifteenth Air Force in Italy and the Eighth Air Force in England. Doolittle would be under him as commander of the Eighth. Eaker would take another command down in the Mediterranean. Roosevelt and Eisenhower both gave their approval. In one fell swoop, Arnold had transplanted the team that had successfully led the airwar in Africa back to England, where they would do the same against Germany in Europe. The problems with the Eighth would now fall into the lap of Tooey Spaatz.

On December 9, 1943, Arnold sat down to dinner with Spaatz and Doolittle and hashed out the details. The three men worked for the next two days on the mechanisms of a new war command. It was agreed that they would operate in England much as they'd operated in the Mediterranean. Spaatz would assume overall command of two air arms in Europe; Doolittle would be his right-hand man for the Eighth. "Our mission is destroying the German Air Force," said Spaatz, and that was exactly what Arnold wanted to hear. "We are looking upon our attacks against Germany as major battles that are phases of a campaign," he wrote. To a military man, that meant just one thing. Campaigns were prosecuted with utmost vigor and focus until a final victory was in hand.[138]

Arnold no doubt pushed back his chair, comfortable in the knowledge that he had experienced men who wanted to kill Germans as badly as he did. "It is a conceded fact that [the invasion of France] will not be possible unless the German Air Force is destroyed," wrote

Arnold to Spaatz. To that Spaatz had but one answer: he would pursue the "maximum destruction of German fighters in the air and on the ground." It would now be like it had been in North Africa: they would do whatever it took.[139] Said Jimmy Doolittle, we will "meet the enemy and destroy him, rather than be content to keep him away."[140]

The reorganization was hobbled by the hard winter weather, and the month of December was unremarkable except for two rather important footnotes. The first had to do with the evolution of auxiliary fuel tanks that could be carried by the American fighters. Where Eaker had expressed skepticism about fighter aircraft as escort, Doolittle was an early advocate of the long-range fighter and believed they were essential to the missions deep into Germany. Recognizing the need to extend the range of the escorts, drop tanks had been developed and improved and were coming into their own. The fighters would have the range they needed to stay with the bombers for the entire length of a mission using a tag-team approach that had such complete overlap that no gaps would be created.

Meanwhile, aeronautical engineers in Fort Worth, Texas, had developed the P-51 Mustang, which the British improved with the Merlin engine. It was a fighter that seemed to rewrite the math in the zero-sum game of aeronautical engineering. In the wizardry of an equation that seemed to defy the laws of physics, the P-51 flew faster and longer and turned quicker that anything before it, even while sporting six .50-caliber machine guns in its wings. It could fly to Berlin and back with auxiliary drop tanks. While the debate about the relative merits of the P-51 versus the P-47 and the P-38 will no doubt continue among fighter pilots for generations to come, the P-51 was an ideal dogfighter, the P-47 and P-38 were sturdy ground pounders, yet all three could reverse missions with ease and did so time and again. Doolittle now had a plane for every combat sortie. It was up to Spaatz to put them into action.

That happened on December 20, when 491 P-38 Lightnings launched a mission to escort a stream of bombers on a raid against the German port of Bremen. The fighters reached their rendezvous point, but the bombers were delayed and most of pilots waited for them, but not all. Four hundred sixty-three of the P-38s stayed in place to meet the bombers, but the other twenty-eight broke free and did what they were not supposed to do, flying ahead of the rendezvous point on their own to find Germans to attack before the Germans reached the bombers.

The fighter pilots had been frustrated by the rules that kept them pinned to the bombers. Their plan was to find the Germans while they were forming up ahead of their bombers and shoot them down before they could mount their attack. The twenty-eight fighters streaked off into the sky and began what they called "freelancing." Their first attempt was somewhat anticlimactic, but from that point on, freelancing became routine, albeit unofficially so. Fighter pilots broke away from their close escort duties and roamed ahead, shooting down unsuspecting Germans as they organized for their own attacks. Like anything revolutionary, once it worked, it was unstoppable. Despite standing policies to the contrary, a small number of pilots on each escort mission would release themselves from their bombers to fly ahead and find the enemy first. Freelancing earned the tacit acceptance of most of the commanding officers who could see in an instant the possibilities for killing German fighters.

It was a glimpse into a future that had arrived.[141]

In January 1943, Spaatz and Doolittle assumed their new commands. On January 21, 1943, Jimmy Doolittle issued his most important order of the airwar. Fighter pilots were formally freed to attack Germans ahead of the bomber streams. At least one squadron out of every group would now be designated a "bouncing" squadron. These bouncers would be free to fly ahead of the formation on hunt-and-kill missions to attack Germans before they attacked the bombers.

They were also freed to stay on the tail of a German all the way to the ground if that's what it took, and, on the way home, they were free to drop down to the deck and attack German airfields. The pilots were no longer there to just protect the bombers; Doolittle and Spaatz ordered them to find and kill the Luftwaffe.

Fighter pilots were now free to be fighter pilots.

CHAPTER 6

ANYWHERE

Upon arriving in England, Spaatz and Doolittle faced a determined enemy with significant air victories and ample aircraft. At the beginning of December 1943, the Luftwaffe had some 4,854 aircraft, including 1,968 fighters on the Western Front. Worse, there was an ever-increasing output of fighters from the Messerschmitt and Focke-Wulf factories, in addition to the development and flight-testing of the Me-262, a new high-speed aircraft powered by jet engines.[142] Against these forces, Spaatz had 2,608 B-17s and B-24 heavy bombers, 964 medium B-26s and A-20s, 1,696 P-47s, 659 P-51s, 809 P-38s, and 259 reconnaissance aircraft.

It would be with these bombers and fighters that Spaatz would exert his will.[143]

Spaatz came to Europe brimming with confidence and ready to do battle. He told Arnold that he'd cut off the supply of new German fighters and take out the remaining Luftwaffe airplane factories with a "few days of visual bombing."[144] Spaatz smartly recognized, too, that any policy of hitting just the German factories would leave thousands of airplanes on the front. By hitting the factories and the airfields together, though, the Luftwaffe would be reduced to a manageable size. "It is my belief that we do not get sufficient attrition by hitting factories," said Spaatz. "Therefore we must place emphasis on aerodromes and knocking them down in the air." Success against the Luftwaffe required a balance, an equal emphasis on factories and airfields, Spaatz was saying, and it was an important distinction that he was trying to make for one telling reason: Until now, the German airfields had scarcely been touched.

Spaatz thus set into motion one of his least heralded accomplishments but no doubt his most important contribution to the war. Spaatz let it be known that he was going to find the Germans wherever they were, and when he found them, he was going to destroy them. If his heavy bombers were what attracted German fighters to come in the air and fight, then Spaatz would use them as bait. If German fighters were hidden under the trees along the edges of airbases, then he'd go down and find them in the trees. It didn't matter. So long as the Germans had fighters that could take to the skies and the pilots to fly them, they were a threat to D-Day, and Spaatz was determined to find them and kill them. Factories, airfields, fighters— it didn't matter, they were all the same. They were all targets.

General William Kepner, commander of the fighter squadrons attached to the Eighth Air Force, was impressed by the immediacy of Spaatz's actions. "The minute Spaatz and Doolittle came here, they directed that I take such steps as I felt necessary to lick the German Air Force. If it meant thinning down the escorts, that was okay with them."[145]

Applying the formula successfully tested in North Africa, Spaatz initiated a whirlwind of changes. The B-17s and B-24s would continue to pound German airplane factories and key suppliers like the ball bearing plants, but they would also bomb Luftwaffe airfields, and the transportation grids over which airframes and parts moved. If that wasn't enough to choke off the Luftwaffe, Spaatz wanted to hit the oil refineries that made their gasoline, too. By using drop tanks to extend the range of his fagers, escorts for the bombers would now be continuous, no more gaps or planes turning back and leaving them naked. One group of fighter planes would come up and relieve another in a tag-team approach that would provide escort over the entire length of a mission with plenty of time for missed rendezvous and unexpected delays. Moreover, from now on, one fighter group would roam ahead and attack any Germans taking off or forming up and, in the most aggressive of all the changes, if no German fighters were seen in the air in the vicinity of the bombers, two thirds of the remaining escorts were now allowed to roam the skies hunting for prey. Finally, everyone was welcome to drop down and strafe ground targets on their way home.

Additionally, but separately, groups of P-47s and P-38s would henceforth be sent on their own missions, effectively turning them into hunter-killers with their own load of bombs and bullets. A tactic quite apart from escorting or freelancing, this was the precursor to the self-defending, multirole, air-to-ground attack fighter of the twenty-first century. The airmen would not only strafe the ground but would bomb it, too.

If not entirely appreciated by the bomber crews, who hated to see their escorts leave no matter how empty the skies were of German planes, these new tactics were a welcome change for the fighter pilots, and they significantly intensified the depth and breadth of the war against the Luftwaffe. Now, more than a thousand additional planes were on the offensive, some with considerable bomb loads plus belts of deadly .50-caliber machine gun bullets. While in the past Luftwaffe pilots watched with some amusement as returning P-38s flew over their bases on their way home, their very airbases were now prime targets. No longer were the escorts pinned to their bombers. American fighter pilots would now sweep the horizon for the telltale pinpoint of black that was the first sign of a German fighter, and if they saw one, they would attack. There was a new partnership in the air, and it came from this new freedom to use combat judgment, the greatest of all the assets of the American aviator.

The benefits were immediate and sometimes unexpected. Nearing the safety of the English Channel after completing a bomb run against a Luftwaffe airfield deep inside Germany, a B-17 pilot noticed a crippled Fort slowly falling down and away from the safety of the formation. In times past, this was the end. But times had changed. The German coastal batteries paused as the spotters saw the cripple and reset their fuses for his lower altitude. "We just knew he wouldn't make it," said the pilot, but others thought differently. A flight of P-51s saw the problem and swept down to the deck to take out the antiaircraft guns. Pushing their airspeed to the maximum, they raked the 88s with their machine guns to prevent the loaders from firing until the crippled Fort was out of range. "As we came across the coast I looked down and watched the P51s at tree top level spitting tracer bullets all over the area. Our little friends had given a very graphic demonstration of how they were quite willing to put their lives on the line for bomber crewmen at anytime and anywhere. The last we saw of him he was safely over the North Sea, heading for home."[146]

With increasing regularity, the American fighter pilots were operating with rules that to the enemy were dangerous and unpredictable and unrelenting. "They were no longer glued to the slow-moving bomber formations, but took action into their own hands," said Galland. "Wherever our fighters appeared the Americans hurled themselves at them. During take-off, assembling, climb, and approach to the bombers; when we were in contact with them, on our way back, during landing and even after that the American fighters attacked with overwhelming superiority."[147]

The Americans were learning, changing, and adapting—but most of all they were being aggressive. "I believe that some of the methods applied in the Mediterranean are applicable here," said Spaatz modestly of the new airwar. What he meant was that it was now all out.[148]

CHAPTER 7

THE CLOCK TICKS

Spaatz's command formally began when he received Hap Arnold's chief of staff, who had flown to London directly from Washington, D.C., to deliver a personal message. When Spaatz heard it, he understood why it could never have been put in writing. The air battles ahead would be violent, Spaatz was told. Arnold accepted that, but he wanted Spaatz to be aggressive and to push. Arnold wanted Spaatz to know that if destroying Germany from the air meant the loss of two hundred bombers in a mission or six hundred bombers in a month, so be it. D-Day was set for May, and D-Day was all important. If that's what it took, that's what it took.[149]

Spaatz's reaction to Arnold's directive is unknown, but it was a significant directive indeed. The loss of six hundred bombers meant the loss of some six thousand men, which was nearly three times the losses of any month so far. It was difficult to comprehend how the American people might take such news if it were to happen, but the message was clear. Time was of the essence, and war demanded much, including the courage to suffer such losses to the end of victory.[150]

Spaatz, though, was up to the challenge. During the transition from Eaker to Spaatz, the attacks had intensified. The Luftwaffe bases in France at Lille, Montdidier, Amiens, Saint Omer, Bordeaux, Cognac, and La Rochelle, and at Schiphol in the Netherlands had all been bombed. Raids against Münster, Cherbourg, Kiel, Bremen, and other targets were mounted as well. On Christmas Eve 1943, the Eighth launched its largest mission yet, sending 670 bombers to hit the German V-1 buzz bombs at their new launch sites in the Pas-de-Calais area. The Ninth Air Force rehearsed operations with its transports and the airborne troops who would be parachuted behind the lines during the D-Day invasion. On New Year's Eve, the skies over Occupied Europe virtually roared with engines. A force of 6,800 airmen mounted raids using 571 bombers, 441 P-47s, and 33 P-51s.

An intricate plan to take out the German fighter factories had been prepared by the plans division prior to Spaatz's arrival. When he reviewed the plan, he liked what he saw and planned to roll it out as soon as the weather permitted. On almost every key dimension, the plan would represent a sharp increase in the war against Germany. It called for seven consecutive days of maximum-effort missions in an all-out application of overwhelming force. No longer would the Eighth fly a single mission followed by a day of rest. Rather, the plan called for more than a week of nonstop flying using every bomber available in England in back-to-back attacks with no rest in between. The targeting strategy would be just as aggressive and would triple the number of factories hit in a single day. An essential element to it all was for combined RAF and U.S. forces to overwhelm the German repair crews and keep the factories down. The Americans would carry out the brunt of the plan with daylight bombing, and the RAF would come back at night to lay down their own bombs. Many of the biggest targets, such as the ball bearing plants in the Schweinfurt area and the sprawling Messerschmitt factory complexes, would be hit three times. The idea was to be absolutely certain that the factories were reduced to rubble, even if that meant that bombs would land on bombed-out buildings. As Curtis LeMay liked to say, the Allies wanted to see the cinders dance.

It would be a bloody week of combat. The targets were the most valuable in Germany, and they would be aggressively defended by every fighter and every flak shell the Luftwaffe had at its disposal. Among them: the four main Messerschmitt manufacturing complexes in Regensburg, Leipzig, Gotha, and Augsburg; the aircraft factories in Kreising, Tutow, Posen, Brunswick, Halberstadt, and Erkner; and the ball bearing plants in Schweinfurt and elsewhere. All together, the factories for Junkers, Heinkel, Messerschmitt, and Focke-Wulf would be bombed.

Spaatz gave the plan his blessing, which was codenamed Argument. It was aggressive, unrelenting, and domineering, all of which suited his style. Indeed, looking ahead, one could scarcely imagine aerial combat attacks more violent than what was about to unfold.

Now he only needed the weather to cooperate.

The Germans came into 1944 concerned but confident. As of January, the raids by the Eighth Air Force had so far been mainly inconveniences, and the damage they inflicted had been bearable. For sure there had been casualties and a significant loss of aircraft, but such was war. On the Luftwaffe airbases there remained a precise and rigid order to air operations, with nothing chaotic or desperate to it. Pilots dispersed to their alternate bases, stood alert, then came back; training squadrons went up and did their chandelles. "I made two or three practice missions daily with my students in [the squadron] formation," wrote German fighter pilot Hermann Buchner in his memoirs. "It was child's play for me to fly with the young pilots, to make them ready for the front."[151]

While on leave, the pilots shaved, splashed on cologne, and stuffed guilders or francs into their pockets, and headed into the nearest town. On one particular night, five pilots made a dash to Paris' Le Doges in the Italian Quarter for a birthday party that went on nearly all night.

TOP-SECRET

HEADQUARTERS
UNITED STATES STRATEGIC AIR FORCES IN EUROPE
Office of the Commanding General

SECRET
AUTH: CG: USSTAF
DATE: JUL 17 1944
INITIALS: R S

AAF Sta 586
APO 633, c/o PM, NY, NY.
17 July 1944

General H. H. Arnold,
Commanding General, Army Air Forces,
WASHINGTON, D.C.

Dear Hap,

The inclosed Special Report, "Effects of Allied Air Power on First Month of OVERLORD Operations", prepared by my Director of Intelligence, General McDonald, summarizes very well the extremely significant contributions made by our Air Forces to the success of OVERLORD.

The latent weaknesses of the German Air Force, created by our POINTBLANK operations, have now been fully exposed by the pressure of recent weeks. It even appears that the effectiveness of POINTBLANK was greater than we had anticipated.

Copies of this Special Report have been furnished Generals Bissell and White, in addition to the normal distribution.

Sincerely,

CARL SPAATZ
Lieutenant General, U.S.A.
Commanding.

3

4

cable supplies.

4. COUNTER AIR FORCE OPERATIONS. The primary mission of air power in major combined operations is to acquire and retain air supremacy - at least over the battle and L. of C. areas. Already it can be said without question that this prerequisite to the success of OVERLORD has been fully attained by our Air Forces. The highly successful POINTBLANK program of USSTAF (hereinafter discussed) had set the stage for the direct counter air force operations conducted intensively by all of The Allied Air Forces immediately prior to and since D-Day. As a result, the G.A.F. has been out maneuvered, out fought and thoroughly disorganized by the weight and efficiency of these operations. In short, the G.A.F. has failed both offensively and defensively in a manner strikingly reminiscent of its collapse in Sicily and Italy. This failure, manifestly, has had a profound influence upon every phase of OVERLORD.

a. Single Engine Fighter Force. On D-Day, it is estimated that the G.A.F. had some 250 single-engine fighters in France. Pursuant to

5

6

9

10

15

24

25

26

27

28

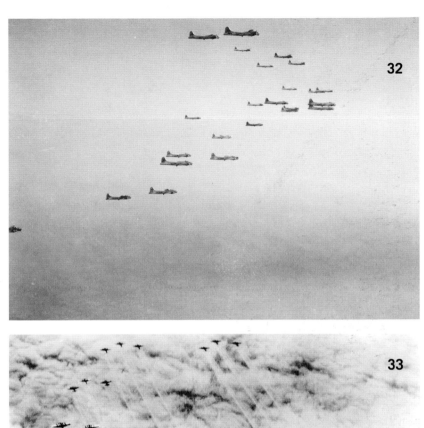

34

35

"When the place started to empty towards midnight," remembered one of the partiers, "we hired the three-man musical combo to stay on until four in the morning to play on just for our musical enjoyment alone."[152] Others used their time off to go home. When they were there, they invariably stood proudly in their Luftwaffe uniforms and had their picture taken with their mothers and fathers, wives and girlfriends, and little brothers and sisters.

Still, it was war. The Germans had overhauled not only their air defense strategies, but also virtually everything else in the military-industrial complex that supported the Luftwaffe. Messerschmitt moved many of its plants well to the east to Prussia and Poland and spread out other production to outlying factories converted from idle textile factories. Clever ideas were put into action to disguise factories. Airfields and autobahns inside Germany were turned into final assembly points, while in other cases, entire production lines were moved underground or into converted mines and quarries. Much of the new jet fighter, the Me-262, was being manufactured inside road tunnels and engineered caves.[153]

As the attacks on airfields increased, German air defenses stiffened. Antiaircraft batteries were transported to the bases, and gunners were brought in. At an airfield in France, the guns from a destroyed FW-190 were mounted on a steel pole with a pair of ammunition belts that fed two barrels. The gun emplacement was a hollowed-out foxhole 3 or 4 feet deep. However jerry-rigged, these guns were as deadly as any Focke-Wulf in the sky, and the airbases were regarded as one of the most dangerous targets a pilot could strafe.[154]

False airfields often were constructed near real German airfields. The decoy fields included mocked-up buildings and dummy aircraft. From a distance, they looked every bit the part, which was exactly the idea.[155]

Across Europe, life was a mixture of war and everyday routine. Farmers farmed, and textile factories made shirts. In France, the nightclubs in

Paris were doing a brisk business; the bakeries and office buildings and factories were open. In most of the major cities, the train stations were crowded with men, women, children, and ever-present soldiers. London was still abuzz with people, and the streets were crowded during the day. Piccadilly Circus was jammed with soldiers and sailors and Londoners going about their business.

Just up the Thames River from London, Tooey Spaatz settled into a comfortable Victorian mansion called Park House on the edge of Bushy Park in Wimbledon Common. Here he lived and worked with his senior staff, an arrangement that suited his command style. Mornings would find Spaatz in his pajamas until 1100 hours, dispatching cables and reading mission reports. He would lunch with his counterparts in the RAF and hold lively conversations in the evenings over poker and bourbon on the topic of air strategies and tactics. "Like some literary characters, Spaatz was inclined to get up very late and work very late," remembered a friend.[156]

Spaatz was a likeable study in contrasts. By all outward appearances, he looked like a pilot out of a World War I photograph, but he was thoroughly modern. In practice, he had an uncanny ability to see airwar in ways others could not, but he never said anything that sounded like bragging. He sported a neat mustache—the only senior American officer in the airwar to do so—wore a fifty-mission crush cap, and displayed a gentle smile with a twinkle in his eye not ordinarily associated with a combat officer. His headquarters, though, were a modern-day Google with people scattered about, including his own staff, who somehow kept up with his idiosyncratic lifestyle. Spaatz liked to play the guitar and sing, and he never shied away from opportunities to do so.

What Spaatz did shy away from was micromanaging his commanders. He delegated day-to-day operations as thoroughly as anyone could, but delegation carried with it its own set of problems. His commander for the Eighth Air Force, Jimmy Doolittle, for example, was already at odds with others, including Spaatz, because of his exceedingly cautious approach to iffy weather.

Jimmy Doolittle's headquarters, not far from Spaatz's, were housed in a fifteen-room home also on the Thames, rented from a retired British couple. But while Spaatz enjoyed working from home in his pajamas, Doolittle preferred to lead from the airbases. He was an immediate hit with his men, many of whom grew up watching him at the air races or reading about his feats in the newspapers. Doolittle was an excellent pilot and a smart aviator, and that went far with the men. He had pioneered instrument flight and helped develop better aviation fuels, which resulted in higher-performing engines. Most of all, he led the famous B-25 raid on Tokyo in April 1942, and to the pilots, that seemed to say it all. "He had just the right mix," said one of his men. "He was a forceful leader and approachable as a man."[157]

The winter of 1943–44 was as bad as any on record, and stormy weather grounded the Eighth Air Force for much of January and February. Of the thirty or so missions launched during the first two months, many were recalled, or the targets were obscured by thick clouds. Two raids in January seemed like a return to the disasters of October: they were savaged by the Luftwaffe, costing Spaatz and Doolittle more than 10 percent of the attacking forces.

In February, the weather remained stormy and cold; just fourteen missions were mounted through February 18, although only two of those amounted to much, and one of these was again savaged by the Germans due to miscues.

The ramps on the bases in England were packed with B-17s and B-24s, and it was possible to launch missions with seven hundred bombers or more, with a like number of fighters to escort them. Unfortunately, because of the winter storms, they were all too often grounded. This put Argument, which Spaatz was so keen to launch, on hold.

On the night of February 19, 1944, the opportunity Spaatz had been waiting for was finally at hand, if only by the slimmest of margins. That evening, Spaatz found himself in the middle of a heated debate. The question again was the weather and whether it was just good enough to give Argument a "go." Spaatz had everything in place to launch seven days of attacks, but he was up against Jimmy Doolittle's frustrating proclivity to cancel missions in the face of bad weather.

As the night closed in on Park House, belts of freezing rain pelted the windows, lending strength to Doolittle's position to not launch the next day. But Spaatz's commanding general of operations, General Frederick Lewis Anderson, argued otherwise. Doolittle had already canceled the plans twice and was opposed to launching the big raid on the next day, February 20. Anderson, on the other hand, wanted to order the bombers into the air at first light. The problem was entirely Spaatz's: the weather forecasters promised hard clouds with icing and a slight chance of finding some breaks over the targets in Germany. They were wretched conditions, but they were flyable nonetheless.[158] "I feel the minutes ticking away," Anderson said to Spaatz. "Our time to do our job is getting critically short."[159]

Spaatz called Doolittle for the latest weather report. It was just after 2130 hours. More than 1,600 bombers and fighters were fueled, bombed-up, and ready to go. The weather, Doolittle reported, was marginal, but the forecasters predicted it would be better the next day than at any time in the previous thirty days. Reported *Time* Magazine of the events as they unfolded that night in his headquarters: "Tooey was anxious to make a start on his greatest assignment: knocking the props from under the German air force. His plan was ready, with six top-priority factories listed for destruction in the first paralyzing blow. 'It's so important that I would risk the loss of 200 planes,' he said. At 11:30 p.m. Spaatz made his decision. Orders flashed out, at bases throughout Britain ground crews tumbled out of their bunks to ready the armada—1,600 bombers and fighters. The attack was to mark the beginning of modern precision airwar."[160]

Spaatz gave the order to go. Argument was on. Pointblank was on track.

CHAPTER 8

FORMATION

"Missions were very exhausting," said an airman from Wisconsin who flew on the heavy bombers against Germany. "By the time you got back, it is anywhere from eight to ten hours. You are always tense. You are scared, you are frightened. You are being shot at. And you are exhausted."[161]

The mission Tooey Spaatz had ordered into the air was to be flown by almost 10,000 airmen, each well trained and of the highest caliber. They rustled awake before dawn, were briefed on their mission, packed their charts and parachutes and guns, went out to an aluminum and steel cylinder of a plane that would be shot at for the next seven hours, and, in a massed takeoff that would put more than seven hundred bombers in the sky, they took their positions on the runway as if they were at their local air strip and they were going for a Sunday ride. It took nerves of steel, but about it all they were remarkably calm.

"Usually it would be totally dark," said Lee Toothman of the Eighth about the beginning of a mission, "but three hundred feet from the end of the runway a search light beam crossed the runway. If you went through that beam you had no alternative but to pull the plane off." Once the bomber was airborne, the pilot held it straight and level until they reached the buncher signal. "After reaching 200 feet, we picked up a vertical radio beam, which we laboriously circled until we reached ten thousand feet, at which time we joined our squadron in a preordained position established by a lead airplane which flew a race track pattern around the vertical radio beam."[162]

Robert Copp, a B-17 pilot, recalled the kinetic display of airplanes and signaling devices that surrounded the planes during the takeoffs: "If you ever saw the take-off pattern, you'd be amazed. Flares are shooting off all over the morning sky, and after I take off, all of the rest of the planes in our group follows us up through the fog. We'd fly back and forth until you picked up all your people and get them in formation."[163]

The order of takeoff was designed to fill in the combat boxes one by one, and that could take several hours depending on the size of the formation. As each combat element was assembled, the lead navigators took over. "One of the toughest jobs confronting me was how to lead a formation of forty-three bombers over a check point, on course, at altitude and exactly on time," navigator John Howland wrote many years later. "Turns had to be slow and gentle. Turn the formation too fast and those on the outside couldn't fly fast enough to keep up. Those on the inside were slowing down to the point where they were ready to stall out."[164]

The cockpit was the busiest place on the plane, although the pilot was so focused on his flying that he hardly knew when the bombs were released. Said a B-17 pilot, "From my perspective in the cockpit, I really couldn't see what was going on down on the ground. I was more focused on what was going on in the air, flying a tight formation, looking out for enemy fighters, watching the engines, instruments. See, you're in a cramped space, a little space. It was a cube. You had about 134 instruments to concentrate on, as well you had a helmet on a flak suit, a Mae West, then your flying [gear], sometimes your electrical suit, your parachute ... you're doing all of this and you're worrying about the oxygen because we had no pressurized cabins, everything was oxygen masks and colder than hell. And then you hear all of that engine noise, the guns shooting, your flak coming up and bursting around you, the fighters coming up and all of their shells blowing up around you. You didn't have a lot of time to look down at the ground and see what was going on."[165]

Some could see the ground, and after they did, many decided not to look again. Above an airfield near the French city of Saint-Lô, a B-17 navigator used his binoculars to identify the corner of an airplane hangar that was his target. They were bombing from the unusually low altitude of 10,000 feet. "A German truck or weapons carrier came roaring across the tarmac at high speed," he said. "I could see the faces of two men clearly as they looked up at us. They came to a screeching halt at the hangar and one man jumped out to open the door. He jumped back into the truck and they drove inside. Just then our bombs struck the hangar and blew it to pieces. The war becomes quite personal at lower altitudes."[166]

The bomb run was a period of nearly total vulnerability. For the bombardier to lock on to the target with his bombsight, the bombers had to fly straight and level, usually over flak batteries. "It was the longest ten minutes you ever wanted to fly," said Copp. "We turned on to the [Initial Point] and from there on it was straight and level with no evasive action." Because he was the lead aircraft, Copp had nothing in front of him except air. Once they reached the timing marker, called the Initial Point, they were unable to do anything evasive. "For the lead aircraft, you give control over to the bombardier and he flies it through the bomb run. You're up in the cockpit and you're just sitting there. You've got no hands on—no control—all you're doing is keeping the airspeed and altitude. That could last three to five minutes over the target." The lead aircraft determined the moment the entire combat

119

box would drop their bombs. Said Toothman of the man that flew in the compartment below him, "Since only the lead plane had a bombardier, everyone else toggled their bombs just as the leader released a smoke bomb. Corporal John Utt was our toggler since he had a perfect view sitting out in front in his Plexiglas turret."[167]

The Norden bombsight was key to the attack. Developed by the Dutch engineer Carl Norden, the bombsight could be gyro stabilized to compensate for the travel of the bomber over the surface of the Earth. It could sight a target with an accuracy of as much as 75 feet. The trick had to do with the inputs. The bombardier was required to sight the target and make adjustments as it connected to the autopilot on the bomber. Too much movement of the plane would throw it off and bombs would fly grotesquely off target during their 25,000-foot fall. One Eighth Air Force pilot summed it up best when he spoke of their misses: "They said we could drop a bomb in a pickle barrel. We couldn't drop a bomb in France." Said another crewman in obvious agreement, "In the beginning, we just couldn't hit 'em! We'd fly over, drop tons of bombs, and a P-38 would come in and check to see where the bombs had fallen for an after-action report. He'd come back and say 'Where'd you guys drop 'em?'"[168] In truth, finding where bombs had been dropped was often a challenge. Through the winter of 1942, only 50 percent of a crew's bombs once dropped could be found by reconnaissance aircraft, so gross were the errors. One bomb crew was scheduled to attack the submarine pens in Saint-Nazaire but instead, by mistake, bombed La Pallice, France, 100 miles away.[169]

The trick was both stability during the bomb run and slaving the gyro as the target was sighted. Both improved with experience. The circular error probable, or CEP, was the probability that 50 percent of bombs released would land within a specific distance from the desired ground zero. In May 1943, the CEP for bombs released by the Eighth

Air Force from the altitude of 20,000 feet was 1,100 feet for B17s and 1,300 feet for B-24s, roughly a distance greater than the length of three football fields. A postwar analysis found that, overall, just 20 percent of all bombs dropped landed within 1,000 feet of the intended target.[170] The oil division war report prepared in the aftermath of the war put these figures in a useful context. For every hundred bombs dropped on a target as large as an oil refinery, one bomb hit a pipeline, two hit production areas, two were duds, three landed on decoy plants, eight landed inside the target area but in open spaces and were largely harmless, and eighty-four completely missed.[171] Wrote one pundit inside the 486th Bomb Group, "As for bombing results. Tsk! Dame Rumor hath it that French, Dutch and Belgian citizens crowded closer and closer to our targets, feeling that the safest place to be was on the target."[172]

Fortunately, bombing accuracy improved. In March 1944, the Ninth Air Force reported, for example, that just 10.4 percent of the bombs they dropped landed within 500 feet of the aiming point; by May, that number had improved to 25 percent, and it was getting better.[173] Moreover, the size of the formations was doing a lot to compensate for the errors. With five hundred bombers over a target, only a few bombers had to make good on the bomb run for a target to be destroyed. The long held-out hope that a massive formation could utterly flatten a German aircraft factory was becoming a reality as the crews gained experience and the formations grew in size. Indeed, more than anything, the large formations that Spaatz could now get in the air would compensate for almost anything.

Anything but the weather.

CHAPTER 9

EXHAUSTION

As word filtered around the airbases that new flight schedules had been posted, the men migrated from their bunks to the mess hall to crowd around the bulletin boards on which the operations groups had posted freshly typewritten pages with the names of the crews scheduled for the morning mission. On February 20, 1944, it hardly mattered who you were; nearly every aircrew in the Eighth Air Force was on the list. The plan called Argument was on. "Operations is bustling with the arrival of late orders from the division," wrote one gunner who saw the flurry of action. "The message center is busy giving and receiving coded messages."[174] Nearly 11,000 men, 1,003 bombers, and 835 escort fighters were scheduled to attack nearly a dozen major German airframe factories in a single mission that would hit multiple sites at the same time. The plans were complicated and involved a diversionary raid to the north that, if timed correctly, might fly entirely unimpeded. The main targets were the very significant aircraft factories that produced the Luftwaffe fighters they faced on nearly every mission. To be bombed were the Messerschmitt, Junkers, and Focke-Wulf factories. With a sky full of escort fighters alongside, the Luftwaffe would have a fight on its hands.

The early-morning departures went smoothly, despite heavily overcast skies that covered most of England and gusting winds that raked the runways. The planes formed their individual combat boxes and moved into positions as they began to stream across the Channel in a procession that stretched some 90 miles. Flying precisely according to plan, the bombers then split up, sending one group north as a feint while the bulk of the force went into Germany. At altitude the contrails were so thick they formed their own cloud deck, while in front, visibility was often reduced to zero by occasional snow showers.

Even so, the weather was much better than expected. It was bitterly cold with clouds and storms that dotted the horizon, but it was still good. As they flew toward the continent, Doolittle's concern about the day's weather proved unwarranted. The bombardiers needed only one good fix to hit a target. Even when clouds covered as much as 70 percent of the surface of the Earth, there were generally enough holes to toggle the 500-pounders. In that sense, the weather on February 20 was surprisingly good, with some of the targets perfectly suited to methodical visual bombing.

German controllers watched the bombers as they approached the English Channel, but they were undecided about where they were headed and what would happen next. The northern force had made its turn, but it could easily turn again toward Berlin; the southern force was by far the stronger of the two, but it wasn't on a track that was particularly dangerous to German industry.

By the time the German controllers figured out a strategy, the fighter groups they launched were scattered by the weather and became disorganized. When they finally found the main American force, it seemed like they were under attack from every direction. The American fighters were all over them. The American escorts tore into the Germans, firing with all of their guns and flying well past their ordinary turn-around points. Rather than being pinned to the bombers, the escorts were flying all out. The dogfights were as intense as any yet, and the fights spiraled all the way to the ground. The Germans darted through the formations launching rockets and cannon shells, but they lacked their characteristic organization. Their attackers were largely fended off.

The disorganized German defenses allowed the main force to reach their primary targets and saturate two Messerschmitt plants with thousands of bombs. Their aim was deadly accurate, and the rain of explosives leveled the giant complex, leaving plumes of smoke curling into the sky.

The bombers winged around and turned home for England. As they cleared the flak fields and passed through the last of the Luftwaffe fighters, it became apparent that they were largely intact. Far from the bleak prospect of losing two hundred bombers in a single day, Spaatz had lost just twenty-one bombers. Moreover, total of seventy-eight Luftwaffe fighters had been shot down at a cost of just four American planes.

All told it was a heaven-sent day. One of Spaatz's friends was in Park House when Spaatz received the details of the mission and heard about the incredibly low losses. He would later say that Spaatz was riding a wave of pure happiness.[175]

Back at the bomber bases, the ground maintainers started their vigil just after lunch, waiting for the return of their bombers. They too expected heavy losses, but to their relief almost all of their planes returned. Still, it came at a price. Of the attacking force of some 1,000 bombers, 234 of the heavies came back badly shot up with forty-seven men onboard either dead or wounded.[176]

Understandably elated by the first day's mission, Spaatz gave the go ahead for the full plan. Unless ordered otherwise, missions would be flown back to back. For the next day's attack, a force of nearly 9,900 men were called on to strike German targets using 924 bombers and 679 fighters. The Ninth Air Force would fly their agile B-26 Marauders and their fighters, both to divert attention from the heavies and to bomb targets of their own. The second day's missions largely focused on German airfields and suppliers of aircraft parts. With almost 700 fighters, they also hoped to lure the Luftwaffe into the sky. "Our goal," said Spaatz of his intent, "[was] nothing less than the annihilation of the Luftwaffe. The strategy [was] to bait them and kill them. Send in the bombers—the bait—to destroy the factories and then massacre the planes and pilots that came up to defend them."[177]

At dawn, the pilots taxied their bombers to their runways and took off for targets, but they found the ground largely obscured by clouds. Still, owing to the sheer number of bombers in the air, clusters of B-17s and B-24s were able to find targets—and when they did, the bombing was good.

Because they had almost no instrument training, the storms and cloud cover stopped most of the Germans from taking off. Those who managed to get off the ground were picked apart by the escorts. The Germans lost thirty-two more airplanes and twenty-four more pilots.[178] The American losses were again slight. Spaatz lost thirteen B-17s, three B-24s, and just five fighters. One hundred and five of the returning bombers were damaged.

For the third day of attacks, Spaatz mustered 14,300 airmen and launched 1,396 heavy bombers with 965 fighters. The massive attack, however, promptly flew into clouds as thick as any the airmen had ever seen. Nearly half the bombers were forced to turn back. The rest found enough holes suitably large to lay bombs across a half dozen manufacturing complexes, but this time, the Luftwaffe was ready for them.

Rather than a dense cloud deck that precluded them from flying, the day's weather was mainly stormy, which the Luftwaffe pilots could fly in by picking their way around the thunderheads. The German controllers vectored in contact keepers, who shadowed the incoming bombers. Here and there, the German controllers saw groups of B-17s cut apart from the others, presumably by the heavy storms. They were prime for attack. When they organized into their attack formations, the Germans struck with a fury as yet unseen. One bomb group saw virtually all of their thirty bombers shot down or badly riddled with bullets, with eight more from their same division shot down. All told, 410 men were lost on 41 bombers that were shot down; 141 others were badly shot up, with 35 dead and 30 wounded on board the ones that got home.

Despite the disarray caused by the weather, two Junkers plants and three Messerschmitt factories were badly damaged. Importantly, the Germans lost another sixty-four fighters against eleven for the Americans.[179]

Despite the success of the first three days, Spaatz was unhappy with the overall results, largely because the weather kept clouding targets. Spaatz wanted the perfect raid. He wanted good weather, heavy bombing, and a knockout blow with a factory laid flat. On the fourth day, he would have anything but. His bombers were completely grounded by storms and heavy cloud decks that covered over much of England and almost all of the essential target areas in Germany. A mission had been scheduled, but it was canceled. Instead, the crews rested while the repair shops patched up their planes.

The amount of damage inflicted on the bombers during the first three days was substantial, but each successive mission was a maximum-effort mission, so there was no time to rest. Sheet metal was used to patch holes, wiring was reconnected, blown tires were replaced. But there was only so much sheet metal to go around, only so many extra engines, only so many rudders and elevators to replace the ones that had been shot off. That so many bombers were able to get into the air each day was a remarkable story that played out in the shadow of the headlines. Fixing bombers involved clever crew chiefs and some old-fashioned horse-trading: "When the serviceable planes had been prepared and gassed up, I would take men off these and they would work to ready the ones that had been hit," remembered Captain Fritz Nowosad, an engineer. "That's when we would start taking bits off our worst aircraft, swapping parts with other squadrons to get as many good aircraft as possible."[180]

Across the Channel, the Germans hastily called meetings to cipher the meaning from the intensity of the attacks. Surveyors reported the damage to the aircraft factories, which was considerable, while base commanders provided an update on frontline fighter losses, which also was considerable. What puzzled them most was the mission tempo. In the past, the Americans would mount a raid and then stand down for several days after it was over. But no longer. This was different. These attacks were back to back, and the targets were almost exclusively airframe factories and aircraft suppliers.

Given the information they had, and based largely on the increased tempo of the attacks, the Germans assumed that the expected invasion of France was near. They promptly beefed up their fighter forces by moving one group over from the Russian Front and shuffling other groups to bases better positioned to meet the bombers. Like hornets stirred up in their nest, the Luftwaffe now waited for someone to sting.

Of course, this was not yet D-Day, but it might well have been. February 24, 1944, dawned bright and cold, the fifth day of the scheduled attacks. Spaatz had 9,998 men in 923 bombers and 765 fighters available for raids that would involve three different bomber streams. The targets for the day included eight major aircraft factories, plus the dreaded Schweinfurt. The weather was clear.

The B-17s and B-24s assembled over England and streamed across the Channel, where they split into their three lines of attack. Ju-88 Junkers immediately maneuvered into position against the first group, which was headed toward the Messerschmitt complex in Gotha, Germany. With the controllers calling out position reports to a cluster of some three hundred German fighters, the Luftwaffe jumped. Once again, steel was thrown across the sky as bombers poured lead into fighters and Germans poured shells into the bombers. This time, the Thunderbolts and Mustangs were simply overwhelmed. Bombers rained down like dying comets. The trail to and from Gotha was littered with the crashed hulls of thirty-four B-24s.

The second group flew into Schweinfurt and unleashed their bombs with deadly accuracy. German resistance was stiff but diluted by the diversions of fighters sent to defend Gotha. Eleven B-17s were shot down.

The third bomber group were poised to attack the factories at Pozan, but they were forced by the clouds to instead bomb the factories at Rostock, Germany. They suffered five losses.

All told, fifty-one bombers were shot down and 161 were damaged, with five dead and twenty injured arrived in the bombers that made it back.[181] Another forty-six German fighters were gone; thirty-one Luftwaffe pilots had been killed.[182]

Living on little more than the Benzedrine pills they took to animate their senses, the pilots were sent up again the next day, their sixth mission in seven days. Incredibly, ground crews were able to patch up 903 B-17s and 24s, and mission planners were able to prepare target kits by working through the night. On the morning of February 25, 1944, the raids would target even more of the heavily defended German aircraft factories. "There will be no let up," said General Frederick Lewis Anderson, and there wasn't.[183]

Once again the American force split into three lines of attack: one bomber stream going after a ball bearing complex in Stuttgart, another against the fighter factories in Regensburg and Augsburg, and the third against a fighter factory in Furth. All three target areas were clear. Seen through the bombsights, the factory buildings were an impressive sight spread over several hundred acres, just waiting to be bombed.

More than five hundred German fighters rose to attack, but the results were a mixed bag. Over Regensburg, a force of 149 bombers escorted by 85 P-38s was sandwiched between accurate flak and a determined force of Luftwaffe fighter pilots who mounted a coordinated attack. In a fight that became a blizzard of deadly bullets and shells firing through the air, the Germans shot down an impressive thirteen B-17s and three P-38s.

A second wave of 635 bombers arrived and smothered their targets while fending off a swarm of German fighters. Against Augsburg, thirteen bombers were shot down, but against Furth, just six were lost. One formation was scarcely opposed.[184]

The results were spectacular. The German factories were nearly leveled by concentrated bombing—by far the most effective bombing so far. Equally as gratifying, forty-eight more German fighter aircraft had been shot down.

More than three hundred bombers came back riddled with bullets, cannon fire, and flak. They brought back two dead and thirty wounded.[185]

It was as strong of a showing as any new commander could hope for., and Spaatz had every reason to feel good. In one week, he rained down more bombs on German targets than the Eighth Air Force had dropped during all of 1942. Every major German aircraft factory had been hit—and hit hard.[186]

The Ninth Air Force came in to help, bringing their considerable force of medium B-26 Marauders and A-20 Havoc bombers into play as well as their own fleet of P-47s. The Ninth flew alongside the Eighth, thus marking the beginning of a crucial partnership that would pay off handsomely on D-Day. Spaatz could justifiably take credit for single-handedly bringing about this welcome turn of events.

American fighter pilots opened a new chapter in the war against the Luftwaffe. Flying with their newly fashioned drop tanks, they climbed into the atmosphere and craned their necks to see the first blip that would quickly swell into the shape of a Luftwaffe Me-109. They bounced anything they saw and etched lines of smoke with their tracers as they chased the enemy all the way to the ground. They proved to be terribly good at what they did, and from that point on, there would be no lack of confidence in them by their commanders. The fighters had turned into effective offensive weapons in their own right, just as Arnold had hoped they would.

Spaatz found it impossible not to overflow with emotion when he wrote Arnold to tell him that the attacks had more than just leveled plants and factories; they had brought the "very existence of the German Air Force" into question. Spaatz called his six days of attacks a "conspicuous success." Arnold no doubt agreed.[187]

German losses were indeed significant, and in that sense Argument accomplished its goal. Some six hundred freshly manufactured fighters had been destroyed on the assembly lines and now lay in the rubble of bricks and glass in the forty-one factories that had been hit, some of which had been leveled entirely. Production was shut down or severely constrained, and for months, deliveries of new fighters slowed to a trickle. In the air, another 355 frontline airplanes had been shot down.[188] All told, the Germans lost 33 percent of their remaining fighters and 20 percent of their pilots, many of them seasoned aces.[189] It was a monumental step toward Allied air superiority on D-Day.

In the aftermath of this week of nearly unrelenting bombing, some of the German high command walked among the ruins. It was as sobering a sight as any had seen. "I have seen Erla-Leipzig and Oschersleben," said Field Marshal Erhard Milch after the February raids on the aircraft factories there. "There is nothing to be seen but bent wires, like a bombed apartment block here in Berlin. Outside there are bomb craters eight to nine meters deep and fourteen to sixteen meters across."[190]

Unlike Anzio or Iwo Jima or the Battle of the Bulge, there was no city or region by which these pivotal days of air attacks would come to be known. The Air Force gamely tried to come up with a name, but in the end the best they could do was put to it an unimaginative moniker that somehow stuck. The air battles of February would become known as Big Week.

CHAPTER 10

LOCUSTS

If Carl "Tooey" Spaatz was the fire that burned in the belly of the Eighth, General Elwood R. "Pete" Quesada was the spirit that infused the Ninth. Young, energetic, and combative, Quesada was one of the senior officers in England who had gone straight into the Army Air Corps, bringing with him no interest whatsoever in artillery or cavalry. Raised in a comfortable middle class family, Quesada's mother was an immigrant from Ireland and his father a Spanish banker living in the Washington, D.C., area. Quesada was well coordinated and exceedingly confident in himself. He was the quarterback of his college football team and a lifeguard during the summers in the Washington, D.C., tidal basin.

But above all, he was an aviator through and through, and a cocksure fighter pilot at that. Along with Spaatz and Eaker, Quesada flew as the third member of the aerial refueling demonstration that took place over Los Angeles in 1929. Tall, dark, and animated by the passion of his Spanish forebears, Quesada was a forceful advocate of airplanes in the aggressive and largely untested role of close air support for ground soldiers. He won Tooey Spaatz's enduring confidence for the gutsy missions his men repeatedly flew in North Africa, including the near total destruction of Pantelleria in 1943 from the air. Quesada commanded the Northwest African Coastal Air Force and was in charge of interdicting German forces trying to reinforce their positions in North Africa. He was a perfectionist with exacting standards; he and his men dominated the Mediterranean air space with such totality that "if a ship got through, we failed," as he once said in an interview.

Filled with an abundance of raw energy if not smooth political manners, Quesada impressed his good friend Carl Spaatz and Dwight Eisenhower alike and was one of the men they brought back from North Africa to England. He was given the Ninth Air Force's main components in England, the IX Fighter Command and IX Tactical Air Command.[191] Now he had 1,600 fighters and 35,000 men to bring to bear against the Germans.[192]

Nazi-occupied Europe remained a sprawling, diverse landscape across which were etched transportation lines and distribution grids consisting of railroads, autobahns, canals, and rivers. Whereas the B-17s and B-24s faced a list of several hundred large, highly visible strategic targets such as factory complexes and refineries that could be bombed from 25,000 feet, the medium bombers and fighters faced a forest of thousands of smaller tactical targets that had to be bombed from below 15,000 feet. According to an intelligence report from April 1944, Hitler possessed three times the rail capacity he needed to mobilize his considerable military forces, four times the train cars, eight times the locomotives, and ten times the facilities to service and repair rolling stock. Much of this traced back to the overcapacity originally engineered into the German rail system when it was designed. But it had to be destroyed.

No doubt anticipating the war that lay ahead, German planners built a web of interconnected switches and spurs that allowed their war machine to reroute traffic along a nearly infinite number of alternate routes between any two points on the map. To keep it functioning in the face of attacks, nearly a million laborers were strategically positioned around the continent to move to wherever they were needed to make repairs. In most cases, after even the most intense and accurate bombing, a cut line could be reopened within twenty-four to forty-eight hours.[193]

One strategy essential to the success of the initial toehold as the soldiers came ashore on D-Day was to isolate the landing areas from a German counterattack so the soldiers only faced the coastal defenses. To do this required cleansing large areas around and leading into the Normandy beaches so that reinforcements could not come forward during the landings. This required an enormous air effort. Planes would have to attack and bomb roads, bridges, depots, marshaling areas, rail road tracks, switches, airfields, fuel dumps, artillery emplacements, German maintenance facilities, field command units, and soldiers bivouacked in tents. Only by throwing the sum total of American air forces into the attack could these geographic sectors near Normandy be reduced to rubble and left bare as a winter field.

Like swarms of locusts descending on crops during a hunt for food, the Allies sent into the skies overwhelming, unstoppable numbers of medium bombers and fighters to attack key targets, including just about every road that led to the Normandy beaches. After that, interdiction missions on D-Day would police the routes heading into the coastal landing areas and attack whatever moved. If tanks were spotted, they would be taken out by air. If a train attempted to move forward, the locomotive would be destroyed and the tracks cut by bombs. Airfields would be post holed and hangars enflamed. Supply depots would be ignited like matches to tanks of gasoline. And if the Luftwaffe appeared in the air, those same warplanes pounding the ground would lift up and engage them in the air.

In Quesada's mind, this was the ever-so-critical but largely untapped value of military aviation. Airplanes could fly pilots over the battlefield, where they could see and destroy tanks that were just over a hill from the ground soldiers. Airplanes could be used to cut railroads and collapse bridges and find and bomb supply depots. But, they would have to attack the ground, and, except for those who flew with him in the Mediterranean, almost none of his pilots in the Ninth Air Force knew a thing about air-to-ground attack. Rather, they were dogfighters. They loved the wide-open spaces of the sky and the world of air-to-air combat, where they chewed up hundreds of square miles of airspace during a single dogfight against a FW-190. That was what they came to Europe trained to do. To bomb a ground target, though, was alien to them. They would need to learn new skills. They would need to learn to cut a needle-thin slice through the air with a pair of 500-pound bombs under their wings as they nosed down toward a target on the ground. "So many of those fighter boys come into the war intoxicated with the glory of aerial dog-fights or the fame of big bombers," said Quesada. "We needed to devise a way to teach a new way of air warfare."

Quesada got to work. He requisitioned a British airfield with a gunnery range and sent his fighter pilots back to school. They were going to become experts in dive-bombing ground targets. He gave his pilots two weeks on the bombing ranges with a syllabus that included dive-bombing at various angles to the ground, optimal bombing speeds, the best altitude to release a bomb, and the best trajectory to do the most damage. Graduation consisted of five practice dive-bombing missions and five strafing missions, each preceded by a briefing and each followed by an in-depth debriefing. "Our job required new ways of doing things, so it was back to school for hundreds of us," said one of Quesada's pilots.[194] It was the sort of initiative that cemented Quesada's place in the hearts of the ground commanders for whose soldiers Quesada's newly trained pilots would be providing air-to-ground support. Quesada's airplanes would open corridors through which the ground soldiers would advance and take out enemy traps that lay ahead. Soldiers could scarcely ask for more.[195]

Some months later, Quesada stood before an assembled group of Allied generals and top-level leaders and gave a top-secret presentation of the air interdiction plans for D-Day. His P-38s were going to encircle the beaches and shoot down anything in the air that had an Iron Cross on its side, while his P-47s would run hunt-and-kill attacks against anything that tried to move forward on the ground inside the perimeter that extended some 100 miles behind the landings.

Winston Churchill puffed his cigar as Quesada built up a head of steam. He would strafe, bomb, and dive-bomb anything that didn't know the winner of the World Series, as he put it, and his P-38s would hunt down and kill any German unlucky enough to penetrate the inner sanctum of airspace over the ships. Quesada's Spanish blood rose to the surface as he spoke, and his confidence was electrifying. Meekly, the first question floated on the air. "Pete," asked an infantry commander, "how are you going to prevent the German Air Force from preventing our landing?" Quesada didn't miss a beat: "There is not going to be a German Air Force there." This piqued the interest of the recumbent Churchill. "Young man," he asked, "how can you be so sure?" Answered Quesada, "Mr. Prime Minister, because we won't let them be there. I am sure of it." Churchill, no doubt slumped inward on himself and with a wave of his cigar, mumbled a growl of approval. Quesada was utterly convincing.[196]

The rules freeing the fighter pilots to be fighter pilots was cathartic, and, in truth, all of the fighter pilots had something more in mind than waiting around for the Germans to hit first. If they wouldn't come up to fight, then they'd go down and get them. As it happened, this was something fighter pilots liked to do. Dropping down to the deck just feet above the ground was as natural to them as punching holes in the sky at 30,000 feet. And while flying over France at 300 miles per hour at tree-top level may have seemed like a death wish to others, to them it was sport. Wrote one pilot in his squadron's history, "On the way back to the base we were 'hedge hopping,' flying 20–30 feet above the ground, lifting one wing, then another to go over some treetops, and just enjoying a good buzz job. I had just flown over a farmer driving a horse and wagon. Both the horse and farmer must have been scared out of their skins because the plane, just barely over their heads, was passed before they knew what was happening. This momentarily took my mind off flying when I noticed the two planes to the right of me suddenly jump upwards and I looked ahead and there I was—heading smack into some high tension wires."[197] The pilot hauled back on his wheel and closed his eyes but snagged the wires anyway. Somehow he still managed to get back home. He nearly died, but that didn't matter: it just made for a better story.

"The term rat-racing on the deck referred to a dangerous game which we all never the less enjoyed greatly, of playing follow-the-leader across the countryside at as close to zero altitude above ground as we could get, at speeds of 200–300 miles an hour," said John Hedenberg, another pilot. "This meant ducking down into valleys, hopping over tree lines, etc. to the maximum degree possible without hitting anything. Needless to say, it was highly risky and sometimes someone would make a tiny, but fatal mistake or fail to see some obstacle. At such times that someone usually got killed rather instantly on an explosion of flames." Such was the case with one of his friends, although there was a code and pilots scarcely thought of the dead. "Too bad, a really swell Joe," said Hedenberg of the pilot who crashed into the ground. And that was that.[198]

Fighter pilots were born with a natural aggressiveness. It was woven into their DNA, something that surfaced during training and stayed with them during their tour. They were restless and irritable when they were not in the sky. When they were in the sky, they liked to fly. When they flew, they wanted to fight. And when they fought, they wanted to win. "The thrill of the chase is hypnotic," remembered P-38 pilot Arthur Thorsen. "Your body tingles. You feel you have wings of your own. You make funny noises to yourself. You strain against your shoulder straps as if that will give you more momentum. You begin to tremble with the knowledge that the German ship ahead of you is yours. You can take him."[199] That was the essence of a fighter pilot.

Robert Powell enlisted when he was nineteen and entered the war as a P-47 fighter pilot. Years later he remembered his time in combat. "Most of us believed we had better aircraft, better training, and a better fighting spirit than the German pilots," said Powell. But he knew the truth, and the truth was that there was nothing like combat to turn ordinary flying into combat-effective flying. Powell met Adolf Galland after the war and made a confession: "I didn't learn to fly until the fight one of your fighters got on my ass." Joel Popplewell, a Kentucky native and also a P-47 pilot agreed: "Every time we went out, even in combat, we learned something new."[200] Gilbert Burns, a Thunderbolt driver, agreed but said that it wasn't the mechanics of flying that changed with combat. Rather, he said, at some point pilots became hunters. "My fifth combat mission changed my viewpoint on combat flying in many ways," he said. "The first four missions I had flown mechanically. The hands and feet flew the plane, the finger squeezed the trigger, doing automatically all the things I had been taught. But the fifth mission got me thinking. I thought about killing."[201]

Fighter pilots had their own techniques, and they talked about them endlessly, usually with their hands to show the relationship of their own plane to the enemy. Such talk flowed like ale in an Irish pub. One would say that speed was how to survive, another a quick and violent move. Hit him with a baseball bat. Dive like hell. Tighten your turn. Come home with your neck sore from looking around all the time. Block out the sun with a wingtip and check that area out. Slice to the inside using rudder. If you lose your wingman, you lose 75 percent of your eyes and advantage. He'll hit you from 1,000 yards if he can—and he can, with cannons. Stay high and fast. Keep the sun behind you. Don't run. Fight like hell. Keep looking. See him first. If you spot a Jerry below you, go down and get him and never let him out of your sight until he's been shot down. Read yesterday's mission report—and figure that the German controllers read them, too, and are adjusting their next plan of attack. Fly good formations. "A guy who doesn't know what his airplane will do, won't have to worry about how to make it do it when he could use the time shooting down the Hun," said one pilot, meaning either learn how to fly combat or end up dead.[202]

On a fighter base, a competitive spirit charged the atmosphere just as surely as there was air to breathe, and not a single pilot would have it any other way. Those who had the touch, those who were the good sticks in the squadron, those who were the leaning forward fighter pilots spared no opportunity to show it off. Said one, "Anyone knows just how good a red hot outfit looks when they take off and land. They look real good. This is all done by practice and don't think they don't feel proud of themselves when they make good landings and takeoffs. I know because I'm in one of those red hot outfits and it makes me feel good as hell."[203]

Pete Quesada's counterpart in the Eighth Air Force was General William E. Kepner, commanding general for the fighters of the XIII Fighter Command. Like Quesada, Kepner was a cradle airman, never seeking a ground billet in the traditional Army, always looking toward the sky. Kepner oversaw a force of 1,500 fighters—nearly the same number as Quesada's—although he mainly had P-51s, which he used to escort bombers and employed for ground strafing. Kepner was there the day Jimmy Doolittle freed the fighters to roam the skies. Doolittle stood before Kepner's desk and gave the fighters license to fight. "We're here to destroy German fighters!" said Jimmy Doolittle. Asked Kepner, "You mean you're authorizing me to take the offensive?" Doolittle smiled. "I'm directing you to." Kepner nodded. *Kill Germans.* They both looked at a sign on the wall next to his desk that said the duty of a fighter pilot was to escort bombers. "Take it down," said Doolittle. "Put up a new one that says 'The first Duty of the Eighth Air Force Fighters is to destroy German fighters.'"[204] New signs were posted on the walls. After living so long in the shadow of the heavies, there was immediate celebration among the fighters. In the briefing rooms, pilots cheered when they heard the news.

Doolittle's decision paid off right away. There was an immediate upswing in combat sorties against the Luftwaffe. The appetite for belts of .50-caliber ammunition, the type used by the fighters, surged 56 percent between February and March 1944, while for the bombers it actually declined.[205]

Further proof could be found in daily combat statistics. Prior to Spaatz's arrival in England in January 1944, the fighters of the Eighth Air Force had not yet destroyed a single German aircraft on the ground. Except for the inconvenience of occasional bombings, a German fighter base was actually one of the safest places for a German to be. Spaatz, Doolittle, Kepner, and Quesada saw to it that that changed immediately. The first German plane lost to a planned ground attack was destroyed on February 4, 1944.[206] Within days, dozens more lay burning on German airfields. Between January and June, the number of strafings and bombing attacks against Luftwaffe airfields grew from just eighty-three missions for the entire prior year to an impressive 6,500.[207] The fighters were fighting, and it was paying handsome dividends.

In addition to strategic bombing and escorting the heavies, air-to-ground attack had opened up yet another thrust against the Germans. The skies were filled with the fighters like locusts, some staying up to dogfight, some coming down to strafe. All attacking the Luftwaffe.

CHAPTER 11

FLAK BOYS

At sea, the shrill whine of a shell traversing the sky gave a sailor some warning of impending death. But in the sky, the ordinary rumble of the bomber was the only noise an airman heard before the blinding flash of an 88 blew his plane apart. In the sky, the terror was not in knowing whether they would be hit, but when. "We never had a foxhole to go in," said Miller. "Our foxhole was our airplane, which was [their] target. There was nothing to protect us except our guns."[208]

The more missions the airmen flew, the more flak they encountered. The more flak, the more death. Flak destroyed bombers in the most terrifying of ways. In fact, flak would soon destroy more bombers than the Luftwaffe fighters themselves were responsible for. So intense was the fire from some of the flak fields that during an attack the explosions from the thousands of shells momentarily altered the very chemical makeup of the atmosphere. Wrote a tail gunner in his diary in the aftermath of a mission, the sky he flew through was almost equal parts oxygen and steel with a greasy residue that suffused the air. "I could smell it through my oxygen mask. The noise was cruel and the concussions were murderous. Every ship in the group must have had flak holes—we had plenty."[209]

Until late 1942, flak had been something of a secondary arrow in the Luftwaffe's quiver.[210] The idea of aerial bombardment by streams of B-17s and B-24s hadn't yet fully materialized as the threat it would become, and flak batteries, while extensive, consisted largely of coastal installations and scattered emplacements around the key factories. It was the ever-increasing size of the bomber streams in late 1942 that made it clear that more guns were needed.

While Hitler rarely allowed his Luftwaffe commanders to talk about air defense, air defense was indeed one of their responsibilities, and he relished the idea of fields forested with 88-mm artillery, of cities surrounded by flak towers, and of briar patches of antiaircraft batteries so thick that at least one plane would catch a burr trying to cross it. In mid-1943, Hitler reacted to the bomber streams by ordering up some nine hundred additional heavy flak batteries consisting of some 5,500 more guns. He manned those with a mix of soldiers and civilians and ordered more than 630,000 men, women, and children to be trained to man batteries in the Western sectors alone. By the time of Tooey Spaatz's spectacularly intense air attacks of February 1944, between 2,100 and 2,400 heavy batteries now surrounded high-value targets, for an incredible total of 10,000 German anti-aircraft guns facing skyward toward the Allied bomber crews.[211]

More than four hundred guns defended each individual manufacturing complex, with as many as six hundred guns surrounding some key airplane plants, oil refineries, and synthetic fuel plants. Some fields had batteries that could carpet the sky with two hundred shells in one volley and could fire two thousand shells in less than sixty seconds. It was nearly impossible to fly against any target worth bombing without triggering a mad race to the guns and a whirl of barrels rising skyward to pour fire into the Allies' fragile Boeings.[212]

The theory behind flak was based on the idea that a shell exploding in the sky would be so violent that close enough was close enough. The basic weapon was an 8-ton artillery piece that fired an enormous 88-mm shell into the sky, packed with explosives and 1,400 jagged metal pieces, any one of which could shred the skin of a B-17 as if it were tissue. Each gun was part of a larger battery that consisted of between six and eight guns and was manned by between forty and 120 artillerymen.[213] The shells were fired upward at the rate of twenty rounds per minute with fuses set to explode after a ten- to twenty-second trip into the sky.[214] The shells blasted out of their 23-foot-long barrels with muzzle velocities so terribly kinetic that they could rip apart a Sherman tank at pointblank.

The 25-pound shells were grooved on the inside to shape the explosion of the 1,400 shards of jagged metal outward in an eruption of utmost violence. A direct hit would rupture a B-17 from the inside out in an angry flash of red; a near miss would create a kill box 20 to 30 yards wide with damage possible as far away as 200 yards.[215]

Flak batteries were almost everywhere the planes flew, including in unexpected spots that claimed crews with their unspeakable violence. Flak guns were hidden inside boxcars left standing in marshaling yards or pulled by trains. They were put on top of flatboats anchored in harbors and in lakebeds; they were built along the coast, around factories, and in wide belts of no-man's lands.[216] Each individual gun was capable of firing shells 35,000 feet up and 12 miles in any direction, indiscriminately blasting large holes in the sky and triggering a macabre sense of humor among the bomber crews.[217] "One comforting feature of flak" wrote one pilot, "is that the German fighter pilots would not risk the hazard of flying through their own flak concentrations to get to you, so you didn't have to worry about fighter attacks while you were being shelled by 88-mm anti-aircraft batteries."[218]

The largest of them all, the 128-mm guns, rivaled anything the land armies had and nearly equaled in size the big guns carried by the battleships at sea. The 128s crowned the enormous flak towers that protected Vienna, Berlin, and other German cities, and they could send shells the size of garbage cans packed with metal and TNT into the formations flying 20,000 feet above them.[219] Rising some 50 feet high, these concrete-and-steel flak towers could shelter hundreds of civilians inside while from the top their guns fired into the sky, reaching bombers miles away.

One operator was so heavily involved with firing that he was caught by surprise when a tail section of a B-24 came crashing to the ground. The B-24 had been hit by a shell from a 128-mm gun blasting off its nose and an inboard engine in one clean shot.[220] One bomber crew was hit by the blast of a near miss. Chunks of metal sliced through the B-17 like a blizzard of knives thrown by some invisible hand. One of the airmen on board described the instant damage and carnage: "A burst of flak hit the plane tearing off the right horizontal stabilizer, part of the right wing, and kill[ing] both right engines," he said. "In the tail section, S/Sgt. Joseph Sawicki was struck by the flak burst that tore away his left arm below the elbow … both waist gunners suffered multiple wounds and each had a broken arm."[221]

As the bombers approached, the gun crews were given a direction, a height setting, a side setting, and a fuse setting by the gun director for the battery. "We put cotton in our ears," said a sixteen-year-old flak boy. "The firing bell sounds for three seconds. The ammunition gunners remove a shell from the fuse setter, pushes it into the breach and fires. A flame shoots out of the muzzle. The barrel recoils. The gun jumps. Effective fire was only possible during the run into the target because the attacking aircraft were not able to alter direction, height or speed. This was estimated to last twenty seconds and only this time was available for the flak."[222]

The German gun crews had merit systems, and they competed for rewards that included extra food rations and gasoline for the winner's family. The flak boys earned medals for shooting down a plane and prizes based on the number of empty shell casings found on the ground around their feet after an attack. Incompetence was scorned. "Working the range finder on our predictor at our battery, we had an adult, a very stupid [one]," remembered a disgusted teenage gun layer after his team lost. "Suddenly in the middle of one of the engagements he threw himself on the ground and covered his head with his hands. Denied ranging information, the predictor could not function and the battery had to cease fire. Peering through the power x32 telescopes of the range finder he had been watching the bombers with their bomb bay doors open and he had seen the bombs falling away. And he thought the bombs were coming for him."[223] The entire crew received a harsh reprimand.

The gun directors had several firing solutions when it came to shooting down an Allied bomber. Barrage fire, an artilleryman's tactic to create a wall of exploding shells through which no enemy could pass, was all too common. The directors would lay their fire across a swath of sky several miles in width and then walk the shells back toward the bombers in overlapping, rolling black puffs of steel. Those who witnessed this kinetic display approaching were quick to say prayers, no matter how often they'd skipped church in the past.

Boxed fire was another way of bringing down a plane. A presighted area would be bracketed by shells and then flooded with bursts until the planes inside the box were chewed up by shrapnel.[224] During one of the attacks on the German sub pens at Bremen, Germany, the gun directors boxed a formation of B-17s. One of the pilots remembered feeling helpless. "Just about at bombs away at 24,000 feet we were caught in what was called a box-barrage of flak. Sixteen German gunners on 88-mm guns, twenty-five pound shells, all fired at the same time to fill a cube of airspace with shrapnel that broke into bits of half inch or so. Pretty deadly stuff to airplanes, equipment, engines, people. We were bracketed perfectly. Within seconds nine of our twenty-two airplanes were in trouble." As they completed their bomb run and made a turn for the Dutch coastline, they encountered even more trouble from the coastal batteries as they headed out into the North Sea. "Crossing the Dutch coast at about 3,000 feet you could look down and see the muzzles of the guns flashing as we went overhead."[225]

Edward Tracy, a B-17 pilot, belatedly realized that radar-guided guns had zeroed in on his plane. Like a fighter pilot, he yanked his yoke to the right and put his bomber into an abrupt dive so the shells would burst above him. It worked. He leveled out and looked back to see that the shells had virtually followed his every turn. "I could see the long, curving contrails that our formation had left in its wake. Angry puffs of smoke were polka-dotting the long contrails left in the sky by our formation, attesting to the accuracy of the German radar-controlled 88-mm flak batteries."[226]

Throughout 1943, flak batteries accounted for just 252 American planes shot down, versus 877 downed by German fighters. The addition of 5,500 guns had an immediate effect. In 1944, flak claimed 1,587 B-17s and B-24s.[227] In the air over Nazi Germany, the Allies were never entirely safe.

CHAPTER 12

BERLIN

The month of March dawned cold and dark with dense clouds blanketing the bases and storms that showered down belts of snow, rain, and sleet. Thin blue lines of smoke rose from the Quonset huts as the men fed their small stoves to keep warm. Across the airfields and around the perimeter tracks, hardly a thing moved. Most of the men were in their bunks catching up on sleep, writing letters, or playing cards. March 1, 1944, was payday for the enlisted men, and they lined up at the bursar's office for their money.

Away from the war, the day began as usual. In London, Paris, and Berlin, bakers opened their boulangeries, children were wrapped in coats and scarves and sent off to school, and train stations were packed. It was the beginning of the third month in the third year of the Allied airwar; there was still not a single American soldier in combat on the ground in Europe.

The drumbeat of D-Day, though, was ever present, and the buildup of combat forces was progressing at an astonishing rate. Jeeps, tanks, and artillery pieces lined virtually every street and alley in England. In the fields, wire fences enclosed small tent cities that would soon bulge with a million men.

For the airwar, the Allies were on track to have a combined D-Day force of 3,400 heavy bombers, 1,600 twin-engine medium bombers, 2,300 gliders and transports, and 5,400 fighters of all types, including some 300 that would be used for assessing bomb damage, forecasting the weather, and providing photographic and human intelligence.[228]

The Germans, though, weren't resting. With every passing week, German flak towers and gun emplacements grew in number, and coastal batteries grew stronger. Steel claws designed to hole landing craft linked up with land mines on wooden staves from Pas-de-Calais to Normandy, and more were laid down every day.

German aircraft factories had been badly damaged during Big Week, but they were not shuttered. Photo-reconnaissance experts concluded that ninety-nine functioning German airfields still threatened the D-Day beaches. Some seven hundred combat-ready fighters were based on these field including the powerful Me-109s, FW-190s, Heinkels, and Junkers.

In addition, there were seventy-five major rail hubs through which German reinforcements could flow to the front, forty-two major German radar installations along the English Channel, and fifty coastal batteries that could pour deadly fire into the ships as they approached the beaches. Hardly noted were the hundreds of other targets such as depots, refineries, roads, marshaling yards, and bridges.[229]

"The thing that has struck me the most," said Spaatz in a letter to a friend, "is the critical time factor. We have very little time in which to finish the job."[230] It was the understatement of the war. If every single day between March 1 and D-Day featured perfectly clear skies, and if three major targets were completely destroyed by near-perfect air strikes, it would still take almost a hundred days to clear the list of these 292 must-hit targets of airfields, radar stations, and coastal batteries, not counting the cottage industry of piece goods shops that manufactured five hundred new planes a month, nor the pressing demands to bomb their launch sites for the German buzz bombs that were spread across in western France.[231] Unfortunately, Spaatz had just ninety days. And the weather was hardly perfect.

The grind of the Big Week missions had taken its toll on the airmen of the Eighth. They were exhausted, they needed food and exercise, and they needed time to sort things out. Hundreds were suffering from "shell shock" or struggling with "war neurosis." Many of them were on the edge of nervous breakdowns. Some had already gone over the line and were in the hospitals, with sympathy hard to find. Sadly, because post-traumatic stress syndrome was still decades from being diagnosed, those who refused to fly were branded as cowards.

After Big Week, the crews rested for two days before they took off again. In their first new missions, they attacked an aircraft factory in Brunswick, Germany, on February 29, and then hit the rail yards in Frankfurt on March 2. Like the Allies, the Luftwaffe was worn down, too, and the bombers were only lightly opposed. Of the 270 bombers that hit Brunswick, just three were shot down. The same held for Frankfurt. Of the four hundred bombers on that mission, just nine bombers were lost, most to flak.

But rail yards were not the targets Spaatz had in mind. In fact, targets were hardly his first priority. It was back to the multiplicity of purpose: airfields, factories, and fighters. Operating under the theory that highest-value German targets would stir up the strongest defensive response from the Luftwaffe, and that American fighter pilots were superior to Germans in aerial combat, it followed that the more German fighters that were drawn into the air, the faster they could be killed. It also held that by attacking targets of national importance, such as Berlin itself, the Germans would be compelled to move air defense fighters away from the English Channel and to beef up the defenses of the interior. Both outcomes were consistent with the objective of gaining air superiority before D-Day. By pinning down fighters to the rear to defend Berlin, away from the invasion beaches and by shooting down and killing as many of the others as possible, Spaatz was inching toward his goal for Eisenhower's invasion. Thus it was for an airman that the cruel reward for the job well done in February was to be assigned to bomb Berlin in March. The capital of Germany, home to countless industrial giants, was now on top of the target list. The airwar's bloodiest day yet was fast approaching.[232]

By March 1944, Berlin was no longer a residential enclave of the German elite, nor was it a city of the arts or a haven for the intellectuals of Germany. By 1944, the streets of Berlin had long since been festooned with flagpoles flying the red-and-black swastika of the Nazi party and lined with soldiers, agents, and party officials moving from one meeting to the next. With a population of some 4 million residents, Berlin was in fact a military target of extraordinary value and the center point for the nation's political and military base of power. Here were headquarters of the Gestapo, the New Reich Chancellery, and the Air Defense Ministry. In Berlin proper could be found some ninety military barracks, military headquarters, training facilities, and depots. The plants and factories around the perimeter of the city made radar sets, instrument panels, radios, navigational equipment, ball bearings, and pneumatic mechanisms for tanks, artillery, and airplanes, as well as the pulse jet engine that powered the V-1 rocket.

To make room for the war effort, some 1.2 million Berliners had been evacuated from the city, including most of the city's women and children. Behind them arrived a flood of laborers and soldiers to work in the factories and to fill the now-vacated apartment buildings, some five to a room, most conscripted from conquered territories.[233] In truth, by March 1944, those who could leave Berlin had left; those who remained elicited little sympathy from Allied airmen. "They are victim of their own leadership," argued Captain Ellis B. Scripture, a lead navigator on a B-17, meaning that they didn't have to go along with the status quo of the Third Reich.[234]

To hit Berlin would certainly draw the Luftwaffe into the sky, but it would no doubt come at a terrible price. The most prized target in Germany was surrounded by some 742 Luftwaffe fighters, with just as many if not more flak guns pointed skyward. If they attacked, it would be an air battle of titanic proportions.

On March 6, 1944, the Allied aircrews were awakened at 0300 hours. The first question airmen asked was, invariably, "How much gas?" A full fuel load meant a long mission deep into Germany.

On March 6, 1944, precisely ninety days before the landings on the Normandy beaches, the tanks were full.

General Jimmy Doolittle was as brave as any aviator in the war, and he had nothing to prove on that count. But he was more of an engineer than a visionary. His leadership was unmatched in areas such as the mathematics of instrument navigation, the carbon structure of high-octane fuels, and the thorny issues of a long-range mission from an aircraft carrier to Tokyo. But he lacked a degree of aggression. General Fred Anderson, Spaatz's operations officer, kept pushing Doolittle to launch more raids and schedule more missions. When Doolittle scrubbed missions on the eve of Big Week, it was Anderson who went over his head to get them rescheduled. And it was Anderson who understood the significance of Berlin.

German controllers were cautiously selective about which bomber formations they would oppose. Having lost one third of their frontline fighters during Big Week, it made sense to conserve their strength for the most important targets. As the missions against Brunswick and Frankfurt showed, a well-defended bomber stream was generally avoided, or, if it was attacked, it was hit where the fewest American escorts flew. The controllers watched for mistakes, stragglers, and stray groups.

Given this, how then to entice the controllers to send up the Luftwaffe when the skies were thick with American Mustangs? The only answer was Berlin, and Anderson knew this. It wasn't about bombing the German capital, per se. It was about drawing the Luftwaffe into the sky in numbers significant enough to further reduce their frontline strength. It was about bait. "We've got to go to Berlin with three bomb divisions," said Anderson. "Then they'd come up."

And then they'd be shot down.[235]

The operations groups laid out a plan of attack to hit Berlin in the same way they hit the factories in February. Massive missions would be launched on consecutive days, each with as many bombers as could fly. To draw as many German fighters into the air as possible, there would be no feints and no diversionary raids. Each mission would follow the same path in and out as the day before. The escorts would fan out ahead of the bombers and hunt down the Luftwaffe, but plenty of them would stay alongside to take up any challengers. Specific military targets were designated for the focus of the attacks, but, in truth, just about all of Berlin was a military target.

Weather remained a problem in March, and storms covered most of Germany, forcing Doolittle to cancel the first day of attacks against Berlin. The next day's weather was no better, and after the bombers launched, Doolittle had them recalled. Anderson was livid. Again he went over Doolittle's head to seek Spaatz's approval to launch bombers no matter what the weather was. Anderson argued that bombing accuracy was largely unimportant. "It didn't matter if Berlin was overcast," he said to Spaatz. "The resulting air battle would result in attrition, which makes it more important than any destruction on the ground." Spaatz fully understood, and on March 6, 1944, there would be no recall. On March 6, the Eighth Air Force bombed Berlin.[236]

The attack against Berlin was to be fully escorted by the best fighter pilots Spaatz and Quesada had. A total of 8,800 men, 810 bombers, and 800 P-38s, P-47s, and P-51s were massed for the raid. The Heinkel aircraft assembly plant, the Bosch Electrical works, and the Daimler-Benz engine plant were the primary targets. The jewel itself was Berlin itself.[237]

On the morning of March 6, the bombers assembled and began to stream out over the English Channel. They made no attempt to disguise their target; the formation stood out so clearly that the Germans hardly needed radar screens to see it. It was 94 miles long and 1.5 miles wide, and it was flying toward Berlin as straight as an arrow.[238]

The air-to-air battle that ensued has since become the stuff of legend. Some thirty-nine German fighter groups came up, into which the P-51s, P-47s, and P-38s turned to attack. The whir of airplanes streaking around the bombers was a bewildering, kinetic mixture of Messerschmitts, Focke-Wulfs, Heinkels, Junkers, Mustangs, Thunderbolts, and Lightnings. "The German fighters came like the proverbial swarm of bees," remembered Allan R. Willis, a B-17 copilot. Below him the guns of some 414 88s on the ground barked their shells skyward while 331 smaller-caliber guns filled the skies with their bullets. Willis was shot down.[239]

Parachute bombs were dropped from above, new surface-to-air rockets were fired up into the combat boxes, and tracer rounds etched lines of smoke as they poured to and from the bombers. Waist gunners swung their barrels as fast as they could, creating clouds of smoke around their fists as shell casings cascaded to their feet. The big twin-engine German fighters came in groups of four, six, eight, and more. They fired their rockets as one, and deadly explosions blasted apart the combat boxes, forcing strays and cripples to drop away; they were promptly bounced and torn apart with cannon fire and bullets.

In the air, the American fighter pilots were as aggressive and as determined as ever, but so too were the Germans. Captain Harry Ankeny watched in amazement as five Me-109s suddenly streaked through his defensive shield and attacked a bomber box he was escorting. A B-17 went down in flames, and neither Ankeny nor his leader was able to do a thing. "Those German pilots have got a lot of guts and I have respect for their abilities," he would later write in his diary. "They are far from being licked."[240]

The slightest crease in the formations invited the fury of the Germans, and the controllers kept vectoring them to the weakest spots. One stream was escorted around the front and in back but was unguarded in the middle. The controllers saw it and vectored one gaggle of fighters to distract the escorts while the main body of Messerschmitts picked apart the middle. Bombers fell like leaves from a tree. Forty-one B-17s and B-24s were shot down.[241]

From below, the murderous 88s fired skyward, covering the air over Berlin with angry bursts of steel. Across the city, concussions reverberated from the enormous blasts of the heavy guns on the flak towers. Life on the ground came to a complete and utter halt. A pair of 128-mm pieces got a bead on the bombers and opened fire from atop a flak tower in the Berlin Zoo. Inside, the tower was packed shoulder to shoulder with frightened Berliners seeking shelter from the American 500-pounders. The guns scored a direct hit, perhaps two. All told, twenty-four more bombers fell from the sky.

The Germans sent forth lightning, but the Americans didn't scatter. "The Forts kept their dignity," remembered a fighter pilot who escorted them. "The gunners just blazed away at the attacking fighters and although the pilot might close his eyes, he held it on the bomb run until he heard 'bombs away.'"[242]

Showing no less valor were the fighter pilots. It was one of their most impressive aerial victories yet. In what amounted to an 8-to-1 victory, the Germans lost eighty-two planes against five P-47s, five P-51s, and a single P-38.

A total of sixty-nine bombers were shot down, and eleven more were written off. A total of 387 bombers came back scarred from the battles with seventeen dead and thirty-two wounded. The missing numbered 695, all lost over Berlin. The worst single day yet in terms of loss of life.[243]

Just as they did after Big Week, the bombers didn't pause to rest on their laurels. Although weather precluded a mission on March 7, the Eighth came back to hit Berlin on March 8. Another 600 bombers launched, accompanied by 891 fighters. They shot down eighty-seven more German fighters.

They bombed again on March 9, but the Luftwaffe was too exhausted and the cloud cover too thick for them to launch a single fighter. The Allies flew unopposed over Germany's precious capital.[244]

The Berlin raids were the bloodiest yet in the war, but they gave American pilots confidence. It was increasingly clear that any target anywhere in Germany could be hit—and hit hard. The bombers had been well defended, and although the losses were high, they were the result of mistakes rather than the strength of the Luftwaffe. Moreover, the loss of more than 160 frontline fighters was a devastating blow to the Luftwaffe's strength, as was the insult of bombs raining down on their capital. Taken together, there was simply no question in anyone's mind that the Luftwaffe could be subdued, if not more. "As we turned for home we knew in our hearts that the end of war in Europe was possible," said Lieutenant Al Brown, a B-17 pilot.

D-Day seemed to be within reach.[245]

CHAPTER 13

APRIL

The fighters and bombers of the Eighth and Ninth spread out across Occupied Europe like killer bees. They bombed and strafed anything and everything German, including rail yards, tracks, airfields, depots, factories, and coastal batteries. Thus began the tedious, risky, grinding work of war. Using B-17s, B-24s, B-26s, A-20s, P-47s, P-38s, and P-51s, the airmen blasted airframe factories, cratered runways, hit German barracks, destroyed maintenance hangars, strafed fields, and shot up any fighters found on the ground. Every mission was completely unique, and every target was buried inside a prickly shell of German air defenses.[246]

German airfields had the highest priority, and the April plan called for the use of the bombers and fighters as aerial plow horses to create an arc of destruction 130 miles wide that would leave a barren, smoking ruins of a no-man's land around the invasion beaches. The tactic was novel and accomplished two of Spaatz's objectives in one plan. First, it destroyed German aircraft. Second, it helped isolate the Normandy beaches. A total of ninety-nine airfields and aerodromes were targeted for the main thrust of the April attacks, and, except for a handful that were turned over to the RAF, the Eighth and Ninth were given the lion's share. Forty Luftwaffe airfields were located in the 130-mile no-fly zone, and fifty-nine were between 130 and 350 miles from the invasion beaches.[247]

As Spaatz and Quesada would have it, the fighters had become offensive weapons in their own right. On one typical April mission, more than four hundred P-47s, P-51s, and P-38s took off to attack Luftwaffe airfields. They were organized as if they were their own bomber stream: two groups flew top cover to protect the backs of the dive-bombers as they descended on their targets. They strafed German airfields in France, Belgium, and western Germany. Eleven German fighters were exploded, and in one raid, twenty-four more were damaged. Not a single Luftwaffe pilot opposed them.[248]

Donald Pressentin, a pilot from Wisconsin, remembered his strafing attacks. Doolittle's rules of engagement encouraged fighter pilots to seek out targets of opportunity and use leftover ammunition on their way home. German airfields were wide-open spaces, leaving American pilots terribly exposed to the 20-mm cannon fire and the machine gun nests that dotted the perimeters around the runways. "When we strafed airfields, we always lost one kid, at least one kid every time we did it," Pressentin said years later.[249] There were a number of ways to hit them, explained John B. Henry, a P-51 pilot. "We got down real low, from about five miles out, and we gave it full throttle. We hopped over trees and buildings, going like hell. Tracers and explosive cannon shells were popping all around us, like a rain of golf balls. It was like juggling a dozen ice picks trying to shoot at the planes, trying to shoot at the gun emplacements, going through all the smoke, trying to keep from crashing into something, moving as fast as we could."[250]

Some of the German aerodromes were just meadows with a few thousand feet of cut grass to take off from, while others were impressive complexes with hangars, towers, and multiple concrete runways. The heavily defended ones had flak batteries as well as gun positions. Arlen

Baldridge flew against both. "Going in on a Jerry airdrome to get a crack at his aircraft was something else. There were times when the Germans used a meadow or a road as a temporary landing strip and parked their airplanes amongst the trees," he said. "Some of our fellows were lucky enough to come across such lightly defended set-ups and to make several kills without having to take an inordinate amount of flak. Not so at an established field; these were heavily defended by very well trained gunners and excellent weaponry."[251]

Attacks took more than training and nerve. At 300 miles per hour, things happened incredibly fast. Reflexes had to be sharp. A pilot's situational awareness had to be high. Several techniques evolved, most learned the hard way. Said Baldridge, "The attacking planes would get down on the deck a goodly distance from the field—come in low and fast as much abreast as possible, shoot up whatever might be more or less in their line-of-flight, and continue at treetop level until they were a long way from the field."[252]

On April 10, B-26s from the Ninth came in to level the German airbase at Wevelgem, Belgium. The Luftwaffe pilots had just enough warning to scramble into the air. While the medium bombers worked it over, one German pilot circled the airfield so he could tell the squadron when it was safe to return. The bombs cratered the runway and destroyed a hangar. After the all-clear was called, the Luftwaffe fighters returned but there were still obstacles to contend with. A landing Me-109 came in and flipped over when his landing gear caught a bomb crater on the runway.[253]

Similar attacks took place all over Europe. The German airbase at Florennes was built on a plateau south of Brussels and east of Lille, France, on a line between the English Channel and the German cities of Stuttgart and Frankfurt. The airfield was carved out from farmland, and the hangars were built to look like barns, although there were certainly no plows inside. When the doors parted, the foreboding shape of a Me-109 appeared. This airfield, too, was strafed and bombed.

The German airbase at Villacoublay, near Paris, was hit by the B-17s and B-24s in an accurate attack that blanketed the runways. Reconnaissance photographs showed bomb damage so extensive that it resembled craters on the moon. Another group of fighters spotted an airfield below them, and even though they saw the Germans scrambling to their machine gun nests, it was too much to resist. They decided to go in line abreast, guns blazing, hell bent for leather, all or nothing. "Every man with a gun on the field was daring someone to try a strafing run. But it was agreed it had to be done."[254]

An American fighter plane carried a minimum of six of the impressive and lethal Browning .50-caliber machine guns in the wings, each rated at four hundred rounds per gun per minute. On a strafing run, a single aircraft became a killing machine, pouring out 120 bullets in a short, three-second burst. A four ship would chew up a German airbase with a carpet of bullets that would splinter wood and punch holes into the skins of planes like ice picks through tissue paper. The smoky trails of the tracer rounds etched lines directly into gas tanks and fuel supplies, which exploded in towering walls of flames. Bullets chewed up ground and flesh alike with absolute disregard.

Adolf Dickfeld was on his base when it came under attack. "Everyone raced out of the barracks and into the slit trenches, and in the next instant all hell was let loose. Fragmentation bombs rained down on us while cannon shells tore up the turf. Bomb splinters raced overhead, howling crazily. Lumps of earth rained down on us. I pressed my head firmly against the bottom of the trench, my hands scratching into the damp earth. A few moments later and the entire affair was over, but on getting out of the trench we grasped the full extent of the destruction. Of the twenty-one Me's standing about the field, seven were burning and splinter damage had left some of the others, including the one I was supposed to fly, unserviceable."[255] As the dazed aviators climbed out of their holes, ammunition cooked off and shells danced around them like the last sparks from a dying fire.

On yet another base, a flight of B-26 Marauders seemed to come out of nowhere. "I heard some dull sounds in rapid succession which I had never heard before," remembered Joachim Foth, a Me-109 fighter pilot based at a Germany airfield near Liège, Belgium. "On looking up I saw to my horror the Marauder bombers which we had been sent up to intercept, dropping their bombs on our airfield. A third shower coming down from the right fell into the middle of the field and the last of these bombs exploded beneath me just as I had become airborne."[256]

Airframe factories remained one of the most important clusters on the lengthy list of targets for the month of April, and they were hit repeatedly during the month. Of particular interest were the factories that made Me-109s and FW-190s. With spring-like conditions having arrived at last, Spaatz wanted missions flown nearly every day, and except for the storms that came and went, he got what he wanted. The Eighth Air Force was joined by the Fifteenth to hit the Luftwaffe factories from both sides, England and Italy. The Eighth focused on the FW-190 plants in northern and central Germany, while the Fifteenth attempted to clean up the remaining Me-109 plants in both southern Germany and the Balkans.

The Luftwaffe rose in strength to fight off the Allies, employing old tactics and new. On April 18, a force of more than eight thousand airmen attacked the aircraft plants near Berlin with more than 780 bombers and encountered a new tactic. The pilots of the B-17s and B-24s were surprised when they got into their target area untouched. For a moment they thought they had landed an unexpected milk run, and for the most part they had—save for two hundred bombers which somehow became separated from their escorts. Seeing the confusion, the flak was halted and more than a hundred Luftwaffe fighters pounced, attacking in airspace that was usually off limits to them. Said an operations officer of the Eighth Air Force after the engagement, "This was the advantage for which the enemy had been waiting. He saw and exploited it with split second timing to the tune of at least ten B-17s. Our fighters did not even see it happen."[257] In fact, the German fighters claimed fourteen B-17s shot down in airspace normally reserved for the flak batteries. No longer would the presence of flak mean that Luftwaffe FW-190s were going to stay away.

The Germans were just as all-in as the Americans. Day after day, the airmen launched grueling missions into Germany. The Eighth attacked twenty-nine vital targets; the Fifteenth hit fourteen, most of them Messerschmitt, Focke-Wulf, or Junkers aircraft plants. They encountered swarms of fighters and explosions of flak and shot down as many Germans as they themselves lost. It was bitter fighting. Neither side gave an inch.

On April 8, a total of 605 bombers launched with more than 700 fighters as their escorts. The factories in Brunswick, Germany, were smothered by bombs, and seven Luftwaffe complexes were hit. Three hundred and forty airmen were lost on the thirty-four bombers. Twenty-three American fighters were lost as well.

The heavies flew again on April 9, 10, and 11, losing more than nine hundred men and ninety bombers during the three days of combat, but badly damaging the Heinkel and Focke-Wulf aircraft factories and a half dozen other fighter assembly plants.

On April 13, more than six hundred bombers attacked Schweinfurt and the Messerschmitt complexes in Augsburg, at a cost of another 380 airmen and thirty-eight bombers, but the plant was nearly bombed into the ground.[258] Four hundred and sixty-six tons fell on one factory, 958 tons on another, 1,017 on a third. One raid was nearly perfect with a tight concentration of bombs hitting the target so thoroughly that it was taken off the list entirely.[259]

On April 20, the heavies bombed the V-bomb sites in Pas-de-Calais and another half dozen Luftwaffe airfields. On April 24, they hit nine more targets with 716 bombers, and on April 26, three more factories with 650 bombers.

Both sides fought with absolute determination, pursuing each other until one was dead or nearly so. When under attack, German gunners would fire until the barrels of their weapons were red hot. Russ Draper was an American element leader on a fighter sweep across Germany. He approached an area of interest and dropped his formation down to treetop level. His timing was terrible. Trouble struck almost instantaneously. His inexperienced wingman promptly flew into power lines and cartwheeled into the ground in a ball of fire as he himself crested a hill, only to find that he was over a German airbase and boxed in by a village to his right. "Experience told me that my chances were slim to nil," said Draper.

Sure enough, ground fire soon filled the sky. Thinking the village would shield him from the bullets, Draper banked his plane across the airfield and pointed his nose toward the red roofs to his right. He pushed his plane even lower zooming into the city until he was flying straight down the cobblestone street that ran through the center of the town. "What I was counting on not happening did. From the hilltops on both sides the air was suddenly filled with curving red golf balls, tracers for the 20-mms, and the streaks that indicated there were plenty of .50-calibers also. The tile roofs were shattering on each side and dust from the concrete walls was flying."

Draper assumed that the Germans wouldn't risk civilian casualties, but they seemed unconcerned about mowing down locals. "I hadn't thought they would shoot into their own town. Directly in front of me were troops marching away from me. I opened fire and they hit the cobblestone street and rolled onto their backs. It all happened so fast I'm not sure of the sequence. The sky was full of tracers, the buildings were literally bursting beside me, there was the roar of the full throttle, the troops were rolling to their backs and firing up at me—all of which must have taken ten seconds."

Draper twisted as best he could, but bullets were flying everywhere. One pierced the fuselage of his plane and found his flesh. "From behind, someone poked me in the back of my right shoulder with the end of a broom handle. No real pain, that is not excruciating pain, just a hard poke. My right hand fell from the control stick." Blood rolled down his sleeve and into his glove. With the prop of his fighter just feet from the cobblestone, Draper pulled up, passed through the hail of fire, and, by some unknown miracle, found a cloud to hide in. Fighting bouts of unconsciousness and a case of hypoxia, he managed to work his way back to England. When they pulled him out of his plane, blood sloshed down his flight suit and pooled on the ground around his feet.[260]

Dogfights were as physically demanding as any hand-to-hand combat, and just as certain to end in someone's death. To win in the air required a blend of utter tenacity and exceptional flying skills. Said one P-51 fighter pilot: "With my roommate and myself, every time we weren't on a mission, we'd go up over western England and dogfight between ourselves and come back wringing wet with sweat just because it wasn't in our best interest to lose out to a German."[261]

Henry C. Woodrum witnessed that to-the-death tenacity when a dogfight suddenly broke out over the rooftops of Paris. Woodrum, a B-26 pilot, had been shot down a week earlier and was hiding on the top floor of an apartment building near the German airfield at Villacoublay. He was awakened by the clattering sound of machine guns. He raced to his window. "Coming straight toward me at not more than 50 feet above the roof was an American P-51 Mustang going flat out. Close behind it were five FW-190s sort of bunched together, flying like bees and all of them were taking pot shots with their 20-mm cannon at the poor old Yankee boy." The planes passed so close that Woodrum could clearly see the Mustang pilot in the cockpit—and even his scarf and his leather flight jacket. The pilot was fully engaged in the fight, aggressive, not scared, leaning forward, and giving no ground to his attackers. The planes were momentarily obscured by the horizon. Woodrum assumed it was over, but then they suddenly reappeared. The Mustang had turned the tables. "Coming towards us from the southwest still at rooftop level were the six fighters," Woodrum recalled, "but leading the pack was a lonesome FW-190 frantically trying to escape the P-51 pilot who was relentlessly hosing him with .50-caliber slugs in short, accurate bursts. Behind were the other four Jerries holding their fire for fear of hitting the first FW-190."[262]

The Mustang pilot shot down the first German and then banked down low and raced through a hail of flak across the airfield. Incredibly, the Germans split their formation, three going left, one to the right. The Mustang pilot peeled off to the right. "As the two planes came over, the thunder of their engines was punctuated by the short, ammo-saving bursts of the .50-calibers," said Woodrum. "Scraping over rooftops, twisting and yawing, they crossed the city and finally the FW-190 began to trail smoke."

Again the Mustang pilot yanked his plane into a turn and again he found a target, firing a burst into the tail of the third Focke-Wulf. "By this time I was going absolutely nuts. It was all I could do to keep from shouting in English. Everybody else was excited too. People came out on the roof tops of nearby apartments and the balconies were full of men and women silently cheering for the crazy, lone American." The three planes disappeared momentarily but reappeared again as they banked across the far side of Paris, the Mustang in the middle. They disappeared again over the crest of the horizon. Moments later, a cloud of black smoke blossomed into the sky.

Around Woodrum, everything immediately fell quiet. The Parisians slowly left their balconies and windows and gave the American a silent farewell with a sad shrug of their shoulders. The family hiding Woodrum came to his side with glasses of wine. Everyone had seen it. "Le Americain pilote," they said and toasted the unnamed aviator with a sad nod. "I just couldn't forget the way the man had flown, dreaming up tactics as he went along, playing it by ear only to have his luck run out a little bit too soon," Woodrum recalled.[263]

But Woodrum and the others had gotten it wrong. Some people on the other side of Paris had seen the final moments. It was the German who had crashed—not the American. Sighs of relief spread across the community, although one was careful not to look a German policeman in the eye lest their pleasure be revealed.

The bombers were hardly resting. They, too, were flying a demanding schedule of missions. In addition to airfields and factories, the Eighth and Ninth were tasked with airstrikes against German rail centers and marshaling yards, although the rail yards were stubborn and oftentimes refused to die. The American bombs curled iron rail and tossed freight cars in the air like toys, but in came the repair crews and the damage was fixed, often by the next day. The process was maddening, the progress slow. The question was simple: who would have the last word: the bombers or the laborers?[264]

The rail yards at Creil, France, were targeted by B-17s and B-24s in March, April, and May. Sixty freight cars were destroyed in March, and 180 more were damaged. Every track in the yard was cut at least once. But German labor crews promptly arrived and returned the yard to active service, so the bombers returned at the end of March and cut the lines again. In April, they came back and scored an impressive hit across lines, but, again, the yard was soon returned to service. The bombers came back once more. It was a story that could be repeated time and again. It drained the resources of the Allied bombers, but there was little to do but attack again.

Better results came at Hamm, Germany. On April 22, a spectacular raid against the yards in Hamm turned steel into grotesque shapes and twisted them into broken angles. Sheds were set on fire, freight cars and liquid transports erupted in pillars of smoke and flames. Some 638 bombers hit the yards with 1,551 tons. The rail yard was crippled for the rest of the war.[265]

During April, the bombers targeted sixty major rail centers, but after dropping some 33,000 tons of bombs, just twelve were truly out of commission.

The D-Day to-do list remained frustratingly long.

D-Day was growing in importance by the hour. The airplane manufacturers, the airfields, the coastal batteries, the beams that swept the skies from the German coastal radar installation, one located every 10 miles all the way down to Spain; the increasing concern about the stakes, blades, hedgehogs, and pole-mounted contact explosives running thick at the waterline of the invasion beaches. The original 292 targets had scarcely been whittled when to that list was added a new and unwelcome German trap. After raiding a target of opportunity, some fighters of the Ninth Air Force absent-mindedly jettisoned their bombs into the coastal surf along the beaches of western France. Giving it no thought whatsoever—jettisoning a bomb load was so routine as to merit only the briefest flick of a toggle to let the bombs go—the pilots were shocked by a surprising and no doubt unnerving sound of concussive, secondary blast. A hurried glance backward revealed geyser of water-and-sand, which could mean only one thing. Just under the surfline the Germans had planted landmines, a dreadful prospect if true and yet another obstacle to overcome to get ashore.[266]

On the April list were the coastal batteries and again the news was unexpected but on this count entirely welcome. Above the Normandy beachhead was situated an impressive array of some forty-five poured concrete emplacements each bristling with guns of between 105 mm and 400 mm. Shells from these powerful weapons would make mincemeat of a soldier and send a landing craft to the bottom in an instant. Neutralizing these batteries was easier said than done. With thick walls and lids of a dozen or more feet of solid steel reinforced concrete, only a direct hit would have an effect, and even then it was to merely chip a few inches of casemating off unless it hit it just right.

These were worrisome batteries, and they had to be attacked. But they were not likely to yield to anything less than a heavy aerial bombardment. To take out these installations, some 4,800 tons of bombs would have to be dropped, roughly the equivalent of 19,000 bombs or the weight of an attack that would require 1,900 bombers. That alone was daunting, but there was more. Allied policy called for two decoy attacks for every one in the Normandy region, a requirement that would mean 5,760 sorties had to be flown all told just to hit the gun emplacements in the invasion area, an impossible number given the prospect that the weight of such emphasis in the invasion area might lead to the conclusion that one of these was the real landing site.[267]

There was, however, some promising news. Reconnaissance flights revealed that eight of these batteries were soft, that is they were under construction and their thousand-ton lids had not yet been fitted. This meant that they were open from the top and with accurate bombing, they might be easily destroyed. This created a window of opportunity that could scarcely be ignored.[268]

In mid-April, these vulnerable batteries were assigned to the Ninth Air Force for precision bombing. Into the air they launched their Marauders and Havocs in clusters of one group of planes per target. They all were nearly wiped out. Winging over the Channel, the pilots flew into a wall of antiaircraft fire. One airplane after the other cartwheeled across the sky in flames. In the end, some 3,500 tons were dropped, but without any measureable damage. Construction was no doubt slowed, but the beaches were scarcely safer. The batteries would have to wait until D-Day.[269]

Trains were targeted in April, and they presented new and deadly risks to the pilots. "Jerry liked on occasion to have a train act as a decoy and suck us into a flak-trap," said pilot Arlen Baldridge. "The Germans even had some dummy box cars that were actually anti-aircraft stations with collapsible sides." On a good day, the pilots would find a train and shoot up the locomotive to bring it to a halt. After that, they'd work on the rolling stock behind it. "After the flight leader busted the engine and the train came to a stop, we set up a pattern and went to work on the cars. Having made a couple of passes without getting anything to blow up or catch fire, I decided to give the string of cars a good raking." Baldridge was so focused that he failed to notice the edge of a small village from which a squadron of German soldiers emerged and began to throw up accurate fire. "They had taught me a lesson," he said of the unexpected encounter. "I tried, thereafter, not to get so carried away with myself, or to become so single-minded as to stumble from an advantageous position into someone else's trap."[270]

A German Luftwaffe pilot on leave to marry his fiancée saw the devastation of the train attacks first hand. He was traveling when his own train came under attack. "At about 1000 hours the train was attacked by cannon from U.S. Lightnings and the locomotive was damaged. The train stopped and remained still while soldiers [heading toward the front] ran to the windows and sprang from the train each running for his life. [I] took my wife by the hand and headed for the open. After about 10 minutes, the pilots ended their handiwork and flew away." Amazingly, the shot-up train was far from dead. Reflecting the incredible recuperative powers of the rail system, the pilot and his fellow passengers soon resumed their journey. "After about three hours a replacement locomotive arrived and on we went."[271]

That same pilot had a second experience with the Allied train busting. He was trying to make his way back to his base by train after being shot down in the air. Like most Germans, he traveled by night. "At the damaged railway station—but still running—the only people in the middle of the night were careworn soldiers, women, and children … and me, a shot-down pilot carrying a sack in which there was nothing worth mentioning. Meanwhile the train came in and the travelers boarded. The coaches were partly damaged, the windows without glass and only paper or cardboard used to repair them. Punctually at 0400 the train departed and we steamed through the night."[272]

Despite the enormous April target load, some targets were bombed twice for good measure. The operations officers called these "tickling" attacks. The idea was to scatter or kill the repair crews that would swarm over a factory or rail yard. It was so successful that more than two hundred tickling attacks were flown in April and May.

As the month finally drew to an end, the airmen were near exhaustion. So far they had flown 43,434 combat sorties against targets in Germany or Occupied Europe, nearly as many as had been flown during all of 1943. During April, the heavies bombed, the fighters engaged the Luftwaffe in the air. Trains, roads, and bridges were strafed and dive-bombed.[273]

Spring brought a glimmer of sunshine and with it renewed spirits. Allied planes were a sorry mess and as worn down as ever, and so too were the airmen. But the good weather was refreshing, and the men were keenly aware that the missions they flew had a purpose. "We kept thinking of the infantry," remembered a B-17 crewman. [274] And that said it all.

CHAPTER 14

INVASION

On December 15, 1943, the air plans sections of the Allied Expeditionary Air Force, the Eighth, the Ninth, and the RAF began planning their combat missions for the D-Day landings. In meetings that would continue for four months and would typically run to twelve-hour days, the disparate air assets and the large-scale movement of men and materiel across the English Channel were tied into fighter screens, air-to-ground strafing, interdiction runs, aerial spying, and heavy bombing by the B-17s and B-24s. Because of the vulnerabilities of amphibious operations, air cover would be essential to the survival of the invasion forces as they crossed the Channel and to the overall success of D-Day. Said one of the invasion planners, "Only through air power can we offset the many and great disabilities inherent in the situation confronting the surface attacking force."[275]

First, a landing site had to be selected. The disastrous attempt to land forces at the coastal city of Dieppe, France, in August 1942 had become a textbook example of what not to do on D-Day. On that day, an invasion force of some six thousand Canadian and British soldiers had used some 253 ships to land on a hard, pebble beach in a frontal attack against the port of Dieppe. They faced an experienced German force of some 1,500 soldiers, and a daunting geography that enclosed the beaches with relatively high bluffs.

They were massacred. About a thousand soldiers were killed, another two thousand were taken prisoner, and three thousand more either managed to escape or never even landed in the first place. German casualties numbered just three hundred dead and 280 wounded.

The concurrent air battle, which was decided almost immediately, was also a disaster. Some 106 British combat aircraft were downed against the loss of just twenty German fighters.

The lessons of Dieppe flowed into the D-Day planning. The first understanding was that by only the slimmest of margins would such an invasion be successful. A cross-channel operation was by far the most dangerous military operation an army could undertake. If the invaders failed to attain a lodgment, they would be pushed back into the sea. Failure would thus be complete and regrouping would almost be impossible. Rather than that, the keys to getting ashore would be surprise, speed of attack, continuous attack, air cover, and aerial bombardment. Subsequent issues such as routes to get off the beaches and move the forces inland quickly would follow.[276]

The number one military consideration in the equation for D-Day was the size of the German army. Russian Premier Joseph Stalin was told that five Allied divisions would get ashore fast enough to engage and advance against twelve German divisions and that the primary planning variable called for putting 150,000 men ashore in the first day. Stalin, though, cast a knowing smile that summed up the imponderables of the attack. "And what if there are thirteen divisions?"[277]

The first casualty of Dieppe was a tentative plan to divide the Allied landing forces and saturate the German defenses by coming ashore on a large number of geographically separated beaches. The idea was to land simultaneously on twenty or more beaches, with the expectation that the German defenses would be overwhelmed in more than half the areas and that a toehold would be gained. The Dieppe evidence suggested, however, that this approach would be fatal. A small, heavily emplaced shore defense had pushed off a landing force four times its size with just a handful of casualties. If this could be done in one place, it could be done in twenty places. The concept was quickly discarded in favor of concentrated landings directed against no more than a handful of beaches with follow-on forces flowing directly behind the lead elements, a classic tip-of-the-spear tactic.[278]

The geographical and geologic requirements for the landing beaches were based on several military necessities that would favor the Allies. The first priority was that the beaches be within the combat radius of the U.K.-based fighters. Anything less and air superiority would be an impossibility. This requirement quickly ruled out as landing zones any coastal areas south of the Bay of Biscay. The second requirement was that the beaches had to be conducive to a rapid build-up of forces and be able to funnel soldiers quickly inland. This meant the sand had to be firm enough to be used by heavy vehicles, that the beach should be as wide as possible to reduce immediate congestion, and that there be a network of roads behind the beachhead so soldiers and vehicles could exit and move inland.[279] Furthermore, LST-class landing ships would need a shoreline against which they could ground their ships and drop their ramps, and the seabed offshore should slope gradually so an artificial harbor could be erected and tied to the ocean floor. This ruled out rocky shorelines or coastal areas with offshore trenches.

The Low Countries of Belgium, Luxembourg, and the Netherlands were one possibility, and they were good ones. They were in close proximity to England, but were ruled out for a number of reasons, not the least of which was their marshy topography and the likely prospect that the Germans would flood much of coastal Holland with seawater.

Equally troubling, Holland's beaches were exposed to the elements, were well fortified, and were easily reinforced by the quick movement of nearby German soldiers. Belgium also was eliminated because its beaches were too small and German defenses in the area were too strong, as was the Brittany coast of France.[280]

Pas-de-Calais was the obvious choice to all but the Allies. It represented the shortest route across the English Channel and was ideally suited for a military operation on the scale of D-Day. Pas-de-Calais had the firm, wide beaches and the accessible inland routes, was under the umbrella of the British fighter bases, and could be hit swiftly with the full force of an amphibious assault. The only thing it lacked was any pretense of being anything less than the very best and most obvious choice for the landings, and that is exactly what made it untenable. For the Allies, Pas-de-Calais was simply too obvious, thus negating any element of surprise.

After screening all the potential beachheads from Norway to Spain, the list largely came down to the sparsely habited coastal area between the French cities of Le Havre and Cherbourg. For the D-Day invasion, the Allies selected five Normandy Beaches between Le Havre and Cherbourg, better known today by their codenames: Utah, Omaha, Sword, Juno, and Gold. These beaches were firm, and they had a shallow seabed offshore. Troops could flow ashore in the hundreds of thousands and from there move inland to Germany. They were well fortified by the Germans, but so too were any of the other candidates that qualified. "The objective of Overlord operations," wrote one U.S. Army historian, "was not to bring about the defeat of the enemy in northwest Europe but to seize and develop an administrative base from which future offensive operations could be launched."[281]

Normandy was that base, and Utah, Omaha, Juno, Gold and Sword would be the landing sites.

With that portion of the plan decided, it was now time to map out the areas and prepare for the cross-channel attack. That and the airplan to help the soldiers come ashore.[282]

CHAPTER 15

SECRET WEAPONS

The grind of combat continued, and the airmen learned to cope with their own limitations. The heavies bombed on any day that the weather cooperated, and the fighters were up as either escorts or ground pounders. Target planning by the American operations staff was thorough, and secondary targets were included in the mission folders so bomber crews would have something to bomb if the primary targets were clouded over. But there were some problems.

Orleans, France, for example, was a central rail hub with tracks radiating out in almost every direction and an important German airfield nearby. Located 130 miles southwest of Paris and some 250 miles from the Normandy coast, the airfield at Orleans was going to be attacked. A small force of twenty-nine bombers took off with more than three hundred 500-pound bombs. As the planes arrived over the target, the bombardiers found the runways and prepared to drop, but as they did, a second group of bombers flew underneath them. Thankfully, the bombardiers held their bombs, but as a result, more than half of the bombs overshot and slammed into an empty field.[283]

Wasted missions, with the attendant dangers from flak and fighters, infuriated Spaatz, but there was little he could do except send out another group to try again.

Instrument flying was taught to the pilots, but skill levels varied considerably. Some pilots had an aptitude for the math required to calculate reciprocal headings; others were confused. Some pilots trusted their instruments even when their bodies told them otherwise; some yielded to their senses and blindly flew their planes into the ground. Pete Peterson, a fighter ace, trusted his instruments and readily did the math of headings and angles, a skill that saved the lives of two of his wingmen. Peterson escorted them down through pea-soup fog that cleared only feet above the ground. "As I descended toward the runway and got to about 50 feet above the ground I could see straight down the runway! I knew then that we could make it in by repeating what I had done. I climbed back up on instruments and picked up Roland Wright who flew off my right wing and started the letdown on instruments. I let my wheels down; Wright lowered his wheels and stayed back just far enough to keep me in sight and follow my instrument flying. I dropped flaps; he dropped flaps. I set my rate of descent with the height and time estimated to touchdown. When I got to about 50 feet I spotted the runway and called it out to him. He picked up the sight of the runway and landed. I did the same thing with Tiede and he landed. I then did a right 360 degree turn about 50 feet off the ground and I landed."[284] Peterson would later learn that the crews in the tower had heard his engine and his tires squeaking on the runway but had never seen his P-51 until he taxied around the perimeter to his handstand. It was the sort of bad weather that persistently plagued flight operations during the winter and spring of 1944.

When things went wrong, the volatile combination of bombs, flammable fuels, and the unforgiving physics of flight combined poorly in large, four-engine bombers. By and large, the B-17s were reliable, but accidents happened, often at the base. "I could hear the eerie wailing of a bomber out of control and spinning down," remembered one officer at an American bomber base. "Then I'd hear the crash and the bombs exploding nearby. If I was the officer of the day, I'd have to go out and pick up whatever was left. I can remember going along and picking out a perfectly dissected human heart from a bush. The twisted remains of a crewman would resemble gnarled tree trunk. It was horrible."[285]

Earl Pate, a pilot who flew a B-17, was the first at the scene of yet another bomber crash. The force of the impact had ignited the fuel tanks, and an intense fire swallowed the B-17 and the men inside. "The stinking nauseating smell of burning flesh stays with you the rest of your life."[286] The men inside had been burned to death.

At one base, the fighter pilots were anxious to get their hands on a new shipment of P-51s. Arlen Baldridge watched as one of the guys in the squadron named Botsford took a new Mustang up for a test ride. On the ramp, the Merlin engine towered over the heads of the pilots, and the big, four-bladed prop spun to life as the engine caught. Grins no doubt broke out among the rest of the pilots as the pilot pushed up the throttle. "Botsford took one of the new P-51s up for a check flight. The engine failed just after liftoff and he made a crash landing in a field just ahead of him." The plane was busted up, and Botsford looked fine—except that his neck was broken.[287]

But that was the way of war. D-Day loomed, missions had to be flown; problems demanded solutions, some with lives hanging in the balance. But then, as if all of that wasn't enough anyway, Hitler came up with new ways to kill them.

Adolf Hitler frequently promised his commanders weapons so effective that they alone could turn the war around. The Luftwaffe generals scoffed at what they considered to be the rantings of a madman, but, in fact, Hitler had a viable, extraordinarily advanced arsenal of sophisticated weapons in the pipeline. It was only due to luck that they didn't arrive in time to tip the balance of the airwar in favor of the Germans, for they were considerable weapons indeed. Foremost among them was the jet.

"I shall never forget May 22, 1943, the day I flew a jet aircraft for the first time in my life," wrote Adolf Galland in his memoirs, speaking of the sleek, new Me-262 twin-engine jet fighter-bomber. "This was not a step forward; this was a leap!"[288] With a 120 mile-per-hour advantage over the piston-engine P-51s and P-38s, the Me-262 could use its blinding speed to attack a bomber formation, lay down deadly fire, and outrace any plane in the sky. In a blink of the eye, air-to-air combat would tilt in favor of Germany. Dog-fighting would be a thing of the past because the Germans would be gone. After his flight, Galland rattled off a few platitudes about speed and maneuverability and then came to the conclusion that meant most in matters of war: "If the characteristics of performance, which the firms had calculated and partially flown, were only partially correct," wrote Galland, "then undreamed of possibilities lay ahead."[289]

One of those possibilities was immediately obvious to the seasoned pilot. "It will guarantee us," he wrote, "an unbelievable advantage."[290]

The engineering plans for the Me-262 called for a single-seat twin-engine jet that would be armed with four 30-mm cannons in the nose. The 30-mm shell, larger by half than the 20-mm cannons already doing so much damage to the American heavies, would be like a baseball bat slamming into a pane of glass. If a bomber were struck just right, an entire wing might be blown off in one shot.

Hitler, though, was unimpressed with this aspect of its armament. "Can it carry bombs?" he asked while viewing a demonstration of the speedy fighter. He was told it could. Hitler welled up with enthusiasm. "For years I have demanded from the Luftwaffe a 'speed bomber,' which can reach its target in spite of enemy fighter defense," he said to Galland. "In the aircraft you present to me as a fighter plane, I see the

'Blitz bomber,' with which I will repel the invasion in its first and weakest phase. Regardless of the enemy's air umbrella, it will strike the recently landed mass of material and troops creating panic, death and destruction, *At last this is the Blitz bomber!*"[291]

Hitler viewed the new jet as the weapon he needed to stop the cross-channel invasion in its tracks. Armed with bombs, it could streak down the beaches and bomb the soldiers coming ashore before any American pilot could put it in their gunsights.

The Luftwaffe disagreed and instead saw the jet as the ultimate interceptor. They viewed it not as a blitz bomber but rather as a fighter that could bring the bomber streams to a halt.

Either way, the possibilities were deeply troubling to the Americans. Spaatz saw the advantage the Me-262 possessed and pressed Arnold for an American jet fighter to counter the German fighter, but more to the point, he also pressed the need to attack the sources of production as quickly as possible. "The Hun has still got a lot of fight left in him, even in the air," said Spaatz, "and we must concentrate to kill him off if possible before he can develop these new threats against us."[292]

With the Me-262, threat was too soft of a word. While the Luftwaffe never reconciled their puzzling refusal to make the jet into a blitz bomber, the Me-262 nonetheless soon was in action. When it appeared in combat, it gave a lopsided display of air superiority against the Mustangs and Lightnings. "We saw them all the time," remembered a P-47 pilot of the new jet. "You just had to be careful. We'd operate right underneath them. They'd be up there 15–20,000 feet and we'd be down their strafing their troops. But you had to keep your eye on them because the first time they come down on you—could they go. I thought if those got into production, we'd still be over there fighting."[293]

The bomber crews echoed that sentiment. "When we got the jets against us, it was kinda rough," remembered a bombardier on a B-17. "I had the chin guns, but that didn't do you any good; by the time the spec was here, it was through your formation."[294]

"It was a magnificent feeling," wrote a German fighter pilot of the jet and what it did for his morale. "Finally the hunter and not the hunted."[295] His first kill was against a P-38 that was flying a reconnaissance mission. Neither the Lightning's speed nor its high-altitude service ceiling were enough to escape the jet. The P-38 was shot down in an instant.

Although Spaatz already had a full list of targets, when intelligence analysts confirmed the information, the jet engine factories and airframe assembly plants for the new jet were added to the ever-so-lengthy list of German sites to be bombed.

Oddly, despite the possibilities that Hitler saw in the jet, the Luftwaffe never seriously considered the jet in terms of the invasion. The Me-262 was used almost exclusively as a fighter.

Hitler's jet-engine technologies powered more than a blitz bomber. In the spring of 1943, reconnaissance flights brought back photographs of what would later be identified as V-1 buzz bomb launch sites, although the images were at first confusing. Twin rails some 300 feet long were anchored in concrete and sloped upward like a ski jump ramp. Examining the reconnaissance photographs under magnifying loupes, the intelligence sections identified twenty-one of these ski ramps. Once they had a visual pattern, they found seventy-four more. Because the German research in rocketry at Peenemünde was by then well known, the intelligence groups correctly concluded that the Germans had created a pilotless aircraft, which were aimed directly at London. Hitler called them vengeance weapons, or "V" weapons.

"Our hour of revenge is nigh!" said Hitler of his rocket bombs. "Even if for the present we can't reach America, thank God at least one country is close enough to tackle." Said Albert Speer, minister of Armaments and War Production, to factory workers making the buzz bombs: "German mills of retribution may often seem to grind too slowly, but do grind very fine …"[296]

During a trip to England, Hap Arnold saw the buzz bomb first hand when a rocket exploded near his housing in London, leaving a crater with parts of it scattered about. "The force of the explosion just about lifted all of us out of our beds," Arnold wrote in his diary. He was taken to the site, where he examined the blast crater. "I judge that the gadget had not more than 1,000 pounds, probably about 500 pounds explosive. It was made of pressed steel, about 26 feet wing spread, jet-propelled, automatic gyro-pilot controlled. This particular 'Drone' came down through the clouds in a dive with a dead engine, then leveled off and made a semicircular course before it hit the ground. Around the crater was the steel cylinder fuselage, bolted together, steel sheet wings, the jet tubing from engine, [and other parts]." Arnold's extensive experience in manufacturing allowed him to make some quick mental calculations. He concluded that without very much effort, the Germans could produce enough of these rockets to fire 14,000 buzz bombs at London every day. "Our answer must be to hit the factories where critical parts are made," he concluded.[297] His nearly exhausted bombers had yet another mission.

Arnold approached the buzz bombs with his usual grim determination. It was easy to see that if left unattended, these rockets could rain down crippling destruction not only on London, but also on the American airbases, or, just as likely, they would wipe out large numbers of the D-Day men and materiel, which were already packed shoulder to shoulder in staging areas across England. The launch sites were small and by no means an easy target to bomb from 25,000 feet, but they were also heavily defended and thus dangerous to attack from low level. Still, with no ground forces operating in Europe, the issue of the V-bombs was on his desk. Arnold ordered replicas of the launch sites built in the Florida panhandle on the bombing ranges of Eglin Air Force Base and then experimented with the best way to destroy them. The best solution was a 2,000-pound general-purpose bomb delivered from low altitude. Such a powerful bomb could wipe out an acre of land and anything erected on it.[298] Two types of missions thus were developed to stop the rockets.

The first were called "Crossbow" missions and consisted of strikes against the rocket research and fabrication facilities at Peenemunde, while the second, called "Noball" missions, were attacks against the launch sites, although in time the names became interchangeable.

On the night of August 17, 1943, RAF bombers attacked the launch sites in the Pas-de-Calais area with 670 bombers. On August 27, the Eighth Air Force hit the V-bomb launch sites with 138 bombers. In December, the Ninth Air Force joined the bombing. Although Spaatz believed that the Crossbow missions were a distraction, they continued to be bombed and remained on the target lists until the launch sites were finally overrun by Allied ground soldiers in the fall of 1944.[299]

The most worrisome secret German weapon technology not yet present in serious numbers was the proximity fuse. Flak shells were blind and dumb. They exploded without knowing where they were or what was near them. It was all mechanical. A gun shot them, and they exploded after a preset number of seconds. If a plane was nearby, it was all the better, but they were "dumb" weapons and simply exploded wherever they were.

The proximity fuse promised to make a shell smart, to let it know where it was and when to explode. A tiny radar set placed inside the antiaircraft shell would beam out a signal in all directions. When it received a bounced return, it would activate the firing mechanism and the shell would explode. If this could be developed in numbers, thousands of German flak guns could be converted into highly accurate, highly lethal weapons that would nearly always find their mark. As it was, flak shells often came close, even sliced through bombers on numerous occasions, but without proximity fusing, they didn't explode.[300] Fortunately for the Allies, proximity fuses were bulky and unreliable and development was halted.[301] Thankfully for Spaatz, Arnold, and Doolittle, that was just one less thing they needed to worry about on the road to D-Day.

CHAPTER 16

WAR PLAN

On April 26, 1944, the Ninth Air Force released the airplan for the D-Day invasion. It was 1,300 pages long printed on both sides of legal-sized paper with more than a hundred maps and charts. In it, every plane, every position in the sky, and every layer from the ground to 35,000 feet, as well as the airspace around the landings for more than 100 miles, including patrol sectors and safe passage routes in and out, was covered. More than 14,000 individual sorties would be flown with the sole purpose of getting more than 150,000 Allied soldiers ashore on the first day of the invasion.[302]

The German opposition was expected to be fierce. Within a day's movement from the Normandy landing sites were battle-hardened German infantry and mechanized divisions, including Panzer tanks of sufficient strength to repel the very best Allied soldiers streaming ashore. The invasion beaches were forested with timber stakes, steel blades, and hedgehogs, and they faced presighted machine gun nests and artillery. Worse, British intelligence estimated that the German Air Force was expected to fly 1,100 to 1,250 sorties on D-Day, a considerable weight of attack that, if successful, could add exponentially to Allied casualties. If the Luftwaffe fighters penetrated the screens in less than a five-minute attack, they were capable of pouring some 250,000 rounds of machine gun and cannon fire into the soldiers and to rake the beaches with more than 2,000 rockets tipped with explosives deadly enough to snuff out a life in one blast. By the end of D+4, a force of 1,615 German fighters would be in position to oppose the advance.

The Luftwaffe were expected to attack two key sectors of the invasion area: over the beaches and along the perimeter wall surrounding the beachhead. Equally, they were expected to go after and try to knock down the bombers that would hit the coastal fortifications in the first preinvasion raid, and to pounce on any Allied aircraft strafing ground targets.

The war plan was divided into an offensive and a defensive plan. The geography around the invasion front was divided into fourteen designated areas, and together they formed a sterile no-fly zone. The outside perimeter was defined by extending an imaginary line through the French cities of Rouen, Paris, and Orleans to the Loire River and then around to Saint-Nazaire on the Atlantic Coast.

The opening salvo of D-Day would begin with the dawn arrival of 1,350 B-17s and B-24s to soften up the beaches. Far and away, this was a crucial phase of the D-Day plan. The bombing would be centered on the forty-five major coastal installations attacked in April that ran along the rim of the invasion areas in a stretch of concentrated fortification some 6 miles long between Omaha Beach and the British beaches of Juno, Gold, and Sword. Each installation was a formidable gun platform in and of itself with a garrison force of some two hundred well-trained, well-armed German soldiers. Around the emplacements were machine gun nests and smaller gun batteries, plus the barracks and ammunition dumps.[303]

One group each of some three hundred-plus bombers was assigned to each of the four landing areas: Omaha, Juno, Gold, and Sword. In an early morning raid, they would knock out these as yet largely untouched coastal batteries just before the soldiers hit the sand and take out the German troop concentrations behind the bluffs, while opening up the barbed wire entanglements barricading the beaches and taking out the unreinforced pillboxes and machine gun nests that dotted the approaches. In essence, it was up to these B-17s and B-24s to open the beaches for the assault. The heavies would walk their bombs up from the high-water mark, across the sand, and as far inland as 4 miles, sweeping up the German gun positions and leaving cratered holes in their wake. The important targets, though, were the as yet untouched guns looking down on the beaches. The bombers would rain down destruction, finishing five minutes before the landings on Omaha, which would start D-Day at precisely 0630 hours.

Immediately behind the B-17s would come 433 B-26s and A-20s from the Ninth Air Force to bomb the fifth landing area: Utah Beach. Their target folders included infantry positions, troop shelters, pillboxes, antitank guns, and 75-mm, 155-mm, and 170-mm guns, plus bridges and rail tracks. The Marauders would be airborne before dawn and would split into combat boxes of eighteen planes to hit each of their targets. As would the heavies, the Marauders and Havocs would lift off as early as 0345 hours. The bomb loads would consist of 120-pound fragmentation bombs to take out German infantry, 250-pound and 500-pound general-purpose bombs, and up to and including 1,000-pounders for the heavy gun emplacements. The bombers would carry a mix according to their individual targets.[304]

From this point forward, the airplan was largely defensive. The fighter protection plan was complicated and mixed in the airplanes of the RAF with those of the Eighth with the Ninth. The British air groups would fly directly over the landings between the altitudes of 3,000 feet and 5,000 feet, while above them, 550 P-47s of the Ninth Air Force would fly patrol at altitudes of between 8,000 and 15,000 feet. If any Germans appeared, these pilots would take them out.

A second group would fly further out to sea. The convoys would be coming across the English Channel in a line of ships that would create a lane of traffic all the way back to England. These were highly vulnerable to air attack. These sealanes would be protected by yet another formation of 660 P-38s.

Inland, surrounding the invasion area, would be a perimeter screen of eight hundred P-51s and P-47s. These fighters would patrol the airspace at 6,000 feet, 12,000 feet, and 17,000 feet as far inland as 100 miles. Anything that moved would be shot.

Between the beaches and the perimeter screen was a kill zone that would be patrolled by 550 P-47s. These planes had preassigned targets that consisted of various chokepoints like road intersections and smaller bridges, but they would largely spend D-Day attacking anything that moved on the ground. These were ground interdiction fighters—ground pounders of the highest order. The pilots would fly the prosaic missions that Pete Quesada had taught them so they could block German reinforcements from flowing to the landings by dive-bombing and ground-strafing their movements. These pilots would be augmented by three additional raids by the B-17s and B-24s, which would spend the rest of D-Day blasting lines of communication, bridges, rail yards, and German concentrations. This left about 1,100 fighters to escort bombers to and from their targets and an additional six hundred fighters on ground alert and ready to instantly respond to emergencies.[305]

Timing was essential. The pilots would fly overlapping cover, so as not to leave any openings in their defenses. The Eighth divided D-Day into three time periods, the first beginning before dawn. No doubt reflecting the activities in the barracks, the day parts were codenamed using terms from poker: Full House, Stud, and Royal Flush. Full House would begin at 0425 hours on D-Day, would consist of escort duties, and would continue in effect until 1000 hours. Stud would begin just after the first wave of bombing when fighters would flood the area behind the beachhead and hit their targets until 1600 hours. Royal Flush would then bring the day to the end as some 450 P-51s and P-47s attached themselves to the final round of bombers and flew combat escort. Another 220 P-47s and P-51s would be reassigned to the perimeter defense.[306]

As with any plan, it would all come down to execution. Practice missions were flown during the weeks prior to D-Day in order to determine the best attack formations and the correct munitions. A formation of six heavy bombers was selected for the attacks on Omaha, Juno, Gold, and Sword. Anticipating bad weather, extra radar sets were requisitioned, and one plane in each of the six-ship formations of B-17s and B-24s was equipped with it. They trained, too. With or without radar, the bombers would drop their bombs from 20,000 feet.

Virtually all of the warplanes that Tooey Spaatz and Pete Quesada had at their disposal would fly at least one mission; some would fly four or five.[307] Because the B-17s and B-24s would be the least accurate of the planes bombing that morning, the heavies would stop five minutes before the arrival of the first Higgins boat at 0630 hours, which was H-Hour on Omaha Beach. If the weather was bad and clouds covered the beaches, a contingency plan would go into effect. This plan called for the Forts and Liberators using their radar sets to drop their bombs, but, because accuracy suffered, a margin of 1,000 yards was added to the bomb-safe line to prevent any bombs from landing on the soldiers. Moreover, the plan also called for the bombing to halt ten minutes before H-Hour. Although reports are silent on this, a 1,000-yard buffer—ten football fields end-to-end—would clearly throw all of the bombs so far past the German fortifications that the

Germans might not be so much as scratched. The plan nonetheless remained unchanged.[308]

The D-Day airwar was to be the greatest air operation ever, the equivalent of three modern airlines taking off at the same time loaded with volatile bombs and fuel and flying in a tightly compacted area with guns blazing below them and antiaircraft fire coming up toward them. It was a smart plan, the product of four months of work, and it was a tested plan with drills and exercises and mock missions. But it was only a plan.

Never before in human history had an amphibious operation of this size been attempted, and not in eight hundred years had any such operation across the English Channel succeeded. The unknowns were too imponderable to consider, the what-ifs too unspeakably dangerous. To pull it off would require not only the fighting spirit of the men, but also no small degree of good fortune. D-Day was a day of enormous consequence for both the Allies and for Hitler's Germany. The hard truth was that it would either be the first step toward the end of the war, or a setback that could derail victory for another year.[309]

CHAPTER 17

COMBAT

Even as the first greenish hues of spring welcomed the fourth month of Spaatz's aggressive command in England, Hap Arnold warned that even from the remove of Washington, it still appeared likely that Spaatz, despite all planning to the contrary, would have a great air battle on his hands on D-Day.[310] This frustrated the impatient airman.

Arnold and his British counterpart, Sir Trafford Leigh-Mallory, had been at odds conceptually with respect to the airwar that might unfold during the D-Day landings. In January 1944, Leigh-Mallory had welcomed the idea of luring the Germans into battle over the D-Day beaches and fighting it out in the skies over Normandy. Spaatz disagreed, considering it too risky and too certain to add to the havoc on the beaches. To Spaatz, the number one job for the enormous airpower massed in England was to give Eisenhower air superiority before the invasion so he could focus on battling inland and not worry about German aircraft above him. The job of Pointblank was to eliminate the Luftwaffe as a threat on D-Day—and to get it done now, not later. "Am not sure whether [Leigh-Mallory] has proper conception of air role," wrote Spaatz in his diary. "Apparently accepts possibility of not establishing Air supremacy until landing starts."[311]

Going into the final month before the invasion, there was a truth, and that truth was that there were no magic bullets to be found. The loss of the ball bearing plants hadn't choked off the manufacture of German engines. The attacks on German airframe factories hadn't eliminated the production of fighters. The railroads seemed to be self-healing, back in business just hours or days after being bombed. Nazi Germany was too complex, too developed, too organic for just one raid, one mission, one good day to bring it to an end. The Reich's self-preservation instincts were too well honed.

Occupied Europe was anything but the Europe of old. The Renault factory in Billancourt, France, was no longer making French cars, but rather lorries for the German Army. The international airports at Orly and Le Bourget, and dozens of smaller ones, had long ago ceased to land airliners. Rather, they had been turned into fighter bases for the Luftwaffe with scores of airplanes spread across the ramps and with ammunition depots brimming with belts of machine gun bullets and 20-mm cannon shells. The same could be said of Schiphol in Amsterdam and the airports in Brussels and Rome. There were fighter bases in France at Le Mans, Lille, and Abbeville, and in Gilze-Rijen, De Kooy, and Den Holder on the Dutch North Sea, not to mention scores more scattered throughout Europe. This was no longer Europe; it was Nazi Europe.

Fighter controllers were deftly maneuvering German fighter squadrons wherever they were needed. Pilots were connected to a vast network of coastal radar sites and air control stations deep inside concrete-and-steel buildings. Farm fields were thick with searchlights to track the night bombers of the RAF and with antiaircraft guns to attack the daylight bombers of the Eighth. The French coastal towns of Bordeaux, Brest, and La Rochelle no longer sported harbors filled with sail boats and fishing vessels, but instead were dwarfed by submarine pens with towering 30-foot walls of curving gray concrete that protruded ominously into their bays with dark, gaping holes into and out of which sailed Nazi U-boats. The beaches on the tip of Île de Ré were crowded with steel reinforced concrete pillboxes. More than four thousand antiaircraft emplacements ringed Vienna, Hamburg, Münster, and Berlin.[312] The Dutch port city of IJmuiden, which connects Amsterdam to the North Sea, had submarine pens and 88-mm flak batteries.[313] Coastal batteries lined the English Channel and faced the North Sea and the Zuiderzee. The shipyards at Rotterdam were building and repairing German warships. Barges on the Danube were under Nazi control. A Nazi radio station had been installed in the Eiffel Tower, and German firms had flocked to Paris to open offices for the economic boon that surely lay ahead.

The years of the German occupation brought about increasingly dangerous lands beneath the wings of the American airmen. The breadth and intensity of the Allied bombings meant that the airmen who came down on German soil were increasingly at risk of being lynched, beaten, or brutally hacked to death. The lucky ones escaped or were quickly captured by soldiers.

The vise tightened, too, on the people of Europe. The red-and-black swastika was found on flags, armbands, helmets, and posters on buildings. Hitler's notorious Waffen-SS, the military arm of the Nazi party, had grown from a few regiments of brute thugs into a well-organized armed force of thirty-eight battalions. Nazi officials controlled the citizenry through repression down to the smallest villages. Nazi law replaced the voting booth, and a deadly bullet replaced trial by jury. As the bombing increased, the violence against civilians grew worse. Just days after D-Day, the 640 people in the French village of Oradour-sur-Glane were machine-gunned down and burned to death, including some four hundred women and children locked in a church, which was set aflame. As cries rang out, the fire consumed them all. So it went.

The German war machine was hardened, experienced, and exceedingly well developed, but there were problems. The Luftwaffe was showing signs of weakening. Replacement pilots had slowed to a trickle, and their qualifications were suspect. German fighter pilots who had been shot down or wounded in previous engagements were clearly too valuable to be sent home, so after they were patched up, they returned to combat squadrons through special staging areas that mixed pilots together in a scene not unlike something out of *Star Wars*. Remembered Hermann Buchner, a Luftwaffe fighter pilot returning to service after being shot down: "I was transferred to the *Frontfliegersammelstelle* [Front Line Pilots Assembly Point] at Dortmund-Brackel ... It seemed that all of the flying branches of the Luftwaffe were represented there. As I got to look around and meet many of the personnel there I spoke to bomber crews, fighter pilots, ground-attack boys like me, transport people, reconnaissance personnel and various other flying personnel. I was put in the second Staffel which consisted entirely of fighter and ground-attack pilots who had received severe burns or amputations as a result of combat—illustrious company."[314]

The air battles were bitterly fought, pitting strategy against strategy with virtually every aircraft available on both sides fully engaged. The results seesawed back and forth as American bombers hit industrial targets and American fighters swept the ground. The German flak had increased in intensity, and the German fighters were well controlled. "The defense of Germany against these attacks has in fact become the prime concern of the German Air Force," said a British air intelligence report. Hermann Goering, the head of the Luftwaffe, completely agreed: "The morale of the pilots is excellent," he said. Both sides were all in.[315]

To defend the vast bomber streams that were coming in at more than 100 miles long, the American escort fighters now patrolled areas rather than boxes, creating a corridor of fighter planes through which the bombers marched. Other pilots continued ahead of the Forts to break up the Germans before they organized in strength. "Under the right weather conditions and an all-out effort, the bombers stretched fore and aft as far as you could see," wrote Arlen Baldridge. "What a terrifying and sickening sight it must have been to the Germans—up to 3,000 planes boring their way toward one of their cities."[316]

George Graham was in a bomber coming home from a maximum-effort mission when he realized the full strength of the American airforce. "Once we reached the rally point coming back no matter where you looked—north, east, or west—all you saw were P-47s, P-51s, P-38s, Spitfires, B-17s and B-24s. The whole sky was black with them and not a single German. It was incredible."[317]

Head-on attacks mounted by the Germans increased in frequency, with devastating results. So thick was the hail of fire from an organized strike that bombers sometimes fell away in flames after the briefest of passes. The Germans came up in line-abreast formations of dozens of fighters, all sweeping in together with guns and cannons clattering. "The combat formations usually consisted of one attacking group and two escorting groups," wrote Luftwaffe commander Adolf Galland in his memoirs. "The former were to attack the enemy's bomber formations while the later gave them fighter protection against the enemy fighters …"[318] The destroyers were to break through the screen of American escorts fighters and go for the bombers. Behind the destroyers, the German Me-109s and FW-190s were ready to attack. "Our orders were to cover the destroyers so they could get through the enemy escorts and reach the bombers," said one Luftwaffe fighter pilot of this formation. "But once they were through to the bombers they had to look after themselves for then the single-engine fighters' orders were to attack the bombers also."[319]

Once the Germans formed up for the attack—thirty or forty destroyers lined up in front of sixty or seventy fighters—a near-perfect killing machine was in place. The line-abreast formation diluted the defensive firepower of the Forts by presenting too many targets for a combat box to focus on. Despite this advantage, the American bomber formations were daunting. "A bomber formation usually consisted of twenty machines, which flew in rows of four planes and which were sideways echeloned," remembered a Luftwaffe fighter pilot. "Our fighters were subjected to defensive fire of at least eight guns per bomber, which with a group of twenty bombers, meant the concentrated firepower of 160 machine guns."

Hitler beefed up the air defenses by rotating to the west combat experienced fighter squadrons based in Italy. He also ordered two of his best fighter pilots from each of the fighter groups on the Russian Front to move back to France.[320] Major Günther Rall, a top Luftwaffe ace, was one of the new arrivals. "It does not take me long to realize that over Germany almost everything is different than the Eastern Front. Combat takes place on the edge of the stratosphere, whereas, in compete contrast, I have scored the majority of my victories in Russia at much lower heights."[321]

The bombing of Germany was taking a devastating toll on German airmen, soldiers, and civilians alike, as well as on Germany's economy. The Germans were forced to divert enormous resources to the Defense of the Reich, resources that otherwise would have been used in combat. According to estimates, some 2 million laborers were conscripted from the occupied territories and forced into the factories to maintain the production of airplanes and tanks while some 2 million more soldiers and civilians were assigned to air defense. Another 3 million workers were tasked with the unwelcome business of clean-up and repair work.[322]

Meanwhile, the American fighter pilots were embracing their newfound freedom, and they swept the skies and ground for German airplanes. Luftwaffe airfields couldn't be hidden, but they could be difficult to see. While returning from an escort mission, a pair of P-51s let down to hunt. Remembered one of the pilots: "We came upon an airfield that was very well camouflaged, even at close range. The planes had netting over them. I fired a long burst on a Me-109 and detected numerous hits and believe I may have hit one or both crewmen on the wing of the enemy aircraft." Indeed he did. German reports issued later in the war recorded this attack. The Me-109 was but a few minutes from taking off. The pilot saw the Mustangs out of the corner of his eye and scrambled out of the cockpit just in time. "At that moment bullets started to fly around us," he remembered. "The Messerschmitt was hit several times in and around the cockpit, the canopy was smashed."[323] One of his two crewmen was standing on the wing, and he simply froze. Three of his fingers were shot off, and he was hit in his buttock.

"The buzzing of airfields etc. is not too safe," wrote an American fighter pilot in his diary, although in this case his own experiences had been good. "I saw an airport out on a peninsula near Wismar, Germany. Decided to give it a try. Went southwest about ten miles, dropped to the deck at 375 mi/hr and headed across the bay right on the water. Pulled up slightly as I neared the field and fired a long burst at a He-111. Lt. Starkey shot a ME-110 and damaged a JU-52. Lt. Conlin fired into a hangar. We joined up over the water and headed back." On that same mission, he had a front-row seat to the bombing done by the heavies of the Eighth. They dropped their load dead-on. "Got an excellent view of the bombing—quite a sight" he wrote. "Not a single bomb hit the town but they really laid it in the airfield."[324] It was the German airbase at Tours, France. The pilot later swept the airfields around Paris and saw no activity.

The game of wits between the German fighter controllers and the American operations planners was one of nuance. The controllers picked when and where to attack and for the most part were good at finding holes in the formations. When they did, the results were predictably bad for the B-17s. On a mission to Bremen, one pilot watched another pilot flying off his right wing. They locked eyes for a moment, but then a round of German 20-mm cannon shells sliced into the Fort. "They blew the guy off my right wing and in fact, his copilot got a direct hit and severed his head and his head rolled along the catwalk and the pilot was looking toward me."[325]

On another bombing mission, the sky was filled with airplanes turning and falling, bullets etching lines between fighters and Forts. "There were fighters everywhere," remembered a gunner on a B-17. "They seemed to come past in fours. I would engage the first three but then the fourth aircraft would be on me before I could get my guns on him. I knew our aircraft was being hit real bad. The fighters came in one lot after another; there were hardly any gaps in the attack. The ball turret gunner, Sg. Andrew Brown complained that the belt links and spent shell casings from the chin turret were raining past his turret so thickly he could not get his sights on the enemy fighters."[326]

One pilot was caught in the grip of centrifugal forces and was trapped inside his falling Marauder. "The ship snapped rolled, which is like a corkscrew," remembered Robert Spillman. "I wasn't scared. I didn't have time to be, but I knew this was curtains. A wing was down. I looked out of the window and saw the ground coming up to us. There was nothing to do but shut my eyes and wait. It's peculiar that at a time like that a man is not worried."[327] Spillman's B-26 slammed into the ground upside down. Remarkably, he and the other two on board survived.

Feelings against the Nazis intensified, and to a man, the airmen knew Hitler had to be defeated. Sometimes his reign of inhumanity was brought home in unexpected ways. Toward the end of the war, an American bomber crew limped down the Vistula River in search of a place to set down their crippled bombers. Despite the terrible damage to their own plane, they were aghast at the sight of what had happened to Warsaw. "There was nothing left. It had been bombed so thoroughly by the Nazis that all there was were ruins and chimneys sticking up here and there."[328] Hitler's brutal machine of destruction had to be shut down.

A shot of whiskey after a mission did much to calm shaky nerves, and it helped many of the airmen get to sleep after the adrenaline rush of combat. But the experience of war went deep, and the results sometimes manifested themselves at that moment when the drive to kill and ready weapons created a volatile mixture.

A fighter pilot described what he saw, knowing full well what it meant: "I flew with one fellow who was already on his second tour. He was a killer at heart. I remember he shot down a FW-190. When he shot down the FW-190, he started circling the parachute. When it got down to 1,500 to 1,000 feet, he flew right under it and his prop wash caused the parachute to collapse and the German hit the ground like a ton of bricks. His reasoning was you'd better kill the SOB because he would be right up there tomorrow and you might not make it. To show how his thoughts were, there was a farmer in the field right near where the fellow landed and he was shaking his pitchfork at us and, hell, he just made a circle around and lifted him out of the patch. Of course he had great reasoning there, that he could raise a son that might have to fight mine someday."[329]

Some pilots became jaded and cynical during their months flying over Europe. Many, of course, didn't make it to their twenty-fifth mission, their ticket home. Replacement pilots coming in from America had little sense of the war that preceded them, and they often arrived with untested confidence that sometimes got the better of them. A crew chief for a fighter squadron remembered a new pilot on the ramp. The replacement aviator came out to the hardstands and looked up at his newly assigned P-47. "I remember a young fellow, nineteen, and him standing in front of a Thunderbolt at our base and saying, 'I'm not going in to that stupid barrel of bolts.' I remember him just about one month later standing in front of his Thunderbolt all shot to pieces, full of holes and the whole works. And his face was ash white, and all he could say was, 'Thank God I was in a Thunderbolt.'"[330]

While the Allied airmen continued to launch bombing missions, it seemed as if the Germans were conserving their strength. Not all raids were opposed. On two missions against targets in Berlin, bombers flew a milk run. "The enemy has been unable or unwilling to send his fighters in strength against these operations," wrote Spaatz in an update to Arnold. "Missions such as the operations against Brunswick and Frankfurt which brought practically no reaction this week, would have been subject to violent enemy opposition several months ago."[331]

Based on his own data, Spaatz felt he was close to dominating the air but not quite there yet. Still, he was confident enough of the situation to make one significant adjustment. It was conventional wisdom that the larger the bomber formation, the safer they were, but with fewer German fighters rising to meet them, Spaatz felt comfortable dividing some of the missions into smaller formations. While risky, doing so would allow for more targets to be attacked on a given day, and with Spaatz's target list, this was more than just useful. Spaatz's plan was to launch eight hundred or more bombers a day, but instead of splitting them up into just three or four groups, he was willing to split them into ten or twelve groups to hit ten or twelve targets apiece.

The mediums of the Ninth Air Force followed suit. In mid-April it was common to send one hundred or two hundred B-26s against a major rail center with P-47s as escorts, but both forces—the mediums and the fighters—were doing so well that the operations planners of the Ninth decided to break them down from groups of thirty-six aircraft per target to four- and six-plane formations. Equally, the Thunderbolts were doing so well dive-bombing that many were released from their escort duties and tasked with their own targets.[332]

The load this placed on the German air defense fighter controllers was immense. On one day alone, the Ninth had planes attacking eighteen targets; the Eighth was bombing seven targets while the Thunderbolts were dive-bombing another eleven. Moreover, when they could, the Thunderbolt pilots were using their drop tanks and causing other problems. When they stalled a train, a few of the P-47s would sweep back around to drop their tanks and set cars afire using their guns to ignite the gasoline. It wasn't a terror tactic: as a result of the flaming, conscripted French rail workers began deserting their trains in unprecedented numbers.

But no advantage lasted for long. As the attacks focused on one area, the Germans shifted their squadrons to meet it. The Eighth and Ninth intensified their interdiction strikes against rail and roads, but as soon as they did, more flak batteries rolled in to counter the attacks and more repair crews came streaming to the west.[333]

In the end, the Allied focus was now on the 130-mile arc. Roads would be cut, bridges dropped, airfields bombed, and communication lines blocked. The D-Day beaches would be as isolated as airpower could make them. If German reinforcements could be stalled, more boys just might get ashore, with fewer casualties.

CHAPTER 18

DICING WITH
THE DEVIL

No secrets were more carefully guarded than those that might reveal an enemy's intent on the battlefield. In a like manner, no combat mission was more completely wasted than one that was based on flawed intelligence. The two had much in common. Military intelligence was a precious asset and in both cases, the intelligence the commanders needed was often found in the reels of film brought back by pilots who flew deep into German territory in unarmed fighters loaded with nothing more than cameras and film. More than three hundred modified Mustangs, Lightnings, and RAF Spitfires were used for precisely that purpose, and their crowning achievement would be D-Day. "All of my missions were unarmed and without fighter escort," said John Blyth, a photo-reconnaissance pilot.[334] It was one of the few sorties flown by combat aviators with just a camera.

Aerial reconnaissance photography was used to gather military intelligence about enemy concentrations and movements, as well as to provide damage assessments following bombing raids. It was one of the most useful tools of the airwar, and it included gathering intelligence used to plan missions. Fine-grain films in wide sheets provided intelligence officers images of such quality that they could zoom in with magnifying glasses on a photograph taken at 30,000 feet and see the fuselage of an FW-190 parked along a tree line. If the bombs missed their targets, the reconnaissance photographs revealed the mistake and a new mission was scheduled. In the aftermath of the first Schweinfurt raid, reconnaissance photographs showed the collapse of key buildings where bombardiers had scored direct hits. The images also revealed the use of heavily reinforced internal blast walls to channel the concussive shock waves away from key components like machinery jigs. Craters dotting the fields around the Messerschmitt factory in Regensburg were counted in the photo labs, and from that the number of misses was calculated and the next mission's altitude and release points were modified. A series of photographs also was taken to study the location of buildings across the more than 1,000 square acres of the Wiener-Neustadt Me-109 fighter plant and to infer which step in an airplane's manufacture was conducted in which buildings. The proper building was then targeted and destroyed.

This was the value of aerial reconnaissance, but there was more, of course. On more than one occasion, clever German tricks were exposed for what they were and needless missions were avoided. Fake airplanes and dummy buildings revealed themselves under magnifying loupes and gave away German attempts to draw the bombers into traps.

Other times, information was gleaned in the most circumspect of ways. A reconnaissance pilot fresh back from a mission stood over an intelligence officer who was using stereoscopic magnifiers to riddle the truth from the tiniest corner of a photograph. From his vantage point, it seemed as if she were frozen in place, looking at a blob of meaningless images. "She was drawing red and black circles around little dots. I asked what she was doing, and she said that this was a base that lays mines. [The dots] are seaplanes. I asked what the red and black circles were, and she said the red circles are seaplanes loaded with ordnance to take out and drop mines and the black circles are ones that are empty. I asked how she knew that and she said to look at the wing shadow. The wing shadow[s] were much closer to the wing on the [seaplanes] that were loaded because those planes were lower in the water."[335]

In the compartments that formerly held .50-cal machine guns, modified P-51s, P-38s, and British Spitfires carried large, bulky cameras, two that photographed at oblique angles and one that pointed straight down. The typical photo-reconnaissance mission required a high-altitude flight that traced a needle-thin line over the face of the Earth. As the plane crossed a designated target, the cameras were turned on and the automatic mechanisms whirred film past the lens.

Because pictures were so valuable, cameras were carried by the bombers, too. Joe Harlick, twenty-three, was part of a photo-reconnaissance crew on a bomber base. As one of his planes landed, he went out on the hardstands to retrieve his film. "Headquarters would give us the flight plan and serial numbers of the Flying Fortresses designated to carry strike cameras," said Harlick. "We had to find the designated B-17s in the dark, and usually the fog, over 7 miles of taxiways and hardstands on the base. Because of blackout rules, we had only a 2-inch slit of light from our headlights on our 4x4 truck. You would have to be within a few yards of the plane before it was possible to see the serial number on the tail."[336] Harlick would climb aboard to get his film as the crew was gathering their gear. The camera bays, though, were often grim reminders of the combat just finished. "The floor of the radio room was the only piece of flat floor in the B-17 and also the warmest. Therefore all wounded personnel if possible were brought to this area. Since our strike cameras were in the pit below this floor, I had many unforgettable bloody scenes of the area forever implanted in my memories."[337]

Reconnaissance pilots were a unique breed of aviator. They were all fully qualified as fighter pilots and good at air-to-air combat, but something about them pointed the trajectory of their lives toward this solitary mission. It took cool thinking and confidence in one's airplane to complete a recon mission—that and the rare ability to operate alone. "Mentally we each of us probably handled it differently, but flying alone and unarmed was quite different than flying with others."[338] A crew chief on a photo-reconnaissance base felt the difference almost immediately and saw it in a cosmic sense. "No, there is no full-blown action on a photo recon base," said the chief. "The drama of an individual pitted alone against unknown opposition, of machines and men working as one organ, of callousness born of necessity; there is the drama of accomplishment."[339]

That drama of accomplishment came with enormous risks, and losses among the pilots were high. The stock and trade of a good pilot was to fly fast and high and get in and out of what was often a hornets' nest of German air defenses excited by a recent attack. "We had nothing but cameras," said one reconnaissance pilot. "The idea was to stay out of trouble, and if you were intercepted, with a P-38, the only thing you could do was to get rid of your drop tanks and go as fast as possible and stay out of the way."[340]

"The Spitfire would climb out of the way of trouble," said another reconnaissance pilot who flew the British fighter. "If a patrol would start to come up where you were and you could see them, all you did was continue to climb, and, if you could stay 1,000 feet above them, there wasn't much they could do about it, and if you continued to climb, you could still get your pictures."[341]

Because German factories often had to be bombed several times, pilots became experts in certain areas of Germany and became the preferred airmen for specific missions. When they covered a target, they were taking their photographs, not dropping bombs. Said one pilot, "We had requests to cover synthetic oil plants almost on a regular basis because they'd bomb the daylights out of them, and then we would go and cover them, and when we got back to the point where it looked like they were producing again, then there'd be another raid and we would hit them again."[342]

Pattern recognition was one of their specialties. A streak of white was a runway; a shadow was an entrance to a tunnel. A "hot" object was something suspicious and cause for extra pictures; something seemingly as insignificant as the glint of a rail spur or a single piece of artillery might reveal a new production facility or a German company on the march.[343]

In April 1944, the reconnaissance squadrons began their D-Day missions. The intelligence sections sent down word that they needed extensive photographic coverage of the invasion area in the Normandy region. They required extensive photographic detail on a number of areas: the intended drop zones, the bridges leading to Normandy, and every single road the Germans might use to try to get to the landing sites. They requested flights over the bridges on the Meuse River; the main rail hub that connected Antwerp and Rotterdam to Aachen, Germany; the German airfields; some 160 miles of shoreline along the English Channel, including the Normandy and Pas-de-Calais areas; and a 120-mile stretch of inland farms that probably would be the drop zone for the airborne assault. Because they needed exceptionally good detail, the pilots were to fly their missions at 3,500 feet. Coverage was to be updated every four days.

It was a tall order—and laced with risk. The low-level flights would expose the pilots to ground fire from any soldier who spotted them. Plus, their backs would be exposed to attacks from above. The Ninth Air Force was given the assignment, and they met it head on. They sent their recon aircraft out on eighty-three missions and generated some 9,500 prints. The pictures were morphed together to create the first photographic mosaic of the invasion area. Not a single plane was shot down.[344]

But it was only the tip of the iceberg. A second recon mission would be far more demanding—and far more dangerous. Earlier intelligence had revealed what appeared to be new obstacles on the invasion beaches, but exactly what they were and what they were made of was a puzzle. The invasion planners wanted detailed photographic information so they could determine what sort of explosives were needed to take them out.

The reconnaissance squadrons were briefed on three coastal areas that the intelligence sections wanted covered. Each area had to be photographed from three different positions. The first pass would photograph the landing areas from several miles out, the second pass at 1,500 yards from the surf line, and the third pass would take them immediately over the shoreline. What made this so different was that they wanted the pictures taken from "zero altitudes."

Ultra low-level flight was nothing new to the pilots. They flew it, they liked it, but there was no room for mistakes. To fly at zero altitude meant that they would be so close to the ground that the cushion of air that pillowed under a fighter's wings was the sole margin for error between the fuselage and the ground. Flying that low put everyone at risk, and even a top-notch pilot might miss a beat and be scattered across the ground before he knew what happened. The British called these low-level flights "dicing" missions, as in throwing dice with the devil, gambling with one's soul. The inference was that the missions were one blink short of suicidal, and that the devil never lost when they played his game. The bravado was in beating the devil.

The first dicing mission for D-Day that pilot Kermit Bliss flew was over the French rail lines and bridges that led to the Normandy beaches. "Now, when the invasion came along, then marshaling yards became very important because they wanted to know where they were moving troops, and we got a lot of what they called dicing mission," said Bliss, a Madison, Wisconsin, native who flew with the Seventh Photo-Reconnaissance Group. "We would get missions to take pictures of marshaling yards at zero altitude. Fly right through it as low as possible. We had two planes that covered sixty-two bridges on the Loire River at one time. They were flying right in the streets. They got pictures of people diving into the gutter as they flew the streets. Then they'd shoot out [in the open] and take a picture of the bridge. One of them claimed a flak tower destroyed because he flew between the two flak towers … and one flak tower blew up the other."[345] One reconnaissance pilot came back with 250 holes in his P-38.[346] Some pilots landed with the branches of trees embedded in their wings. One pilot dipped a wing and accidentally creased the surface of the English Channel but regained control and flew on as if nothing had happened.[347]

The dicing missions down Omaha Beach and Utah Beach proved to be one of the most important contributions the reconnaissance pilots would make to the D-Day landings. According to an official history, they flew Omaha Beach only high enough to "clear the obstacles on the beaches."[348] The detailed images they came back with were astonishing. On eleven separate missions, these aviators took off and headed out toward the English Channel, then dropped down to the wave tops to fly in under German radar. They sped up to 375 miles per hour and headed toward the coastline of France, lifting their noses only enough to clear the sand. The margin of error was deathly slim. One pilot simply disappeared over the English Channel. It was presumed that he caught a wave and cartwheeled in. A second pilot was hit pointblank and vaporized by the flak. Naturally, if a pilot was shot down and captured, he would be unable to reveal anything important to the Germans: even the pilots had no idea where the landings would take place.[349]

Lieutenant Garland A. York flew the risky third pass straight down Omaha Beach between the high-water mark and the low-water mark. He pushed his plane as fast as it could go while his cameras clicked away. The photographs he came back with were incredibly detailed. As he flew down the beach, German soldiers scrambled for cover. In one photograph, the whites of their eyes were clearly visible.[350]

Gun emplacements on the bluffs were identified and added to the target folders. The mysterious structures on the beaches were determined to be Czech hedgehogs, antitank obstacles made from steel that would require satchel charges of high explosives to remove. York's pictures also provided the first detailed images of the tree logs that were planted in the sand and cocked seaward. The photographs revealed that they were topped with deadly Teller mines with 20-pound impact charges, some attached to hidden trip wires. One intelligence section did the painstaking calculations of shadows and distances and realized that the obstacles had been presighted by the machine gun nests on the hill. That information was factored into the plan of approach by the Navy for the engineering battalions.[351]

"Probably in no operation in history did the air forces do a more thorough job in this respect than in Overlord," said one Air Force historian. "A total of 400 visual reconnaissance sorties were flown by the Ninth Air Force between 15 May and D-Day, in addition to 140 weather reconnaissance sorties."[352]

The recon photographs made it possible to build scale models of Omaha Beach and use them in preinvasion briefings. The models proved to be exceedingly accurate, something the demolition experts discovered when they landed. Remembered one of the engineers. "We were isolated a few days before the invasion in a fenced enclosure—no passes outside for anybody—and briefed very thoroughly on that part of Normandy Beach we'd be landing on. For the briefing, we had low- and high-altitude aerial photographs provided by the Air Force's 34th [Photo] Reconnaissance Squadron. There was also an extremely accurate scale model of Omaha Beach, complete with natural features, trees, houses, and other buildings, and even such German military installations as were known to be in the vicinity. We memorized the landing site and studied the obstacles in the photographs until we knew everything backwards and forwards. Later, when we did land, we discovered just how accurate the model had been; the coast looked just like it, right down to the last detail."[353]

On D-Day, the reconnaissance pilots were as busy as any of the fighter pilots. Their eyes in the skies helped slow the advance of the Germans as they directed attacks based on their visual observations. The photographs they brought back revealed hidden concentrations to be attacked. "Enemy aerial photo reconnaissance detects our every movement," said one exasperated German officer after the war. "Every movement, every concentration, every weapon, and immediately after detection, every one of these objectives is smashed."[354]

While most of the reconnaissance pilots flew unarmed, the converted P-51s had guns. In that odd way things sometimes happen, it would be a reconnaissance pilot who would shoot down one of the first German fighters destroyed in the air on D-Day.*

---

* The reconnaissance planes had their own nomenclature. The P-38 was the F-4 or F-5, depending on the build, while the P-51 was called the F-6. The "F" designated a fighter aircraft while the "P" in P-51 designated a pursuit aircraft. (Stanley, 80. World War II Photo Reconnaissance.)

CHAPTER 19

MAY 1944

"The Germans are getting very crafty and have been bouncing flights," wrote a P-47 pilot in his diary. "Five P-47s were shot down just off the enemy coast and there have been similar incidents. All pilots are really watching out from now on."[355]

As May 1944 dawned, German and American air forces were engaged in violent combat mitigated only by occasionally bad weather. The Luftwaffe was weakened, but by no means had it been rendered ineffective. A new wedge formation of Me-109s was tried on the B-17s with good results, and the controllers were now targeting Quesada's dive-bombers by vectoring German fighters above them while they were most vulnerable.

Across the Channel, England swelled as war materiel flowed through her docks and out to the assembly areas. Conversations were thick with talk of invasion; the only scuttlebutt now was where and when.

On the American airbases, the barracks bulged to overflowing as more and more replacement crews flowed in. So numerous were the bombers and fighters that hardly an extra inch of empty space remained on the perimeter track.

Here, too, talk of invasion coursed through the air like electricity. Remembered Wilbur Richardson, a ball turret gunner, "Something occurred that made everyone really start talking about this invasion that should be coming up soon. All crewmembers had to carry their sidearms, their .45s, at all times on base. We were told to do this because they expected German paratroopers to come in and louse up any invasion plans that were being put together."[356] The German paratroopers never arrived, but that was the least of the problems. The Germans shuffled fighters to and from their designated dispersal bases, sometimes keeping a group on the ground for only half a day. Some Messerschmitts were moved north, some Focke-Wulfs to the east, and then they were all moved back again. American intelligence officers were forced to make educated guesses about which airfields were active and which were not, but most of the guesses were wrong. D-Day was on the minds of the Luftwaffe, too.[357]

Meanwhile, the war that Spaatz and Quesada had declared on the Luftwaffe was now playing out on an even larger stage. With D-Day fast approaching, the eyes of Roosevelt, Stalin, and Churchill were focused on the Allied air forces. Spaatz and Quesada responded by flooding the continent with their warplanes.

As Eisenhower took command of the Allied Expeditionary Forces, the controlling command for the D-Day invasion forces, he also took control of the bombers and fighters and was responsible for any changes to the target lists. On May 1, 1944, he issued a new directive to step up the attacks on the rail yards. In it were thirty more targets.[358] Quesada took his cue and launched his fighter sweeps and dive-bombers. Employing their well-trained 40-degree and 60-degree diving angles, waves of P-47s struck the marshaling yards and train stations with deadly accuracy.

On May 7, the target folders swelled again when fourteen auto bridges and ten railroad bridges over the Seine were moved up to first-priority status. Eisenhower was determined to stop, by all means possible, the advance of German reinforcements that surely would follow the landings. By D-Day, all of the bridges on the Seine below Paris had been dropped or damaged.[359]

The heavies were flying as hard and as often as weather would allow. On the morning of May 7, Spaatz launched 922 bombers against targets in Berlin and in Münster, along with 754 fighters. That afternoon he put up a second raid against various rail yards. Heavy cloud cover largely grounded the Luftwaffe, though, and losses were light.

On May 8, however, the combat was as bloody as any. Whatever advantage the Eighth had gained seemed to melt away under the gunfire of the Germans. The Ninth launched 450 Marauders and Havocs against bridges and airfields, while Spaatz went back to Berlin with more than 743 bombers and 731 fighters. Some four hundred Luftwaffe fighters assembled to attack Spaatz's bombers, while from the ground the flak batteries darkened the sky with bursts of black, smoky shrapnel. At 25,000 feet, fragments of steel sliced through the thin skin of the bombers and scattered hot metal into the cabins. The roar of engines mixed with the *crrmmmp* of bullets slapping against fuselages. Inside, the gunners were shrouded in the smoke as shell casings piled up around their feet. Messerschmitts, Focke-Wulfs, and Heinkels circled and attacked. A big plane like a Boeing could take a lot—there were plenty of spaces where a round of cannon fire or machine gun bullets could pass through harmlessly—but one bullet in the right place and they were done. Today, the airmen needed all the help they could get.

One by one the bombers fell away as chunks of metal blown off by cannon fire scattered through the sky. A B-17 winged over, spiraled out of formation, and exploded. Sheets of flames completely covered a B-24 from the top turret back to the tail. Inside, the crew was burned to death. Shells found their mark and burst through cabins, finding flesh and taking lives. The grisly carnage inside mixed with choking dust as planes slipped out of their formations and spun to the ground. A total of forty-one bombers and eighteen fighters went down, with another 199 chewed up by the gunfire.[360]

Despite the losses of May 8, the airwar went on. On May 9, 1944, The Airfield Plan was activated and more than a hundred Luftwaffe bases came under attack. The B-17s and B-24s became aerial plow horses and laid down tens of thousands of tons of bombs on the grass runways and Luftwaffe fighter bases across Western Europe and Germany. The strikes had been held back to deny the Germans a chance to rebuild their forward airfields before D-Day. On May 9, the Eighth hit eleven major Luftwaffe complexes with 797 bombers and 544 fighters, while the Ninth sent its B-26s against another half dozen. The next day, they savaged the Luftwaffe complex at Abbeville. On May 11, the Ninth put more than three hundred mediums into the air. From Brittany to Holland, twenty-six fields were pummeled by dive-bombers, and another twenty fields were hit by the mediums. The German airfield at Beaumont-le-Roger, located along the Paris-to-Cherbourg rail line, was hit four times.[361] At Wevelgem in Belgium, a German pilot was shot down in the landing pattern and nearly burned to death in his plane. A German crewman manned a makeshift 20-mm cannon stripped from an FW-190 and shot down a Spitfire. At the airfield near Nancy, eleven Me-109s were set on fire on the ground, five more were damaged, and two ground crewmen were killed during a strafing attack. A German pilot returning to base was just inches from safety when he was strafed as he jumped from his cockpit onto his wing. He was killed.[362] One American pilot bombed an airfield and as he did, he noticed the shadow of a Me-109. He pulled his fighter around to see if it was a decoy. Coming in for a second pass, he emptied a burst into the German plane. It was no decoy. As the Messerschmitt billowed black smoke into the sky, the pilot raced across the field before yanking up into a near-vertical climb to the safety of the sky.

Casualties and near misses mounted, and the chaos of combat proved deadly. One American fighter pilot was on a strafing run when he ran through a string of telephone lines and then clipped the tops of some trees surrounding a German airfield. By force of will alone, he made it home. Another pilot swept in so low that the concussion from the bow wave of his fighter set off landmines. He was hit by a piece of shrapnel, but he too made it home.[363]

The American planners went to great lengths to avoid civilian deaths, but the bombing was now heavily focused on transportation routes, and railroad stations were increasingly at the center of the attacks. Owing to more than a million leaflets dropped across western France, civilian railroad traffic ended on May 20, 1944. The Eighth and the Fifteenth promptly leveled the train stations that had before been untouched.[364]

For all of the violence there were moments of unexpected chivalry. Hermann Buchner was in the fight of his life until he gained a decisive edge against a B-17. "I opened fire from 1,000 meters away and then at 500 meters I added 20mm cannon fire. The hits were good; the rear gunner was no longer firing and the way to success was open. On the fourth attack I aimed for the inside engine and the shots were as good as the previous ones; the rear gunner was still not firing. Some of the crew jumped with their parachutes one by one from the rear gunner's position, six or seven men. I no longer had to worry about its defensive fire so I flew up to its left side and signaled to the pilot that he should get out. He looked at me but made no move to leave the plane."[365] The bomber eventually flipped over in the air and broke apart near the tail section. Buchner saw the two pilots finally jump. They landed near the German airfield and lived to survive the war. Buchner landed, refueled, and took off again.

Wounded bombers were fair game, and the crews of the cripples knew that they had little hope of getting home unless they somehow went unnoticed by the German pilots. Most bomber crews believed that by lowering their landing gear they were signaling their surrender, but accounts differ on this point. Some aircrews recalled moments when the air-to-air combat simply ended in a draw, usually when the bomber and fighters spent the last of their ammunition. Remembered a bomber pilot on a raid against targets in Kiel, Germany: "Feathering a propeller over enemy territory is like writing the boys at the mortuary for space on their slab. All of the fighters see that you are a crippled and immediately set upon you for the kill." On this occasion, he was one of the few exceptions to the rule. "We had only three half-hearted attacks from then on out to the coast, and these pilots must have been very green, or else I had become hardened to it all by the time. Off to our left I saw one Me-109 do a slow roll and then head for home. His maneuver meant, 'Well boys, it's all over for this time. See you soon.'"[366]

For all of the activity and all of the combat missions, Spaatz still had one target that he desperately wanted to bomb. From the earliest days of his command, Tooey Spaatz had been as anxious as Hap Arnold to see the skies over Germany clouded by a force of a thousand American bombers. Strategic bombardment was the vision that had drawn both of them into the Air Corps, to earn their pilot wings from the Wright Brothers, as Arnold had, and to pull off risky stunts, as Spaatz had. Spaatz believed that his heavies could still pound Germany into submission by attacking key industrial sites such as factories and manufacturing complexes and in particular, the German oil refineries. Unlike the ball bearing plants, which had largely proved to be futile, the refineries would directly contribute to Pointblank by drying up precious fuel reserves for the Luftwaffe. With no oil, there'd be no gas.

Eisenhower wasn't interested in oil. He wanted the Normandy beaches sealed off. If the Germans couldn't get to the invasion front, they couldn't attack, and if they couldn't reinforce the soldiers on the beachheads, he might get through. Eisenhower turned down what would be known as the Oil Plan, a plan to bomb German oil refineries, in favor of the Transportation Plan, which called for the bombing of rail, roads, and bridges. That said, on May 12, Spaatz was allowed to attack a few refineries. The results were spectacular.

The chemical complex at Merseburg, Germany, was one of the largest like it in the country. It was home to the IG Farben Leuna Works, a large industrial complex that consisted of 250 buildings spread over some 3 square miles. Leuna was Germany's second largest chemical works and second largest synthetic oil refinery. It was here that they made sodium cyanide, tetraethyl lead, sulfuric acid, nitrogen, methanol, ethylene, caustic soda, ethyl chloride, ammonia, chlorine, and calcium carbide—all of the essential ingredients for bombs, ammunition, and fuels—as well as where they converted coal to gasoline. So important was Leuna to the German war effort that some six hundred guns surrounded this vital complex.[367]

Albert Riedel, fifteen, was a flak boy serving in one of the gun batteries around Leuna. Riedel was well trained, patriotic, and remarkably capable, even as young as he was. "The regular soldiers did their best to give us good training," said one of his friends. "We were confident of our ability as gunners."[368] Unbeknownst to Riedel, on May 12, a major attack was on the way, and his oil refinery was the target. A total of 886 B-17s and B-24s had climbed into the air with an escort of 780 fighters. Like a column of defiant soldiers, steady and unflinching, the bombers had crossed over the Low Countries and were flying into Germany. When it was clear that Leuna was the target, the air raid sirens wailed. Said Riedel, "We leapt from the wall to our guns."

This time, the advantage was with the Allies. "The attack lasted an half an hour, bombing the Leuna works in several waves," said the young gun layer. "The air was full of swishing and roaring sounds. The silhouette of the Leuna works disappeared behind the fountains of earth thrown up by the bombs."[369] Riedel's gun emplacement was nearly hit, but only clumps of earth and splintered wood showered down on their heads. The pace of firing was so fast that scarcely anyone had time to breathe. In the span of the raid, one gun in Riedel's battery got off 106 rounds.

The air battles over Leuna were as deadly as any in the war. Some 430 Luftwaffe fighters came up to meet the bombers and shot down forty-six of them, but the Luftwaffe lost more than a hundred of their own fighters.[370] Moreover, the bombardiers found the refineries. "The only thing I saw between us and the target was a lot of falling bombs," remembered a B-17 crewman.[371] A total of 1,718 tons of bombs hit Leuna with astonishing accuracy. Flames soared more than 20,000 feet in the sky, and the plant was reduced to charred, twisted steel. Spaatz was pleased.

By May, rail traffic in France had been reduced by only 33 percent, and Allied intercepts indicated that the Germans still had three times the capacity they needed for the movement of their military. Quesada thought his fighters could do something about that.[372] Recalling the song about a train popularized by Glenn Miller, he ordered sweeps against the locomotives and called them "Chattanooga Choo-Choos."

Quesada divided western France into seven zones and gave every squadron one zone as their personal hunting ground. Winging over from above, the pilots attacked with determination. They bombed passenger trains, freight trains, encampments, and personnel carriers. They cratered roadways, bridges, major intersections, and airfields. They met the Germans in the air and strafed them on the ground. "I called for the flight to go down and believe me, the boys were really flying good that day," remembered P-47 pilot Glenn Duncan. "We came across the 'drome in a good four ship line abreast each individually picking a likely target."[373] One of them got a German staff car as a bonus. They watched as it shuddered under the hits of the

.50-caliber machine gun fire and then lifted in the air and was tossed back. Said Spaatz, gutsy fighting such as this "opened the door for the invasion."[374]

Attacking ground targets taught pilots to think defensively, to see things in new ways. A bend in the road might hide a gun battery. A house that looked too quiet was often a false front for another gun battery. A thin line of smoke was a locomotive. A fluttering tree line was the *whoof* of a heavy gun firing.[375]

By D-Day, Quesada had silenced the whistles of some 475 locomotives.[376]

The escorts now numbered more than seven hundred fighters per bomber mission while Quesada's dive-bombers mounted their own raids with nearly as many fighter-bombers. Through the end of May, bombers and fighters roamed the face of Occupied Europe seeking German aircraft wherever they could be found. On one day of combat, five hundred fighters dive-bombed and strafed a dozen airfields while four hundred B-17s and B-24s cratered German marshaling yards. On another day, 140 Forts hit the V-bomb sites while six hundred fighters dive-bombed bridges. So it went, unrelenting attacks. Tutow, Leipzig, Oldenburg, and repeated attacks against Pas-de-Calais were mounted, hitting airplane factories, parts suppliers, airfields, and transportation synapses. In the final week of the month, eight hundred or more bombers launched each and every day, with a like number of escorts and half as many mediums.

Spaatz was now battling for—and winning—control of the airspace over Western Europe. The statistics were revealing. Since assuming command, his all-out bombing and strafing had cost the fighter arm of the Luftwaffe a total of 2,262 pilots and an equal number of aircraft and destroyed dozens of airfields, forcing the German Air Force to pull back many more of their fighters from the invasion areas.[377]

In April, American fighter pilots destroyed more German fighter aircraft on the ground than had been destroyed in the air during all of 1943. In May 1944, American fighter pilots shot down 596 Luftwaffe planes in aerial combat, setting a dogfighting record. Apart from the overall statistics, taken together, one-by-one, mission-by-mission, the Eighth and Ninth had destroyed more than a thousand Luftwaffe airplanes in the sixty days leading to D-Day. Better still, more than half of the Luftwaffe's best pilots were gone, too.[378]

Spaatz was now all about attrition. The attacks deep into German air space and the five major raids on Berlin in May had nothing to do with the fall of Hitler. At this point in the war, Spaatz could scarcely care about the damage to factories. He wanted planes, pilots, and airfields. He was focused on D-Day.[379]

As a young man, British Field Marshal Bernard Law Montgomery had attended St. Paul's School in London, a boys' preparatory school of much accord founded in 1509. In May 1944, St. Paul's lecture theater was in use not by young men on their way to college but rather by an audience whose considerations that day would possibly change the world. Filing in to take their seats were Prime Minister Winston Churchill, Allied Supreme Commander General Dwight D. Eisenhower, and Generals Omar Bradley, Courtney Hodges, George Patton, Lewis Brereton, Quesada, Spaatz, Doolittle, and their British counterparts. The last person to arrive was King George VI.

Inside the theater, wall-sized maps had been positioned around the room, each clearly visible from a considerable distance. Placed in the center of the theater, and perfectly illuminated, was an oversized scale model of the D-Day invasion beaches. Cigar and cigarette smoke drifted upward as Eisenhower took the stage. In his slightly high-pitched voice, the Allied commander welcomed his audience to

St. Paul's and outlined the purpose of the meeting. On this day, the plans for the invasion of Europe would be unveiled. Each division, each tank, every soldier, and every movement down to the minute the first ramp would splash down into the surf of the Normandy beaches would be presented for all to review. Said one officer who attended the meeting, "It was a curious experience to see so great and vital a secret written so large and revealed to so large a crowd."[380]

Pacing in front of the enormous maps and walking around the scale model, Montgomery started things off, and he was at his best. Holding his audience spellbound, he outlined the sequence of events that would put more than 150,000 men ashore. At dawn, the infantry combat brigades would hit the beaches. Following them would be combat engineers, including those of the Ninth Air Force, who would start construction of the first airstrip. Montgomery pointed to the phase lines on his maps, which showed his expected advance on D-Day, D+1, D+2, and so on. He made it clear that he intended to take ground quickly and move inland with the utmost speed.[381]

British Air Commander Sir Trafford Leigh-Mallory came next and gave a brief overview of the airplan. Some 14,000 sorties would be flown by bombers, fighters, troop transports, and gliders, with the first missions beginning at D-1 and continuing at maximum effort for more than two weeks after the landings.

Spaatz followed Leigh-Mallory. Although he commanded the most powerful bombing force in the world, Spaatz lacked Montgomery's zest for speaking, and he delivered a wooden review of the Eighth's responsibilities on D-Day. He used a written speech, which he delivered poorly, but the facts were there.

Pete Quesada came up next. The dark-haired air commander explained his new dive-bombing techniques and then detailed how the coordinated fighter groups would block the merest hint of a German warplane. Churchill puffed his cigar as Quesada followed up with one forceful detail after the other. He then answered that fateful question asked by Churchill, saying "There is not going to be a German Air Force there." Then he yielded the floor.[382] But before he walked off he had one request: he had 10,129 bombs on hand, but he could use another 53,000.[383]

By the conclusion of the presentation, the attendees were overwhelmed. D-Day would be the bloodiest day in a war that had gripped their countries in battle for almost four years. Hundreds of thousands of young men were already dead or wounded, and yet here was a plan that would add thousands more to the list. It was impossible to imagine a day of combat more vicious and more certain to kill and maim than this terrible day on which each leader had just placed his personal seal of approval. Said one of the men who attended, "When the briefing was over, there was no conversation, no laughter. No one lingered and we filed out of the cinema as though we were leaving church. Old friends seemed oblivious of each other. Expressions remained solemn."[384]

Spaatz closed out the month of May by hitting the oil refineries one more time. Captain Bernard Nelson, Jr., a navigator from California, remembered it well: "We bombed the Lutzkendorf Oil Refinery in southern Germany on May 28, 1944. We flew almost 10 hours on that mission. This refinery would take coal, grind it into powder, add a small amount of gasoline to it, mix in hydrogen, and use it to power the German army vehicles. It worked. However when we hit the refinery from 25,000 feet in the air the explosion was tremendous. The hydrogen was so volatile that there was a huge fireball that shook our planes 5 miles up in the air. It was amazing."[385]

And thus came to an end an amazing—but deadly—month of combat.

CHAPTER 20

DECEPTION

One of the most brilliant contributions made by the British to the ultimate success of D-Day was a plan to deceive the Germans into believing that the invasion of Europe would begin in the Pas-de-Calais area of western France.

Under a program called Operation Fortitude, U.S. Army General George S. Patton took command of the First United States Army Group and prepared for the invasion of Europe in two landings. In Edinburgh, Scotland, one army massed its strength for the invasion of Norway, while a second army assembled in the south of England for the invasion of France. Expansive tent cities began to spread across the landscape, tanks rolled in, an oil refinery and storage facility were built—and promptly bombed by the Germans—and the daily workings of an army in preparation for an invasion clogged the airways with message traffic.[386]

Of course it was all a ruse. While the Germans believed that Patton's success in North Africa made him the logical choice to lead the invasion of Europe, he would not be the leader of D-Day. Rather, his credibility as the presumptive commander was the cornerstone of an elaborate plan to deceive the Germans into believing that D-Day would take place some 300 miles north of the intended landings in Normandy. The smoke that curled up from the barracks, the airplanes that came and went, the lights of jeeps that inched their way among the barracks were all meant for the eyes of spies and the occasional reconnaissance flight by the Germans. The thousands of men assigned to run these phantom armies down to the ever-so-convincing details such as a shortage of towels broadcast in lightly encrypted radio traffic, the transfer of one group of soldiers from one place to another, also broadcast in lightly encrypted messages, were all designed to lead the Germans to the wrong conclusion. Most importantly, the bombs that landed on Germany were dropped in a pattern of attacks that pointed away from the Normandy beaches.

Operation Fortitude was a finely organized plan of fakes and feints that had been concocted by British intelligence services and approved a year before the appointment of the real D-Day commander, Dwight Eisenhower. "In wartime," said Winston Churchill after briefing Roosevelt on the plan during their meetings in Tehran in December 1943, "truth is so precious that she should be attended by a bodyguard of lies."[387] Fortitude was that bodyguard of lies. Its sole objective was to "persuade the enemy to dispose his forces in areas where they can cause the least interference" to the real invasion.[388]

Operation Fortitude was divided into two plans: Fortitude North, which was designed to telegraph that an invasion would begin in Norway and thus force the Germans to keep soldiers stationed there, and Fortitude South, which telegraphed that the invasion would start in the Pas-de-Calais area. Inside Fortitude South was a subset of secret plans codenamed Quicksilver, which in turn contained another subset of plans governing the Allied air forces called Appendix B.

Appendix B was the lynchpin to it all. With rare exceptions, the Germans were unable to mount reconnaissance flights over England

and thus were unable to see the fake tanks and tents. Fortitude therefore relied on evidence they had access to, such as radio intercepts, but nothing speaks louder in war than bombs and bombing patterns. In this was found the heart of Fortitude. Appendix B contained the written guidelines for an overall scheme that called for each of the flying arms of both the British and American air forces to use their combat airplanes to enhance the charade using their bombs. While the tactical specifics were up to the commanders, the overall concept was to vigorously bomb targets in the fake invasion areas as if a real landing would take place there. Equally, it was imperative that the pattern of the real bombings never pointed to Normandy. It was a feint within a feint.

The airplans prepared by the Ninth and the Eighth Air Forces included a method of bombing that would generally point to an invasion in Pas-de-Calais while also making certain that the tempo of real missions didn't inadvertently point toward Normandy. It was a delicate balance. Directly bombing the landing area of Omaha Beach might help the Germans to correctly deduce that this was where D-Day would begin, but to avoid all of Normandy was a signal in and of its own. The coast of France was thus divided into two areas at Dieppe. North of Dieppe was the decoy area; south of Dieppe was the real area. Two bombing missions were to be flown in the decoy areas for every one in the real area; moreover two of the same types of targets had to be bombed for every one in the real area. For example, if the heavies attacked a coastal battery in the Normandy region, they had to attack two coastal batteries in the deception area. If they bombed one rail yard in Normandy, they had to bomb two rail yards in Pas-de-Calais. Moreover, knowing full well that the Germans were analyzing everything they did, roughly ten missions had to be flown to the northwest of the Seine River for every mission to the southeast.

The British loudly objected to the American application of Fortitude. The RAF was flying as hard and as often as it could with a heavy target load. The loss of more men during missions that neither paved the way to the collapse of Germany nor aided the landing of soldiers seemed crazy. It was a "wildly extravagant method," huffed RAF Air Chief Marshal Harris, but Eisenhower, now Supreme Commander, wouldn't budge. Despite the fact that the build-up in England was obvious to all, counterintelligence indicated that the Germans had no idea when or where the invasion would take place. However extravagant Harris thought it was, the decisions to maintain a 2:1 ratio prevailed.[389]

Blinding the eyes of the German High Command to the first movement of airplanes on D-Day was on the May target list but also within the control of the deception plan. German radar stations along the western coast of Europe stretched from Norway to Spain and represented a serious threat to the invasion forces. They needed to be taken out, but there were so many of them, all ringed by flak batteries and closely defended by German Me-109s. It was possible to narrow down the list to the radar stations between Normandy and Pas-de-Calais, but to do so would also narrow down the focus of the Germans to that stretch of coastline. Instead, the target list was extended down to the Channel Islands on the western side of the Cherbourg Peninsula and up to Oostende, Belgium. Even so, there were forty-two radar processing centers and 106 radar installations to bomb. On May 25, more than 800 heavy bombers, 250 B-26s, and 250 P-47s took off with 400 escorts. They winged their way toward their targets and dropped 500-pounders and 100-pound fragmentation bombs. After the heavies passed through, wave after wave of fighters banked down and dove on the radars. Oddly, they met very little enemy opposition.

On May 27, more than 900 B-17s and B-24s came back for a second time with nearly 700 Marauders, and 1,200 fighters. This time they met deadly opposition. Up and down the English Channel, German flak batteries poured shells skyward and German fighters ripped through the attacking bombers. More than 240 airmen went down on 24 bombers with another 200 airplanes badly damaged. The fighters lost eight of their own with another nine badly battle damaged. Before it was over, the Allies had to mount more than 16,000 sorties to take out 150 installations but some 80 percent of the targeted radars were blinded.[390]

Lest anything inadvertently allow the enemy to pierce the veil, the reconnaissance pilots participated in the deception plan, too. Beginning in mid-May, the Ninth started flying eight missions daily north of the Seine to create a pattern of photo-reconnaissance operations in an area of no interest whatsoever to the Allies except insofar that it might serve to confuse the German analysts and further point them to Pas-de-Calais. The pilots were flying visual reconnaissance and rarely taking pictures, but they were also sitting ducks on missions that were almost entirely useless except for the deception. Partly because they were flying in weather that grounded other fighters, including the Germans, they suffered few losses.[391]

Training flights played to the watching German eyes, too. Newly arrived fighter pilots were routinely sent up for familiarization flights that sometimes included shallow penetrations of Occupied Europe. To be convincing, these flights had to lead to and from Pas-de-Calais as often as they did toward Normandy. To make the deception complete, the High-Speed Air Sea Rescue Services faked training sea rescues under these bogus routes.[392]

The Fifteenth Air Force had their part, too, and it was a plan within a plan. The idea of shuttle bombing between the airbases in Italy and airfields in Russia had been bandied about for months, but it wasn't until D-Day neared that the Soviets opened an airbase for a trial. The first raid was launched on June 2 with some 130 B-17s. The bombers took off from Italy, struck their targets in Germany, and landed in Russia. The mission sent its own signals to the Germans, but that it coincided with D-Day served mainly to distract them from the what-ifs of D-Day to the what-ifs of this new tactic.[393]

41

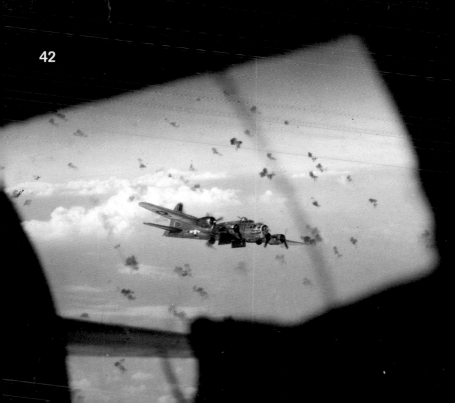

42

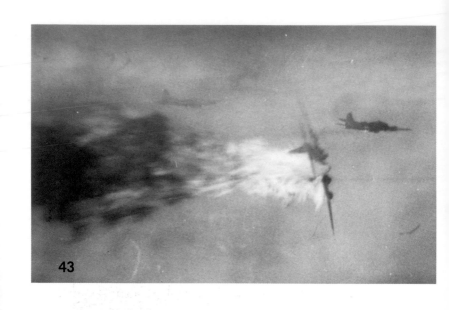

43

44

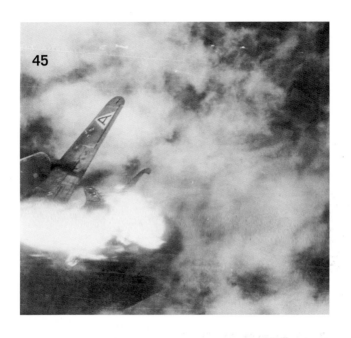

47

48

49

50

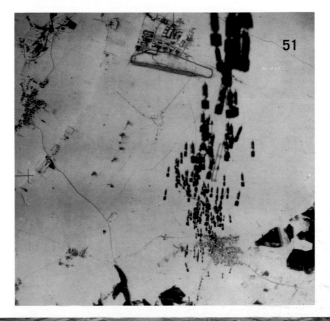

53

54

55

56

58

59

60

61

62

FORCE - GAINST TARGET: 1ST WAVE 388A, #2-388B, #3-452A, #4-452B, #5-96
#6-96B (2 50, LD. & LO.) #7-96B (HI, 30) #8 -380 -452 & 388 (2 MIN
BETWEEN WAVES)...ESPECIALLY ACTIVATE...ALL TYPES OF RAF AND USAAF A/C
IN TARGET AREA. 9TH AF MEDIUMS, AND 1ST DIVISIONS. FIGHTER BOMBERS
1ST DIV, ON TGTS BETWEEN 0-40 & 0, 2ND DIV. HITS TGTS BETWEEN 0-30 & Q-2
BOTH DIVISIONS WILL CONTINUE TO 4900. TURN RIGHT AND RETURN AT PORTLAND
BILL... TAKE-OFF: A-0210 B-0225 RUNWAY DIREC: NE-SW SURFACE WIND:
5807 WESTERLY....TURN RIGHT TO 310 DEG. CLIMB TO 6,000 TURN LEFT
GROUP ASSEMBLY: PLACE BUN. #19 (MENDLESHAM) 96TH A - LEAD-12,000
HIGH-11,500: LOW-11,000 96B - LEAD-7,500: HIGH-7,000: LOW-6,500 5AXX
ASSEMBLY ROUTE: BASE TO BUN. 19 (0412) TO BUN. #21 (5237-0044C) (0403)
TO HORSHAM ST. FAITH (0410) TO SPL. #4 (0459) TO BARTRY (0419) TO
HARROW GATE (0531) TO BEVERLY (5543) TO SPL.#4 (0553) TO SRAFFOM (0507
T) TO DARTFORD (0633) TO COAST .0634.......AT BUN IN 150 M.P.H. I.A.S.
AND 300 FEET PER MIN... ZERO HOUR: 0725   KEITHREF   ROUTE OUT: COAST
(0416) TO TARGET (0715)......BOMBING ALTITUDE: WAVE #5 & #7-15,000
WAVE #4 - 14,000   BOMB LOAD: 452 X 4 5,000 - LD. LO OF 96A, 96B
96B -- 38 X 100 & HI OF 96A SALVO......TURN FROM TARGET: RIGHT
SECONDARY TARGETS: GLEN   LAST RESORT: #1 & #2 - 2ND
COMMON...ROUTE OUT: TARGET TO PORTLAND BILL TO 4
CONTINUE TO 48001, TURN RIGHT AND WITHDRAW SOUTH
AND GUERNSEY ISLANDS THEN TO PORTLAND BILL.... TARGE
29,52 RIGHT AFTER T.O.... LAST POSSIBLE TIME OF TAK
FIGHTERS: SUPPORTS, 24 SQDS P-51 AND 8 SQDNS P-47:
CALLSIGN: BALANCE (NO NUMBER)... MISC: 2300 GALS
BOMBING ALT. WAVE #5,#5,000, #6 14,000, #7 15000, T
SQUADRONS - 2 MIN, IF VISUAL ASSEMBLY SHIP T.O
LEFT UNDER 4,000 HEAD OUT FOR BUN #19 (MENDELSHAM)
THERE, IF OVERCAST, USE OVERCAST PROCEDURE, COME OVE
ALT. HEAD OUT FOR BUN #19, ASSEMBLE THERE: STAY BES
FIELD: ASS. ALT. OVER BUN #19 = 96% LEAD -12,000: 96B
11,000: 96B LEAD-7,500: 96B HI-7,000: 96B LOW-6,500:
SHORT BOMBS ARE LIKELY TO FALL ON LANDING CRAFT OR F
BOMBING MUST BE DONE WITHIN TIME LIMIT: LATEST TIMES
ARE THE ABSOLUTE TIMES WHEN BOMBING MUST CEASE ON TH
ATION ARRIVING LATER WILL BOMB SECONDARY OR LAST RE
MADE ON ANY TARGET... IFF WILL NOT BE USED AFTER DE
COAST EXCEPT BY A/C IN DISTRESS....SIGNAL A RED FLA
IGNATION OF RCB... A/C STRAGGLERS NOT CONSIDERED
ABORTING A/C WILL TURN RIGHT FROM BOMBER CHANNEL AND
IN AT PORTLAND BILL.... GUNS WILL BE MANNED BUT NOT
SHIP UNABLE TO LOCATE FORMATION WILL JOIN ANY FORMAT
MAKE FLIGHT PLAN AS INDICATED.

63

HEADQUARTERS   6-A-2
45TH COMBAT BOMBARDMENT WING
APO 559   5 June 1944

NIGHT ASSEMBLY PLAN FOR SPECIAL MISSION

This Wing will put up twenty 6-ship squadrons. This will include Pathfinders

18-ship groups will be formed if possible. Otherwise 6-ship squadrons will
proceed to target and attack by squadrons.

As many IFF aircraft as are available will lead groups. Squadron leaders
and deputy leaders will be best crews available.

Weather at base or target will not stop mission. Take-off will be accomplished regardless.

Each group will have a leader and deputy leader. Third squadron will be
led by an experienced flight commander.

Maximum number of bombs will be carried.

45th Wing will start take-offs one hour and fifteen minutes prior to time
4th and 13th Wings start take-offs. Same as 3rd Wings and 2nd Division will be
taking off and assembling at same time as 45th.

388th Group will assemble over Genance 10.
96th   "   "   "   "   "   9.
452nd   "   "   "   "   "   11.

(INCOMPLETE) ...will be supplied.

Groups will assemble over their own Bunchers. Then squadrons of 96th and 452nd Groups will proceed to
Bunchers 19 and 11 for group assembly.

Groups will depart bunchers enroute to Horsham St. Faith 1½0 minutes after
first airplanes of "A" Groups take-off in order to clear area for 4th and 13th
Wing assemblies.

Waves will follow each other at two minute intervals in following order:
Wave "A", 388th "A", 452nd "A", 452nd "B", 96th "A". 96th "B" 11th Squadron
with "B" lead and low squadron and 8th wave consisting of one squadron each from
452nd and 388th Groups.

Individual airplanes will join any squadron or group if unable to find own
squadron or group.

                                   -213-

64

65

ROBERT L ALBINE S SGT
MICHAEL J BALCA S SGT
ELMER J BETHKE S SGT
JOHN L CROCKER JR S SGT
DONALD R DECKER 1st LT
FREDERICK B GATENS 2d LT
ROY G JORGENSEN 2d LT
JAMES M LIDDELL 2d LT
AIR CORPS
FEBRUARY 20 1944

66

Like the shuttle bombing, some real plans were modified to enhance the deception. The D-Day plans called for many of the American fighter aircraft to move forward to temporary staging bases where they'd be refueled before taking off for the invasion, but this needed to be practiced. On May 29, a mission was flown to simulate this preraid staging, but the fighters simulated the bombing of the northern perimeter of Pas-de-Calais. More than 1,100 fighters took off on missions that day with some six hundred of them moving to the staging areas where they refueled and flew to Pas-de-Calais. It was exactly what they would do on D-Day if the landings were in Pas-de-Calais, but it was a practice mission cloaked in yet another bodyguard of lies. Two P-47s were shot down.[344]

The second part of the deception was to begin on June 1, 1944, with the launch of Operation Cover. Operation Cover was designed to condition the Germans into falsely believing that the attack by the thousands of bombers and fighters that would take off on D-Day was nothing more than just another maximum-effort mission. To pull off that misdirection, a full-scale attack had to be flown just days before D-Day that would mirror D-Day in most parts but amount to nothing so that when the real thing arrived the Germans might see it as just another fake. The second part of Cover was to reinforce the idea that the landings would take place in Pas-de-Calais, and that would be accomplished by bombing that area with the intensity a German military commander would expect if it were being softened up for the invasion. The key part of this was that it omitted the 2:1 ratio.

After these events, all of the June missions leading up to D-Day were designed to reinforce the idea that Pas-de-Calais was the invasion area by sending 60 percent of the bombers against targets in that area while the other 40 percent hit targets in Germany. On D-2, half of the American forces would rest while the other half would narrow their focus to raids on Normandy and Pas-de-Calais. If at any point the Germans saw through the deception and gave off a signal strong enough to convince Eisenhower that his cover had been blown, the plans would be thrown out the window and the heavies would immediately begin to bomb Normandy with everything they had. Interestingly, the Normandy fortifications would not be hit until the morning of D-Day.[395]

If there was genius in Spaatz's in-the-air-and-on-the-ground approach to attacking the Luftwaffe, if there was genius to Quesada's dive-bombing missions, then there was equal brilliance to Eisenhower's insistence on deception. The bombing of the Pas-de-Calais area that so often frustrated the British by favoring any target 2:1 over Normandy had confused the Germans to the point of paralysis.

As May became June, Eisenhower was even more alert to deception. Said Eisenhower of the extra strain this put on the already stretched resources of the Eighth and Ninth, "I cannot overemphasize the importance of maintaining as long as humanly possible the Allied threat to the Pas-de-Calais area."[396]

And so they did, even on D-Day.

CHAPTER 21

JUNE 1944

On June 2, Spaatz activated the Cover Plan and put more than a thousand bombers in the air in all-out raids of bombers and fighters as if it were the day of the invasion itself. They attacked more than a German dozen airfields, rail yards, and, in heavily concentrated raids, the coastal batteries along Pas-de-Calais, but not a single landing craft hit the beaches—despite appearances that an invasion was on. The Germans, who were as on edge as the Allies, had jumped into action but within a few hours felt foolish.

On June 3, two groups of more than five hundred American bombers hit the antiaircraft batteries directly overlooking the beaches in the Pas-de-Calais area. A total of twenty-one targets were bombed, including the heavily reinforced four-gun battery at Berck-sur-Mer, which was reduced to a rock pile by a near-perfect concentration of 500-pounders.

On June 4, more than 450 bombers launched a similar raid.[397] The Cover Plan was right on schedule.

Although the deception remained in place, it was impossible to hide the build-up and its attendant activities. The sense of moment was heightened by the arrival of war correspondents and newspaper photographers. While they didn't know what day it would happen, they all knew D-Day was coming soon, and they wanted to be on the airbases when it did. The well-known journalist Ernie Pyle arrived at one base, newspaper mogul William Randolph Hearst at another. One writer noted a "great upswing in morale" as D-Day seemed to near. "The base hummed with activity as all personnel were in the throes of hurried planning and preparation for the big day."[398]

The plan, though, was to keep things as normal as possible, which created some odd timing. One group of pilots flew a heavy schedule of missions through June 3, but then went on leave on June 4, missing the real invasion all together. On June 5, hundreds more left on their scheduled leaves. After a long night at the local pub, one airman would later remember that he slept through D-Day entirely.

Replacement pilots arrived on June 2 and 3. Orientation flights introduced them to the countryside, with landmarks pointed out as if they were an auto club tour. One air group received an entirely new commanding officer. He arrived on June 5 to take over. Two airbases had training sessions on the rainy days between June 1 and June 4. Uniforms were pressed, men arrived, men were sent home. Such was the ordinary ebb and flow of life so crucial to secrecy. Such were the smallest of details that protected the truth with a bodyguard of lies.[399] Nothing seemed out of the ordinary, not to German spies, and not even to the men who would be carrying out the invasion.

Preparations for D-Day required the start of a new mission that carried with it some risk of revealing the invasion sites. Almost any land route from Germany to the Normandy beaches had to cross either the Seine River to the north or the Loire River to the south, but because the bridges over the Seine carried roads that went to Pas-de-Calais just as surely as they went to Normandy, cutting those bridges hadn't given away a thing. Not so with the Loire. The only reasonable explanation for bridge cuts across the Loire would be a landing in the Normandy area, and for that reason they'd been left alone. No longer. On June 2, a pair of P-38s lifted off to photograph the targets for the operations officers who would prepare the plans to drop the bridges into the river.

Two reconnaissance pilots by the names of Chick Batson and Hubert Childress were given the risky flights. They took off and raced across the English Channel. They crossed inland into France and then flew over trees, rooftops, and even a few pleasure boaters as they winged their way up a tributary leading to the Loire River. They neared the first bridge and immediately came under fire. "Shells burst around them and tracers followed their every move," wrote a unit historian. "The two pilots felt they disturbed a hornets' nest at every bridge." They bobbed and weaved up the river, whisking through towns with their wingtips just feet from buildings. They needed to photograph four bridges at Tours, but there their luck ran out. "Back and forth the planes roared at rooftop levels scattering civilians and stirring up the angry gunners of the flak batteries. Tracers were everywhere." One had their name on it. Jinking as best as he could, Childress felt a thunk against the fuselage of his P-38, and one of his engines began to stream smoke. His day was over. The second pilot kept the needle on his airspeed indicator pegged to the right and covered the last of the bridges alone. Together they photographed twenty-six bridges, all of which were promptly fed into the Plans Division for attack.[400]

No doubt the Allied commanders were going over everything twice, and Tooey Spaatz was no exception. But Spaatz couldn't shake the feeling that something wasn't quite right. A May 30 decryption of an Ultra intercept spoke of only ten fighter groups of about four hundred single-engine aircraft remaining in Germany. By all counts, there should have been more than 1,100 fighters based in Germany. So where were the rest?

Most of the airfields inside the 130-mile arc were empty, or nearly so, but Spaatz worried they had gotten something wrong. He sent the reconnaissance crews back in for another look and scheduled raids on the eight fields that troubled him most. But even then, he still worried.[401]

The Luftwaffe continued to deal with their pilot attrition by using increasingly inexperienced replacements. Where before new German pilots had arrived with months of training and extensive flight experience, by June they were arriving at the forward bases with scarcely enough experience to take off. In truth, a good day for training was also a good day for the bombers, so training was given short shrift against air defense.

The problems this created were obvious and troubling. A group of Me-109s was scrambled to intercept an incoming flight of American bombers, but the replacement pilots could scarcely get airborne. One Messerschmitt pilot took off from his side of the field but was so disoriented by the cacophony of a squadron scramble that he died before he got to meet the bombers. Observed another pilot, "He passed too close to one of the other Me-109s and ran into the propeller wash as the formation was climbing at low speed. The fighter rolled onto its back and spun into the ground. It smashed into a house beside the airfield; the pilot and four people living there were killed."[402]

Allied crew chiefs learned how to paint their airplanes. Orders came down from London to paint all Allied fighters around the wings and the aft section of the fuselages with distinctive stripes of alternating black and white. With the expected counterattack by the Luftwaffe, these "invasion stripes" would help gunners on the ground distinguish between friend and foe. Straight lines were not a requirement. In fact, some enterprising maintainers found buckets and brooms and painted seventeen planes in one day, however wobbly their lines were.

As would be expected, the pilots in the ready room were curious about the strange stripes going on their planes. Pilot Howard Hightower was there when he noticed the new livery going on his aircraft: "I believe June 4th was a Sunday. About mid-morning someone came into our ready room and said the flight crews were painting white and black stripes all over our planes. Well, we all went out, got on bicycles and rode over to where the planes were parked. I found my crew chief and asked him what was up. He said, 'Beats the hell out of me, Lieutenant! They said to paint them like this and that's what we're doing.'"[403]

On the morning of June 5 in the Paris office of Luftwaffe meteorologist Colonel Walter Stobe, aides hurriedly finished the 5 a.m. weather report, which would be disseminated to all German forces in the West. The forecast was more or less the same as it had been the day before: rainy and overcast with occasional thunderstorms and winds gusting to 20 to 30 miles per hour.

Field Marshal Erwin Rommel's aide, Captain Helmuth Lang, delivered the reports to Rommel just before 0600 hours. Through the glass of the double French doors leading outside, Lang could see twigs and branches strewn across the rose garden, casualties of the storm that had blown through the night before. Lang was able to report that American heavies had bombed the Pas-de-Calais area again, but none of the Forts was down in the Normandy region.[404]

It was a miserable day. Rain drizzled everywhere.

The bases in England were unusually quiet on June 5. "The weather was so bad we played poker throughout the morning and into the afternoon," said Hightower.[405] Despite the gloomy weather, a sense of anticipation filled the air. The invasion stripes, the talk in the barracks, everything seemed to point to something big: "Invasionitis spread like a flood," said one pilot.[406] But storms rumbled through the sky, ruling out this day as the big day.

The rain didn't stop the ground crews who had bombs to load and belts of ammunition to lace into the wings of the fighters. Throughout the day, bomb racks, fuel trucks, jeeps, and maintenance men moved about the hardstands and prepared planes. Hunching a shoulder against the driving rain, the ground crews could only wonder. Wrote a historian for one of the bomb groups, the implications seemed obvious, but no one was sure. "We in the 68th Squadron were to have 18 ships ready, and the other squadrons were to have a like number available. This would indicate that 70–75 of the 90–95 ships were scheduled. Ordinance started to work early on the bomb loading, armament on the guns, and mechanics on the ships—everyone else on everything else. Later in the barracks there was considerable speculation regarding tomorrow. Could it be the big day? Pro and con, each had an opinion."[407]

As the gassing of fuel tanks and loading of bombs continued, a group of P-47 pilots were returning home after a late-afternoon attack on Killem, France, just a handful of miles inland from Pas-de-Calais. As they cruised over the English Channel, they each lowered a wing and craned their necks to have a better view of what was happening below. Through the misty rain they could see that hundreds upon hundreds of ships were at that moment steaming into the English Channel in a convoy of such enormous size that it seemed to cover the water with ships of all sizes, but mainly with troop transports and destroyers. Not a word was murmured, but they knew exactly what they were seeing. "As soon as we landed, our crew chiefs told us that

D-Day was on and we were to go to our bunks and then go to the mess hall and get a sandwich and be at a briefing at midnight."[408]

A number of important rail yards were situated near the Normandy beaches, but they were surrounded by small French villages. They needed to be bombed, but doing so would result in a tremendous loss of civilian lives. It was not a decision Spaatz felt he could make on his own, and so the matter was taken up with President Roosevelt.

When asked whether to bomb the rail yards, FDR was firm in his resolve that nothing would stand in the way of the ultimate success of the invasion: "However regrettable the attendant loss of civilian lives is, I am not prepared to impose from this distance any restrictions on military action by responsible commanders that in their opinion would mitigate against the success of Overlord or cause additional loss of life to our Allied invasion forces."[409] The yards were attacked that day.

While Spaatz and Roosevelt were contemplating the loss of civilian lives, D-Day commanders were keeping an eye on the weather. British Group Captain James Martin Stagg knew precisely what weather the Allied commanders wanted on D-Day, but he wasn't sure what magic could conjure up such perfection— especially considering the dreary weather of late. The Navy wanted a mild onshore breeze, but not more than 10 or 12 miles per hour. The Air Force wanted clear skies, but if not that then no more than 60 percent cloud cover. For his part, Eisenhower wanted a moonless night with a tide at the extreme low end of the tide tables. It was no good. Said Skagg, "When I came to put them together I found that they might have to sit around for 120 or 150 years before they got the operation launched."[410]

After months of intense air operations, D-Day would have to be flown in the rain.

The beginning of D-Day was ever so abrupt, and it happened without any notice whatsoever. A soldier at an American airbase near the British village of Leiston was about to pass through the gate for two days of leave, but just as he walked up, the gates were locked. Melvin Applebaum witnessed the event. It was June 5. "It was around 11 bells in the morning and the M.P. on guard at the gate leading into Leiston began to move about restlessly," he wrote. "A G.I. rode up to the gate on a bicycle, well showered and wearing O.D.s with a musette bag slung over one shoulder. He grinned at the M.P. in friendly fashion, producing his pass. A shake-up date with the loveliest wench in London, he confided and winked significantly. The M.P. nodded knowingly and warned, 'Well, you have to work fast on 24 hours.' Just then the field phone rang and the M.P. picked it up … 'Nobody leaves this base!' he said. The G.I. started to protest then changed his mind and rode back towards his area, looking forlorn."[411]

At 1300 hours, the loudspeakers came to life and broadcast a notice for all to hear. The base was now on lock-down, said the announcer. The bases were officially closed until further notice. Local British workers from nearby villages could go to the base exchange to buy soap and cigarettes and other overnight necessities. Extra cots quickly appeared.[412]

Across the Channel, there was no way of knowing that the American bases had been locked down. Quite to the contrary. It was war, but nothing special had happened.

The game of wits involving deception had not been one sided. The Luftwaffe was employing a deception plan of its own, an elaborate shell game that not even its squadron commanders fully understood. By moving its fighter groups around its many airbases in no particular pattern, it was almost impossible for the Allies to determine which German airfield was occupied and which was not. This was more than the ordinary dispersal plans for daily combat readiness. Over the course of the past several months, German fighter groups had moved from field to field with a regularity that to the average pilot seemed tiring and excessive. But it was all part of a plan.

The German High Command was well aware of the near-daily American reconnaissance flights. They knew their own activities were being observed and that information about the locations and strength of their deployed fighters was being used for target planning by the British and American intelligence services. By moving their squadrons around, an airbase would look empty one day and occupied the next, or not, depending on the frequency of the recon flights.

A German pilot was shot down after D-Day and taken prisoner. As he was being questioned by British intelligence officers, it dawned on him that his interrogators had no idea of which fighter groups were based where. It was only then that he realized that the near-constant shuffling of airbases ordered by the High Command, the shuffling that at times was so annoying to the pilots, was actually a ploy. "This last snippet [of information] gave me a great deal of satisfaction," he wrote, speaking of the mistaken information the British had. "Our recent moves from one landing ground to another suddenly made sense."[413]

It did not make sense to Pips Priller. German Colonel Josef "Pips" Priller was one of the Luftwaffe's most decorated fighter pilots and a seasoned ace. On June 5, he commanded a group of 124 FW-190s and Me-109s based at the expansive German Luftwaffe complex in Lille, France, just 50 miles from Dunkirk, 110 miles from Dieppe, and 150 miles from Le Havre, all potential landing areas. The morning's weather report called for several days of rain, which by simple observation seemed to be correct: storms had rolled in over the airbase, and the coastal beaches of Normandy were soaked.[414]

Priller's unit was one of the most experienced, battle-hardened fighter groups of any of the frontline German air forces. In the event of an invasion, they were to be the leading edge of the Luftwaffe response. Under his command he had two groups of Focke-Wulfs and one squadron of Me-109s. His planes were in fine working order, they had ammunition, they were properly staffed with ground crews, and he had excellent pilots. As a fighting force, they could bring enormous firepower to bear against any invasion, and, considering the resolve of their leader, Priller, they had that intangible "X" factor in their favor as well: they were motivated German fighter pilots ready to do whatever it took to stop the landings.

Although history has scarcely noted it for what it was, in what can now be seen as a stroke of incredibly good fortune for Eisenhower, the German High Command decided to shuffle its forward fighters again, on June 5, a process that usually took about two days to complete. While there is no evidence the Allies knew about this reshuffling, and the plans to invade were certainly already in motion, what would happen next would be of incalculable value on D-Day. Priller was ordered to move his force of 124 combat-ready fighters to three German airbases that were well inland from the invasion beaches—in most cases an hour's flying time away from Normandy. The pilots would leave immediately and would be followed by Priller's ground crews, which would be moved by truck. The shuffling would begin on June 5 and wouldn't be completed until June 7.[415]

Unaware of any master plan, Priller was irate. The feeling that an invasion was imminent was as prevalent on the German airbases as it was on the American bases. To move fighters away from the coastal areas seemed counterintuitive. Priller wanted to get into battle. He was poised to meet the soldiers on the beaches. He wanted to fight. "If we're expecting an invasion," Priller said sharply to his group commander who was on the other end of the phone, "the squadrons should be moved up, not back."[416] The weather, his commander patiently argued, was far too bad to be concerned about any imminent invasion; Priller would have plenty of time to regroup his forces.

A dejected Priller gave the orders, and for the next several hours more than a hundred German fighters were fueled and armed and took off to bases away from the coast line, inland to the German airbases at Metz, Mont-de Marsan-Biarritz, and Nancy, France.[417] In light of the disastrous bombing that would take place the next morning, it was a blunder of the first order. But no one yet knew that much. As the last airplane disappeared into the cloudy skies, the dejected commander walked out to the now-abandoned airfield. Two airplanes were left, his and that of his wingman. "If the invasion comes," Priller said to his wingman, "they'll probably expect us to hold it off all by ourselves. So we might as well get drunk now."[418]

Which they did.

CHAPTER 22

D-DAY

Rain dripped from the nacelles of the powerful Wright Cyclones as the last light drained from the sky. Bomb carts and jeeps seemed to be everywhere as lights winked off in the darkness. A quiet hung over the airbases that belied the violence that was about to unfold.

The air battle that would begin in a matter of hours was about to pit men not yet twenty-five years old against a German air force that was one of the most experienced combat forces in the world. Some 20,000 American pilots, copilots, radio operators, bombardiers, navigators, and gunners who had been trained and brought to England for this moment would be launched into battle. "The electricity was so thick you could hear it, smell it, feel it," remembered one sergeant. "We felt like we were sitting on a live bomb with the fuse sizzling."[419]

In fact, preinvasion nerves were rattling on both sides of the Atlantic Ocean. General George C. Marshall's residence was located inside the Ft. Myer Army base located in the Washington, D.C., suburb of Arlington, Virginia. Marshall's residence was called Quarters One, a handsome three-story house with a broad-breasted lawn lined with shrubs and flowers that sprouted in the summer and painted the garden with spectacular colors. When the weather was right, Marshall and his wife Katherine would lunch at a handsome round table set in the back of the garden against an apple tree that had four trunks. Quarters One was the official residence of the chief of the staff of the United States Army. Near his house was the residence of his close friend Hap Arnold. On D-Day eve, both men were in Washington. Both men no doubt went over the events of the past six months in their minds. The bombing missions against the German fighter factories. The strikes against the rail yards and the bridges and the roadways. The attacks against the Luftwaffe airfields. The risky reconnaissance flights down the beaches, the ground pounding behind German lines, the dog fights, and the deception plans. Thousands of men flying combat to prepare for this day. More than two hundred aerial combat missions, with some 160,000 aircraft sorties, all since the first of the year and still counting. Some 156,000 tons of bombs dropped on Germany. Had it been enough? Had it worked? There were no shortcuts to the answer. Just D-Day.

On the night of June 5, Marshall received the telex he knew would inevitably arrive. Although he was both relieved and resigned to whatever might happen, the beginning of D-Day marked the beginning of the unknown, the beginning of what would be for him several agonizing hours of silence during which so many lives—and the future of the war—would most certainly be determined. "Halcyon plus 5 finally and definitely confirmed," said Eisenhower's coded message to Marshall. So many questions would soon be answered. The invasion was on.[420]

Across the pond in London, also on the night of June 5, Spaatz had dinner with Eisenhower and then went to visit the headquarters of Deputy Air Commander General Hoyt S. Vandenberg, a close friend. He stayed with Vandenberg until four in the morning and then returned to his own headquarters in Park House.

Somewhere out in the dark, 6,939 ships packed with 175,000 soldiers were sailing across the English Channel, swells and waves pitching the smaller ships up and down as rain swept their decks. A broken cloud deck skimmed the Normandy region at 2,000 feet with a second deck, which was nearly solid, at 12,000 feet.[421] Although the conditions were no worse than forecast, the skies were thick with tricky weather and embedded thunderheads that would certainly pose problems.

England was blanketed by unsettled weather with scud running across the airfields in layers that made for an exceptionally dark night punctuated by sudden bursts of rain that in some places was heavy. Shafts of lightning splintered the clouds over the Channel, but for the most part, the type of turbulent weather that would ground the planes held off. It was rough weather, but not severe. The pilots would be on instruments most of the day, but there were enough breaks in the clouds to hold out hope for successful bombings. Thus they had their first answer: they could fly.

At 0100 hours on June 6, the Allied bases in East Anglia came alive. Lights flickered on, men rubbed sleep from their eyes; their sleep had seemed far too short. "We went to bed and lights were finally put out at after 11 o'clock," wrote a Nebraska airman who was a ground crewman in a P-38 squadron in a letter to his parents. "At 1:20 we were roused rudely by the CQ's whistle—and finally dragged out of bed, got onto our bikes in the darkness and rode in the rain."[422]

One by one, the airmen dressed, hunched a shoulder against the sloppy night, and made their way to the briefing huts where they took their seats. Before them was the familiar 20-foot-wide map of Europe that previously had revealed missions to Berlin, Merseburg, Schweinfurt, Regensburg, Tutow, Münster, Hamm, Brunswick, and Rostock, and countless missions to the Pas-de-Calais area, as well as numerous others. Today it would have a new narrative to tell, a new mission to fly. "The blackout curtains were still tightly drawn and the air was thick with cigarette smoke," remembered one airman. "This must be the pay-off."[423] No doubt they grumbled, smashed down cigarettes, lit another, and talked about D-Day, but no one yet knew for sure the extent of the operation. "I knew the invasion of Europe was about to happen and I wanted to be a part of it," remembered Captain Bill Reeder, a B-17 pilot from Nashville, Tennessee. So, too, did the rest of his squadron.[424]

Across the Channel, an early-morning quiet blanketed the town of Nancy, a small French village some 200 miles inland from Omaha Beach. The sky was overcast with ragged clouds at 1,500 feet. A light rain had darkened the streets, but otherwise it was an unremarkable morning. Bedded down in the local guesthouses were the pilots of Luftwaffe JG2, among them Wolfgang Fischer. Fischer had landed the night before with a group of a dozen fighters. They pushed their planes under a bank of tress that edged a plateau above the airfield east of the river and then went into town for the night. As dawn broke on June 6, 1944, the town square was suffused with the pleasant smell of freshly baked breads as the proprietor of the local bakery pulled trays of baguettes out of his ovens.

The German airfield at Villacoublay lay within walking distance of Louis XIV's palace in the village of Versailles, a dozen miles southwest of Paris down Avenue de Paris. The airbase was home to German Me-109s as well as a flight school and several advanced aeronautical manufacturers essential to the operations of the Luftwaffe. A national highway ran neatly down the center of the field, so Villacoublay was actually two airfields: Villacoublay-Nord (north) and Villacoublay-Sud (south), the larger being Sud. Lining the fields were impressive hangars, each crowned by large, cantilevered poles out of which radiated suspension cables that held up the roofs.[425]

Villacoublay was about the size of a modern commercial airport. It had hardened runways, plenty of ramp space for the Messerschmitts, and fields large enough for squadron take-offs. The town around the airbase was an attractive French village with three-story apartment buildings crowned with burnt orange roofs and generous balconies, some facing the airfield. On a warm day, neighbors could talk to each other across their balconies, their conversations occasionally interrupted by the thunder of engines as a German Messerschmitt or Focke-Wulf swept overhead.

Spaatz believed it and could feel it, but he could scarcely risk the life of a single soldier on it. The Luftwaffe was subdued; he truly believed that. Their airfields were in pitiful shape, their factories were in rubble, the railroads that would bring new parts forward to the underground factories were in a constant state of repair. Moreover, he was certain the deception plan had worked as well as anything could. He truly believed he had the Luftwaffe right where he wanted them and that his forces would prevail. But he nevertheless prepared his airmen for the biggest air battle they would face. However weakened by the attacks on the radar installations along the coast, German radar would certainly see the bombers and the fighters. Just as soon as they had a fix on a target area, they'd start alerting their own fighters and the battle would be on. Spaatz's heavies would have to fight their way to their beaches and then face the coastal flak, so he knew he would incur losses in the morning. The fighter screens would be hit by the Luftwaffe along the perimeter, and those air battles would cost him more men. The German planes that had evaded detection inside the 130-mile no-fly zone would launch, and around those fighters more skirmishes would take place, ending favorably, he hoped, for his own men.

That was his scenario. That was how Spaatz played it out in his head. But war is unpredictable, and the Germans no doubt had plans to counter every one of his own.

And so it began.

Over the farms of rural England, the quiet of the night was interrupted by a deep-throated sound that grew in strength until it reached a peak that instead of falling off like the bomber formations of the past remained strong and unwavering. Awakened by the noise, the townspeople went outside to see what was going on. From horizon to horizon, 1,600 Douglas transports crowded the sky, each blinking their red and green navigation lights as they passed overhead. One of General Pete Quesada's staff members was hurrying down a road when they flew over. He stopped and got out of his car to look. It was a "carnival, a mélange of colored lights, a giant, brilliant Christmas tree," he said.[426] The first wave of airborne troops was heading toward France.

An airman on a base who saw the spectacle remembered a sky simply filled with planes pulling their gliders: "We heard the aircraft overhead, the Dakotas hauling the airborne. We all stood outside and looked up against the semi-dark sky. There were so many of them it just boggled the mind."[427]

At the Allied command center in Uxbridge, England, rapt eyes swept the flickering lines on the radar scopes. Ready hands were poised over the radio and telephone sets that would instantly connect command center to command center, and, ultimately, to the front. A team of British women silently moved symbols across the face of a map as reports came in from the airbases. The battle commanders watched and waited, cigarettes and cigars in hand, the air thick with a mix of nervous energy and plumes of pale blue smoke.[428]

Eisenhower, Spaatz, and Arnold were expecting the worst. "At the very best," Eisenhower wrote in a memo, "we are going to have here lively air opposition." Arnold had said as much to Spaatz six weeks earlier. He expected a "great air battle" during the first three or four days. British intelligence agreed and even put some numbers to that: 1,250 German sorties would be mounted against the invasion during the next twenty-four hours, and some 1,600 German fighters would be in the battle within four days.[429]

While the airbases in England were still completely dark, light poured across the ramps each time the doors to the briefing huts were opened. Inside, the rooms were packed with men anxious to see the details of the day's mission. "I don't believe I got more than five hours of sleep a night for the three-and-a-half months leading up to D-Day," said one airman. But the day would be worth it, of that he was sure.[430]

The curtains covering the large map in the briefing room were finally pulled back to reveal a line that ended on Omaha Beach. The room exploded in cheers. Pilots slapped each other on the backs as excitement charged the air. "This was it!" said John Hibbard, a radio operator on a B-17. "Everyone was bursting with excitement and pride because we were all to be there to help those doughboys assault the enemy beaches."[431] Todd Webb of the 68th Bomb Squadron knew this meant that the days fighting alone in the skies were over. Soldiers would now be on the ground, in Europe, fighting the Nazis. "This day brought the news the whole world has so long awaited. At long last the invasion was under way," he wrote. To a man, they all wanted to get into the action and bomb the Germans. "Everyone was anxious to make a flight on one of the missions being flown this day, in order to see firsthand the biggest armed event in the history of man."[432]

"As pilot of the lead crew for the next mission, I was called for a special 'pre-briefing' at 9:30PM the night of June 5, 1944," recalled Harry Paynter, a B-24 pilot. "The group CO told us that the next day would be the one everyone had been waiting for—D-Day." Paynter was briefed on his target, hack time, and other mission details, but it was all a blur. "You can imagine the flush of excitement that rushed over me. For a minute I couldn't hear what was being said. I don't even recall what we were told that night except that we were told not to tell anyone else the news until the regular briefing was held the following morning."[433]

The mission details unfolded in stages, and even though the bases were locked down, security remained tight. "[We] received our final briefing at 0130 hours," said John W. Howland, a lead navigator on a B-17. "Only pilots, navigators, and bombardiers were allowed in the briefing room. All personnel were pledged to secrecy until the planes were in the air and the mission was underway. Only then could the location of the target be released to the crew."[434]

Robert Schaffer was a bombardier. He remembered the attention his group received before they departed on their mission. "Never will forget when they told us we were to be the first to bomb ahead of the troops just before they landed. They read us all kinds of messages from all the Air Corps generals. We were up all night getting minutely prepared. Took off two in the morning. Flak was light. Mission was very successful. There was a full moon. I have never seen as many boats of all descriptions as there were crossing the Channel. Quite a sight. Quite a show."[435]

The fighter pilots were up, too, and being briefed on their mission. "On June 5, 1944, at midnight, our pilots were briefed as to the nature of the invasion that was to begin in a few hours. This was what we had been waiting for, the moment had arrived," remembered a P-47 pilot. "All was silent, but each man was tense as he listened to what our part would be. As the plan unfolded we were told our upcoming support of the Allied armies, the escort of paratroopers, and patrolling the beachhead areas; we knew we were in for long hours and sleepless nights. But who cared about all that as long as we could give Jerry his just due, everything was all right."[436]

In fact, the airmen were about to embark on a battle that would build a special bond with thousands of soldiers they would never meet. Their battle was the Battle for D-Day, a battle to protect the soldiers on the beach. "We knew we were good pilots," said one. "We were ready for it."[437]

So, too, were the Germans.

Pete Quesada called his squadron commanders together for their formal briefing. He delivered the welcome news that D-Day had arrived, and, with his energy nearly overwhelming the small hut, Quesada urged his men to greatness. This was their moment, he said. They were warriors, and this was their day. "I had never heard such a pep talk before or since," said one of the men in attendance. "By the time he finished talking, I wanted to forgo dinner and rush back to my base and start the invasion."[438]

Colonel Donald Blakeslee, the head of an American fighter group, briefed his own group of P-51 pilots. It was a rousing speech, a coach exhorting his team to victory. The soldiers were going to have a rough time of it, he said, and he was going to make sure they made it ashore. His pilots rose as a group and cheered as Blakeslee's adrenalin-charged voice reached a peak. "I am prepared," he said, "to lose the whole group."[439]

In the predawn darkness, D-Day illuminated East Anglia as brilliant shafts of light suddenly burst up into the sky and lit up the night. "All of the searchlights in England—the ones they had used for antiaircraft—all of them were just going back and forth pointing their way to the beachhead," remembered a Wisconsin airman.[440] It was a sight worthy of a letter home, or so thought Sergeant Robert Sand, who saw the lights blink on and wrote to his parents to tell them about the kinetic spectacle. "On the horizon a searchlight springs to life and swings in great beckoning circles. Two more flashed on, sending fixed shafts of bluish light to the roof of the sky. Dark clouds cover the moon and the countryside is darker than ever."[441]

B-24 pilot Paynter and his crew were awakened at 0200 hours. After the briefing was over, they headed out to their planes. It was then that the weight of the moment hit them. "My own crew hardly spoke as we rode out to our B-24," Paynter recalled. "No one seemed to feel we'd be in much danger, rather I think it was [our] fear and concern for those in the invasion forces who'd be hitting the beaches that day. They were the ones I was thinking about."[442]

Three safe-passage corridors had been established for the planes headed toward Normandy, including one that went directly over London before pouring out over the English Channel between Portsmouth and Eastbourne. The airspace would be so terribly congested that the traffic in the corridors would be one way only unless a pilot was forced to turn around before reaching the Channel. "If there are any aborts," said one of the men briefing the aviators, "leave the formation before crossing the English coast and fly back under 14,000 feet."[443]

If a plane couldn't make it back and the pilot had to ditch, landing in the Channel would be no easy feat, either: Boat traffic, too, was one-way only. "We were to ditch into the English Channel and await a landing craft to pick us up out of the water, at which time we became not airmen but infantry," said one airman. "We were to hit the beach with the first, second, or whatever wave fate provided."[444]

Ever so slowly the bombers and fighters began their crawl around the perimeter tracks, bursts of flames erupting from their exhaust stacks and propellers spinning in wide, flat arcs. The rumbling planes sounded a symphony of war. With wind and rain whipping past their canopies, the first wave of fighters taxied into position for takeoff. "It was still dark," recounted Lieutenant Colonel H. Norman Holt. Holt was in a group of P-38 pilots who would escort the ships crossing the Channel. The flood of airplanes was a sight he remembered more than forty years later. "The red and green navigation lights dotted the taxiway as each ship wormed its way into position. One or two [of the planes] roared as pilots checked their engines for power. Ground crews stood around their planes while waiting for their pilots to take off. The pilots got a little bit of a boost out of that sort of a cheering section to urge them on. But the pilots are not grandstanding for attention—they are only appreciative of the concern shown by the crews for their safety. The first two started down the runway. Gathering speed they staggered into the air with extra belly tanks full of gasoline and a 1,000-pound bomb under each wing. We were off to play our part in the show."[445]

"I remember it was raining pitchforks," said another pilot. "None of us had ever taken off in the rain in the daytime in formation; now we were going to have to take off in the pouring rain at night. Well, Colonel Duncan [our wing commander] saw that we were worried. He put his finger on the map at Cherbourg, and he said, 'It's ten after one. Ten minutes ago our paratroopers landed—and we're going to take off if it snows.'"[446]

In pairs of two aircraft, the pilots pushed up their throttles and lifted off into the sky. Hundreds and hundreds of P-51s and P-47s and P-38s began to wing over to their sectors. Remarkably, there were only two accidents. One Mustang pilot lost control of his plane and slammed into the side of the watchtower. Another pilot became disoriented in the clouds and flew into the ground.

The B-17s and B-24s began their take-offs at 0155 hours, and for the next three hours and thirty-four minutes, they assembled in the sky forming groups of six planes. A total of 1,361 planes took off, 1,198 of them to attack the beach fortifications over the landing areas with the rest hitting targets near the city of Caen. Every tool available to help organize the formations was in use, but the weather obscured most of the sky and it was ink-black dark, save for the searchlights. Tom Parsons, a crewman, wrote in his diary that day: "After briefing we went to the planes (which were already lined up for us on the perimeter) and as soon as time came we took off. Of course, a great amount of difficulty was encountered in making formation since it was very dark (about 2AM) and there was a terrible overcast." Parson's bomber actually collided with another bomber; the damage was insignificant and largely confined to the rudder, but it was no doubt a terrifying moment in the clouds.[447]

Together the bombers banked to the east and passed over the English Channel, precisely on schedule. Although they were picked up on German radar, they encountered no fighters, and what flak they came upon was entirely ineffective. They turned south. Below them the clouds were solid as they streamed toward Normandy.[448]

At sea, the invasion forces began to move toward their landings. The fire from the shore was intense. Well off Omaha Beach, hundreds of Higgins boats pulled alongside their mother ships and took on their men as the first wave began to move in. German shells exploded in the water around them, sending geysers of white froth into the air, many finding their mark and sinking boats before they made it all the way in. The Forts and Liberators arrived and winged in toward the bluffs with their escort of fighters. It was their job to take out the machine gun nests and the big guns well in advance of the first boats hitting the sand. They flew in at 20,000 feet loaded with 2,944 tons of bombs and were perfectly spaced to cover the coastline from Omaha to Sword. They carried a tested, well-planned mix of 100-pound general-purpose bombs, 120-pound fragmentation bombs, 500 pounders, and 1,000-pounders.

Although entirely unopposed and thus undistracted in the cockpit by German fighters or flak, they missed entirely.[449] "It was a day of frustration," remembered a crewman on a B-17. "We certainly didn't do as we had planned."[450]

As they feared, the clouds were heavy over the D-Day beaches, and the bombardiers were forced to use radar to sight their targets, which also meant they were required to add an extra 1,000-yards to the bomb safety line. Under the best of circumstances, that would have resulted in a circular error of such magnitude that only the occasional shorts and the creep back of bombs would have had any chance of hitting the guns that were now firing on the ships. Compounding the problem, at 20,000 feet, none of the men could see even a hint of the ground, which naturally gave them concern. But after months of flying skin-tingling missions, they knew that errors were part of the game. Some would later say the bombardiers held their releases for another 30 seconds rather than risk a single 500-pounder dropping on a landing craft. Doolittle was certainly one of those who said as much. "I suspected they added a 'fudge factor' to their aiming points," he later wrote in his memoirs.[451] The closest any bomb came to the German batteries was between 300 and 400 yards off target, a distance that meant the raid did no damage at all. Considering the safety line, it was no surprise that most of the bombs landed as far as 3 miles inland. Tragically for the Americans, the Germans overlooking the beaches had no idea that they also were being attacked from the air.[452]

Of the entire force of 1,198 bombers, 1,083 released bombs. The inbound force split into four groups and attacked Omaha, Juno, Gold, and Sword. Against the gun emplacements on Omaha Beach were tasked 329 bombers, B-24s all of them. The B-24s bombed Omaha for nineteen minutes, ending their raid at 0614 hours, just eleven minutes off schedule. By 0630 hours, when the first Higgins boat dropped its ramp, the bombers were more than 50 miles inland.[453]

The bombing was ineffective, and on Omaha Beach, the consequences were particularly bad. Unaffected by the very attack that was meant to silence them, the big German guns kept barking their deadly projectiles 25,000 yards out to sea, and the German machine gun nests on the bluffs launched unobstructed fields of fire across the sand. Inside the crowded Higgins boats, the American soldiers rocked left and right as the waves spit over the bow ramps while they motored toward the beach.

The first wave of soldiers had almost no chance. The Germans poured fire into the men coming ashore with such devastation that a retreat was nearly ordered.

Meanwhile, the fighters climbed through the clouds and spread out into their patrol sectors. Each group went to their assigned positions. Some formed the perimeter wall that would cordon off the landings from the interior, some flew escort, while others found ground targets and bombed away. Said one fighter pilot, just twenty years old at the time, who was covering the landings, "Our job was to go over Omaha Beach at 3,000 feet and circle it, so that if enemy fighters came in to strafe the beach we'd shoot them down. And then there were other groups that would be at 5,000, 8,000, 12,000 [feet]; they were stacked just like that ... Here I am, three thousand feet above the beach. I could see the ships starting to come in the daylight, and all of a sudden a blanket of fire from the ships to the shore, and then from the shore to the ships. And then I saw the landing barges." A cloud passed beneath his fighter as the ramps on the landing craft dropped and the soldiers surged into the surf. Interlacing fields of machine gun fire brought them down, one young soldier at a time. The helplessness he felt was inconceivable. Some boys coming ashore scarcely advanced a step before being shot dead. "It was a slaughter," he said, and that was all.[454]

Howard Hightower had a similar view as his group of P-38s flew top cover over the Higgins boats as they motored toward the landing area. Hightower admired the orderly line of their advance, each boat packed with thirty-six combat soldiers. "I remember we flew cover over a group of small landing craft. They appeared to be 12–14 feet wide, 40–50 feet long, square nosed, low-sided and filled with men. The boats were in excellent formation with several boats abreast and stretched out for a fair distance." He craned his neck to look down and saw the men below him nearly face-to-face. "As I flew over the gray water this fog and scud shrouded day I looked down at the men huddled together in their boats and they in turn watched us, turning their faces upward as we passed near. When they did this, you could see a solid patch of white faces in the dullness that surrounded them."[455] His squadron completed eight D-Day missions that day.

The Marauders and Havocs headed toward Utah Beach. They took off at 0343 hours, but things started poorly. So bad was the weather that two bombers collided in the clouds and crashed, killing all on board. Moments later, two more rammed together; both crashed. Four ships were down, and they hadn't even reached the English Channel.[456]

The attack against Utah Beach went much better. The mission called for a low-level pass with a mix of bombs to take out troop concentrations and soften up the defenses before the men came ashore. Unlike the B-17s, the Marauders had no radar so coming in below the cloud cover was a necessity. While that would ensure a high degree of bombing accuracy, it would also expose the aircrews to every manner of ground fire for the entire bomb run. That brought back bad memories of a similar mission with a similar flight profile over Holland earlier in the war when virtually all of the Marauders had been shot down. "We were told it was our job to prepare the ground to the best of our ability to enable the infantry to get ashore, to stay ashore and fight and win," said an officer in the Ninth. "I just couldn't get the thought out of my mind of these poor devils in Holland on that low-level raid. Here we were about to do the same suicidal thing with hundreds of Marauders."[457]

Dangerous, yes. Suicidal, no. Despite the fact that they were sandwiched between a layer of clouds above and German gunfire below, the Ninth did a spectacular job. Picking their way through the weather, the B-26s and A-20s formed their combat boxes and reached their targets at 0515 hours. Unlike the B-17s who were above the clouds and never saw the invasion, they could see everything. As they arrived on the scene, a ferocious gun battle was under way between the Navy ships and the German shore batteries. Tracers streaked through the sky as lead poured from one side to the other, never letting up. Said a B-26 pilot, "As we approached the coast, we could see ships shelling the beach. One destroyer, half sunk, was still firing from the floating end. The beach was a bedlam of exploding bombs and shells. I imagined many of those young med huddled in the landing craft, doubtless scared to death. I could see what they were heading into and I prayed for those young men."[458] Unsaid was the thought that likely crossed everyone's minds: how could anyone survive the fusillade of steel flying through the air below?

The B-26s came around for their pass and were greeted by a hail of bullets. One bomber was hit in the wing, and an engine erupted in flames. Two more shells punched into the fuselage before the pilot broke it off and pulled up so the crew could bail out. Another bomber, an A-20, took a direct hit in the bomb bay and was blown in half. All aboard were killed. Another Marauder flew directly in front of a machine gun nest on a bluff. "I have this frozen image of a machine gunner set up by a bastard firing at us," remembered the gunner in the top turret. "For a short second I looked right down the barrel of that gun. We were accustomed to heavy flak but this was the most withering, heavy, and accurate we ever experienced."[459]

With tracers whizzing past their cockpits and flak bursting all around them, they lined up for their passes and let their bombs tumble out. So low were they that the concussions from the explosions sent them bouncing into the air. "It was like driving a car down the ties of a railroad track," said a flyer.[460] But the attack was remarkably effective. German gun emplacements split open under the deadly accurate bombardment. Pillboxes and machine gun nests were silenced, as were German soldiers huddled in shelters waiting to fire on the soldiers streaming ashore. The airborne infantry witnessed their arrival. "As dawn broke," remembered a paratrooper on the ground, "we could observe one of the most impressive sights of any wartime action. Wave after wave of medium and light bombers could be seen sweeping down the invasion beaches to drop their bombs."[461]

The after-battle report was careful to give the Navy its due for the shelling they laid on Utah Beach, but the Marauders were given ample credit, too. The bombs dug craters for the infantrymen and sent spears of shrapnel into the Germans, killing hundreds upon hundreds of soldiers who would have otherwise fired down on the landing craft. A total of 289 B-26s smothered their targets with 523 tons of 250-pounders. Two 75-mm cannons, two 50-mm antitank guns, and an 88 were reduced to so much steel, details that indicate tremendous accuracy. Utah was so pocked by shell craters that it looked like the surface of the moon.[462]

The first wave of Marauders returned to base at 0800. They ate, refueled, bombed up, and headed right back out.[463]

Inland from the beaches, word of the invasion raced through the German Army units. The French countryside sprang alive with soldiers roused into action and mobilizing toward the beaches. Radio sets crackled to life as Germans streamed from their tents and barracks. Men strapped on helmets, grabbed guns, and at a sprint dashed to their trucks. Bursts of black smoke shot above their tanks as engines rumbled to life. Trucks pulling artillery pieces turned onto the roads leading to the Normandy beaches. Reinforcements were on the move.

Above them, the P-47s arced through the sky in brilliant flashes of steel and bore down on the movement below as Full House, Stud, and Royal Flush were carried out. As they expected, the Germans were poised for battle, and the return fire from the ground was murderous. The sides of rail cars dropped down, revealing antiaircraft guns that began to spit their shells pointblank into the fighters. Ground soldiers spun into the ditches and started firing skyward from their backs. One P-47 had its tail shot off in a battle with some tanks. Another burst into flames while strafing a truck convoy. An armored vehicle claimed a P-51 when some small-caliber fire sawed off a wing. Some of the pilots were too anxious and came in too low or were unable to pull up before the blasts from their own bombs blew them out of the sky. A dozen P-51s were so focused on their strafing that they failed to notice a swarm of Me-109s that arrived. It would be one of the most successful German counterattacks of the day. Four Mustangs were shot down.[464]

Others found the mark and got a bead on German emplacements. "We had to see what we could do to help the boys advance," wrote Lt. Col. Holt. Holt and his P-47s got into the air before dawn and formed up before they crossed the English Channel. As the sun lightened the clouds with the first shafts of daylight, they caught a glimpse of the invasion. "Below us, for a three or four mile stretch, we could see innumerable water craft of all sizes, shapes and types. There seemed to be thousands of them! Battleships standing offshore were firing broadsides over the other craft. Their firepower was helping pin down and hamper return fire from the enemy shore. At the shoreline, landing craft were spewing out men and equipment at an astonishing rate. We could see them scattering like kids from school."[465]

The primary target for Holt's group was an inland German gun battery. As it came into view, Holt cried out tally-ho and led the formation down. Their bombs found their targets. The mission was so quickly completed that it left the group with ammunition and time on their hands. They asked for a new target, but none was readily available, so they were told to hunt for targets of opportunity. "We noted one battery had just fired. Expertly camouflaged we would not have seen it had not the concussion of the gun blown the surrounding shrubbery and camouflage nets to attract our attention." Holt banked toward the target. One plane after the other laced the area with deadly .50-cal bullets. "The gun did not fire again."[466]

But the Thunderbolts still had bullets and plenty of gas. Muzzle flashes from a hedgerow caught their attention, and once again they rained down a hail of deadly fire until the German guns were silenced. Their senses were sharp, and the adrenalin raced through their bodies. They took the fastest route home. "All of us wanted to get back, refuel, re-arm and get in another sock at the Nazis."[467]

The fighters and dive-bombers swept down on their targets and dropped bombs, strafed, and relentlessly attacked anything that might interfere with the invasion or that could keep the Germans pinned down. In groups as small as two planes and as large as twenty-six, they streaked down from above and hit targets on the ground. In addition to Luftwaffe airfields, they bombed seventeen bridges and ten marshaling yards and attacked three convoys. They flamed 216 trucks loaded with Germans soldiers, 21 locomotives, 76 wagons hauling material forward, and 85 trains. They bombed radar towers, barracks, troops in fields, staff cars, two tugs on rivers, and nineteen armored vehicles, which were reduced to smoking hulks. They encountered small-arms fire and heavy guns and often flew with bullets streaking past their canopies. They rarely pulled off a target before a plume of black smoke was climbing into the sky.[468] "Every corner of the Reich was ablaze," said a German fighter pilot who led a squadron of Me-109s. "It had become a playground for Allied fighters and bombers. They attacked day and night, giving the nation no rest."[469] He described the threat from above as being nearly impenetrable. "Spitfires, Lightnings, Thunderbolts and other aircraft kept a constant watch over our airfield and we were unable to take off."[470]

The Germans encountered men like Holt and squadrons of fighter-bombers during the entire day, which considerably slowed their advance. They were blocked by rail cuts, bridges that had been felled, marshaling yards that were in disarray, and bomb craters that pocked almost all of the major roadways. "The Allies won their premier objective in the transportation campaign," wrote an Air Force historian. "They were able to build up their forces in Normandy from across the Channel faster than the Germans could reinforce theirs from adjacent areas in France."[471]

Reconnaissance pilots launched at 0600 hours and picked their way over to Le Havre to gather photo intelligence on German positions.

They turned toward the invasion area and dropped down to 1,000 feet, descending through clouds and light rain. Two of the pilots failed to see a German airbase that was immediately below them. "Suddenly little red golf balls started floating by my wings—light caliber flak," remembered Clarence Shoop, one of the pilots. Shoop was with pilot Norris Hartwell flying in an in-trail formation of two fighters streaking along at some 300 miles per hour. They banked away as hard as they could. "I yelled at Hartwell and he turned one way and I turned the other. The air was pretty full of lead for a few seconds. I snapped a few pictures and discovered later that we had flown over Caen/Carpiquet airport." Shoop and Hartwell escaped, but the German airbase spooked them. They turned to the north and swept up the beaches, running their cameras until they were in the middle of the landings, where crossfire made it too dangerous to continue. "There were Allied fighters everywhere," said Hartwell. But fighters weren't all they saw. One of Hartwell's pictures showed an old woman kneeling in prayer in her garden.[472]

Although Shoop and Hartwell had been surprised by the Germans, some of the other pilots turned the tables when they themselves surprised a flight of German fighters who were making a break for their airbases. It was a lucky break, and they made the most of it. Thanks to their quick reactions, they got the drop on four of them. They wheeled into position and let go short but accurate bursts from their .50-caliber machine gun fire and shot down three of the Germans.[473]

Another crew was not so lucky. On an unrelated mission, two other reconnaissance pilots were flying in formation checking the rail line between Chartres and Châteaudun and looking for German soldiers. The sky was cloudy, but the visibility on the deck was good. The two pilots, named Cosby and Wicker, were flying at maximum speed. Cosby led the way, but flak and gunfire from the ground immediately surrounded both of their cockpits. They yanked and banked and avoided any hits, but suddenly they flew out into an open area and were immediately in the clutches of 20-mm cannon fire. They both pushed their throttles to maximum speed, but there was little hope. A unit historian wrote their epitaph: "As they roared down the tracks across the field, cameras clicking, light flak began exploding around them. Cosby, leading the way, looked at his wing man just in time to see Wicker's *Bluebell 2* disappear in a burst of black smoke."[474]

The Eighth Air Force had no way of knowing how poorly their first mission had gone as they launched their second raid just hours after the landings began. This raid was mounted by a force of five thousand airmen and more than five hundred bombers, but again the clouds were dense and weather blanketed the target areas in heavy storms. The second round of bombing was as ineffective as the first, and two bombers were lost to a midair collision. There was no German fighter opposition or effective flak. Of the 528 B-17s and B-24s that mounted the second raid, just thirty-seven released their bombs, with little to show for it.[475]

Later, another seventy-three bombers launched a third raid, but when they got over their target—Caen—they again encountered solid clouds. Even so, fifty-three of the bombers released anyway. There were no losses.[476]

The Eighth launched their fourth bombing mission at the end of the day. The weather remained stormy, and heavy clouds and intermittent rain showers socked in most of the targets. A total of 736 B-17s and B-24s made the run, out of which 553 were able to see enough through the holes in the clouds and drop their bombs. Of those that dropped, 116 were forced to hit secondary targets, most of which, they would later learn, had already been attacked by other units. It was frustrating. The crews so genuinely wanted to do more, but the weather made operations difficult at best. In the official report on this final mission, the assessment of the overall bombing was at best lukewarm.[477]

Back at the bases, the flight lines were thick with activity and transformed by the nearly nonstop pace of operations. Planes landed, refueled, rearmed, and took off again. Pilots grabbed sandwiches, took naps, and were briefed on their next mission. On the hardstands, something always needed to be worked on: repairs, avionics, fuel, bombs, bullets, tires. Rather than pedal back and forth, the ground maintainers came up with a timesaving solution of their own. The fighters carried drop tanks, which were packed in large crates. "The men, to be closer to their planes, built homes out of the belly tank boxes and lived besides their planes," wrote Kent Miller of the 356th Fighter Squadron. "It seemed that overnight on the line a small city had been built by the men." The men called their new home "Belly Box Apartments." Some had lights, many had radios, and at least a few claimed to have showers.[478]

Ready rooms became second homes for the pilots, and throughout the day they were packed with men in flight suits. "Iron cots were all over the place," remembered a ground maintainer. "The news radio was tuned in constantly for latest reports of Allied progress."[479] On some of the cots sprawled exhausted pilots trying to grab quick naps. Around them, men came and went, the air thick with stories from the missions. Wrote Todd Webb in the history of the 68th Bomb Squadron, "Combat crews say they had never seen anything like it, when the clouds opened up and gave them a glimpse of what was going on in the English Channel; thousands and thousands of all kinds of boats ... infantry men on the beaches looked like pin points moving about."[480]

In addition to Hap Arnold's own observer, who was flying in a B-17 over the D-Day beaches, Doolittle wanted to see the invasion, too. A superb aviator, Doolittle could pilot any aircraft in his command, but he chose a P-38 Lightning because of its distinct silhouette, one that was readily identifiable by the Allies and thus less likely to be shot upon. He flew with another officer, and together they reached the skies over the landings before they became separated by the clouds. Alone, Doolittle dropped through a hole in the clouds and saw the fleet.[481] Remembered Doolittle: "The scene below was the most impressive and unforgettable I could have possibly imagined." Ships stretched before him as far as he could see. Shells raised fountains of water around the landing craft. Men flowed ashore. Doolittle spent some two and a half hours in the air before landing. He hurried over to Eisenhower's headquarters to deliver a first-hand report. "Of course, I proudly emphasized the fact that the Luftwaffe had not been able to interfere. The impression I had was that everything was going smoothly everyplace except at Omaha Beach, where I saw many landing craft blow up beneath me."[482]

In fact, Doolittle was correct. Most of those who flew that day saw little in the way of enemy opposition. Lieutenant James M. Chapman, Jr., a pilot, was tasked to bomb the port of Cherbourg. The mission, he wrote in his diary, was successful. They were met only by light flak and no German fighters, but he was surrounded by Allied aircraft coming and going. "Seemed as if the sky was covered with planes of every type," he wrote. D-Day, he believed "should be successful."[483]

John Hedenberg, a fighter pilot, agreed as he wrote in his diary: "Down to the beachhead again today. Still no enemy air activity."[484]

A reporter from *Yank* Magazine was allowed to observe the comings and goings of the bombers at an Eighth Air Force base in England. "The ground crews worked with a little more zest than usual," he wrote. "For more than a year now they had loaded bombs and checked engines and guns with nothing to show for it except what it said in the papers. But this invasion made a milestone in the two long years of bombing." The reporter felt it in the air as he moved about the hardstands, saw it in the smiles and in the boisterous talk among the men: the troops coming ashore, the end for Adolf Hitler, the first step toward going home. "It was as if their pin-ups in the barracks were beginning to stir out of their paper frames and would soon talk for real in the accents of the girls back home," he wrote.[485]

He was struck, too, by a surprising irony. The very men who were making the news leaned in to the radios to hear the news. No doubt it was the same at every airbase in England. "The pilots in the officers lounge listened intently to a radio speaker talking an awful lot about D-Day but saying very little. The pilots were very interested even though they themselves were going to fly today and were in effect part of the invasion operation. They listened to someone off in London giving them the low down." The reporter walked around and listened to comments from the crews coming back from missions. One pilot seemed to sum up the enormity of it all. Despite the fact that the English Channel was some 150 miles long and as wide as 20 miles, he simply shook his head. "It's dangerous ditching in the Channel today. There's no room in the water."[486]

Nor was there any room in the air. "The biggest hazard then was the possibility of colliding with another Allied aircraft," wrote a fighter pilot. "I understand at times that day there were over a thousand aircraft flying over that small strip of Channel water between the English coast and that of France. Making that worse, there was an overcast at around 1,500 feet most of the day, so all of those aircraft were compressed into that small piece of airspace."[487]

The Luftwaffe's plan to fly in reinforcements was to be triggered by the code phrase "Threatening Danger West," but the German High Command was unwilling to commit the reserves until they were certain that this was the invasion. So far, the raids on the morning of June 6 fit the ongoing pattern of American attacks in terms of numbers and targets; the day's attack didn't strike the Germans as anything completely unusual. German coastal radars picked up the air activity over England sometime and by 0500 hours, the fighter controllers had seen enough to conclude that a major strike was underway and that it was headed to the south. This attack, however, was more or less the same as any American raid. As part of the deception plan, Spaatz had routinely launched coastal raids of more than a thousand bombers each with a like number of fight planes as escorts and with diversionary raids by the mediums of the Ninth. Just two days before, a force of more than a thousand bombers had hit Pas-de-Calais, a force not much different than this day's.

Thus, as the controllers watched the invasion force come across the English Channel, they had no reason to view this attack with exceptional alarm. Moreover, the American formations were flying away from Berlin, so the heavy concentrations of fighters reserved for the defense of the Reich had no reason to be alerted or sent into the air. "The German Command actually groped in the dark until the moment of the landing," Adolf Galland wrote in his memoirs.[488] With only sporadic communication from the West, they remained undecided even as the fighter controllers started to take local action. Threatening Danger West would not be formally issued until June 7.

As the attacks clarified and pointed to the Normandy region, the German controllers ran down the list of available squadrons and started to put them on alert. Because they were as keyed up to D-Day as the Allies, in their alerts they included a warning that this might be the invasion they had long expected. At 0500 hours on June 6, Col. Pips Priller was awakened and received the news. "The invasion has started," he was told over the phone. "You'd better get up there."

Priller exploded in a rage. His fighters were now inland, save his own Focke-Wulf and that of his wingman, Sergeant Heinz Wodarczyk. His squadrons had pulled out the day before for bases well to the rear, but the ground support personnel for those aircraft were still with him there at Lille. "Where are my squadrons?" he asked. They didn't know.

Communications were spotty at best. "We don't know yet exactly where your squadrons have landed but we're going to divert them back to the field of Poix." Poix was an airbase near Amiens, one of the many German bases that dotted the French countryside just inland from the Pas-de-Calais–Le Havre area along the English Channel.[489]

The news reached Wolfgang Fischer and his men next. Around the town square in Nancy, the morning quiet was suddenly interrupted by the sound of screeching tires and urgent honking as men sprang from cars with cupped hands and yelled "Invasion! Invasion!" At first, the words made little sense to the pilots, but as they sorted out the sounds and understood the meaning, they all sprang from their beds as one.[490]

Word spread quickly through the Luftwaffe, and a military response began to form. At 0700 hours, Priller's Second Group had been found and notified. They departed from their airbase south at Mont-de-Marsan and were en route to the airbase at Vraux, west of Paris. They would later be redirected to Poix.[491]

Other squadrons were found and notified, and they too began to move. At 0800 hours, the controllers reached a fighter group in Compiègne, France.[492] At 0830, another group of fighters located in Salzwedel, Germany, was activated and put on readiness. At 0843, that group was instructed to take their forty-five Me-109s from Salzwedel, 90 miles southwest of Hamburg to the German airfields at Evreux, France, 50 miles inland from Omaha Beach, and to St. Andres, France, 60 miles west of Paris.[493] A third wing was reached, this one in the German village of Lippspringe. They were instructed to move their FW-190s and Me-109s to Quentin-Clastres, France, 100 miles behind Omaha Beach. Yet a fourth wing got their instructions and took off from Götzendorf, Austria, deep to the east, and flew to Connerre, France, 120 miles southeast of the invasion, adding their Me-109s to the total.[494] Priller's group of 124 Focke-Wulfs and Messerschmitts were now in the air and en route to the airbase at Poix, near Pas-de-Calais, about 120 miles from the landings.

Satisfied that they'd done what could be done, the German fighter controllers waited for their planes to report from their forward airfields, which ultimately proved to be nearly impossible. As the Germans moved up, they moved into the no-man's land of destruction. Thirty-four German airfields within 130 miles of the invasion front had been bombed by 3,915 Allied aircraft with 6,717 tons of bombs. Four of those fields were now completely destroyed, and fifteen had been reduced to burnt-out hangars and cratered runways. In addition, at least fifty-nine other airfields outside of the 130-mile arc had been attacked, including aerodromes and fields in Holland, Belgium, western France, and western Germany.[495]

It was into this landscape of destruction and disarray that the Germans now flew. Said Galland, "It all happened in a great rush and under a nervous strain ... the intermediate touch-down fields were overcrowded ... the destination of the units often had to be changed in flight because the intended landing field had been put out of action at the last moment ... almost half the units got involved in dogfights on the way to their action stations ... there were an incredible amount of crashes ... the repair squads were so overtaxed they were unable to get a sufficient amount of aircraft back into service ... soon everything was in a hopeless chaos."[496]

In truth, it was chaotic, but it wasn't entirely hopeless. The Germans improvised and did it well. An American pilot shot down earlier in the week was in hiding on a partisan's farm in western France when a section of German fighters suddenly flew overhead. "We were examining the vineyard when a sudden roar of engines filled the air. Out of the mists of dawn a 36-ship formation of Me-109 fighters, with a large bomb slung beneath each glistening green and gray belly, swept low over the farm as they assembled from a near-by airdrome." He was startled by the planes, and he understood what it meant, but he was scarcely concerned. "With the fighter cover we'll have over the Channel I'll bet not one of those bastards gets back to base."[497]

Exactly which unit those Germans belonged to remains unclear—a great number of planes were headed in the direction of bases near Paris—but they weren't the only crews to get airborne, and they weren't the only ones to successfully reposition that day. Indeed, the same clouds that had frustrated the B-17s were in fact playing into the hands of the Germans.

Although accounts differ, it seems reasonably certain that some 317 fighters survived the airfield plan and were now available to fly combat missions (417 if one counted the night fighters).[498] Considering the orders issued that morning by the fighter controllers, at least 200 of these German fighters were now in various stages of mobilizing in response to D-Day.[499]

The weather—and not a little resourcefulness—benefitted the Germans. "If I were the German operations officer and Providence had promised me to allow me to select the weather in which to make my defense, these were the conditions I would have chosen," said American General Laurence Kuter. "Here was the perfect concealment for German airmen. They could dive out of the dense cloud upon the packed Channel below, bomb or strafe any ship, and climb back into the protecting clouds in a matter of seconds." Kuter spoke from firsthand knowledge. He had been asked by Hap Arnold to circle the D-Day beaches as his personal observer. Kuter's B-17 moved in and out of the heavy clouds for most of the morning.[500]

On Omaha Beach, the advance had been nearly halted. The first wave had been met by withering machine gun fire, and the second wave had fared little better. So heavy were the casualties that General Omar Bradley was uncertain whether to press the attack or withdraw. Had Priller's 124 fighters been at Lille, they might very well have tipped the scales in favor of retreat, but such is speculation: they were in no position to counter the landings that morning.

Not so Priller himself. Priller remained as determined as ever to get into the fight, and so he started an attack on his own. At Lille, he and his wingman, Sergeant Wodarczyk, hopped into their planes and with a full load of shells and bullets started their engines and turned onto the runway.[501] Armed and loaded, their plan was to stay low to the ground until they reached the coastline and then use the clouds to conceal their approach. "We're going in alone," Priller said to Wodarczyk, "and I don't think we're coming back."[502]

At 0900 hours, the two pilots took off from the north field at Lille and headed toward the Normandy coast. They flew as fast as they could and as low to the ground as possible, hoping the ground clutter would camouflage their flight. It seemed to work. As they crossed over the German airfield near Abbeville, they saw Allied fighters patrolling above, but they were well hid and no one came down.[503] Near Le Havre, they flew out over the ocean, pulled up sharply, and melted into the clouds, still undetected. It was only a matter of minutes before they knew they'd made the right decision. "There is everything out there— everywhere you look," said an excited Priller over his radio. "Believe me, this is the invasion."[504]

No doubt shocked by the armada that lay before them, they nonetheless remained determined and began their attack. Winging over, Priller and Wodarczyk began their dive, leveling off at about 50 feet over the ocean. As the surf line of Sword Beach swelled in front of them, they took aim on the men coming ashore and let loose with their guns. Their shells exploded everywhere at once, slamming into sand and flesh in a blur of bullets. Both planes fired continuously as they flew up the beaches, reaching Omaha Beach just before their guns dried up, at which point they pulled up and in a power climb clawed their way back into the clouds. On the edge of Omaha Beach, Navy Lieutenant William J. Eisemann watched the attack. He remembered the two German planes were "at less than fifty feet and dodged through the barrage balloons."

Incredibly, Priller and his wingman had flown through the tightest fighter screen in the history of military combat aviation to attack the D-Day beaches. They had flown straight down the sand, strafing as they went, and without so much as a bullet hole escaped unharmed and made their way back to the German airbase in Creil, France.[505]

Priller wasn't the only one to attack. Wolfgang Fischer's orders were to reposition his dozen FW-190s to Creil to rearm and then launch their own attack. "We were informed our Focke-Wulfs were to be fitted for rockets," he wrote in his memoirs. "We were told that we were going to have to use [them] against the Allies invasion shipping." With a pair of seven-foot long rockets tipped with explosive warheads under their wings, a flight of twelve warplanes could do considerable damage.[506]

The armorers took two hours to retrofit the Focke-Wulfs for rockets, during which time the pilots were briefed on the techniques to fire them. Their target was Gold Beach. With a thunderous roar, Fischer's men took to the air and climbed into the overcast as they winged toward the coast. As they flitted in and out of the clouds, they could see Spitfires and P-51s and Thunderbolts, any of which could have turned and attacked. But their luck held, and they remained unseen as they came in over the ships. "The sky was seven-tenths clouds," said Fischer. "These were ideal conditions for our purpose."[507]

Using speed to their advantage, the Germans flew out over the beachhead and the ocean, where they made a daring 180-degree turn. As they came around, they lined up with the ships, which were headed in the direction of the landings. Fischer found a ship and watched as it grew in his windshield. He fired. "For a second I was enveloped in brilliant ball of flame and the noise of a thousand howling devils assaulted my ears," he wrote. "Never having fired a rocket before in my life, it gave me one hell of a fright." One of his rockets streaked down but missed, exploding harmlessly in the ocean in the wake of a

Victory-class cargo ship; the other found its mark and exploded against the stern. All twelve Focke-Wulfs successfully launched their rockets.[508]

Still near maximum speed, they saw the invasion beaches. They dove down ever closer to the water and lined up on the soldiers streaming ashore. From 700 feet or so, they emptied their guns. "As I crossed the beach at a height of 300 meters I let fly at the mass of men and material packed below. After the spectacular and noisy fireworks that had accompanied the launch of the two rockets, the thumping of my cannon, drowned out by the roar of the engine, sounded like the harmless popping of a cap pistol."[509]

After strafing the beach, the fighters pulled back into a climb and made a frantic dash for the clouds. Behind them was a hail of gunfire, but, incredibly, their luck held and in a moment, they were in the clouds and on the radio with German fighter control, which gave them instructions to land at a racetrack near Senlis, France, 30 miles north of Paris and some 110 miles inland.

Just as Priller had, Wolfgang Fischer's twelve fighter pilots had done what was by all measure impossible. They had pierced the fighter screens, dodged the gunfire from the ships, attacked the D-Day beaches, and had escaped unharmed. They arrived at Senlis, no doubt exhausted from the effort, and reported in. The ground maintainers rearmed and refueled the fighters before pushing them under the trees at the edge of the track.

Incredibly, Fischer spent the rest of the afternoon of D-Day sunning himself beside the swimming pool in town. He remembers watching a lone P-51 circling above, but his planes were never attacked.[510]

American fighter screens were tested repeatedly throughout the day as bitter air battles burst out suddenly and ended just as quickly. For the most part, the defenses held. Captain Bert Marshall, twenty-five, intercepted a section of Stukas dashing toward the beaches. He quickly banked his P-51 and got behind them, putting one of the Germans squarely in his gunsights. Marshall was on just his third combat mission ever, and would become one of three Texans to shoot down a German plane that day. "They were probably going after our boys and vehicles on the beachhead," said Marshall of his dogfight. "There were two of them in front of me; I took the one on the left and started firing when I was about 200 yards behind him." Drilling the fighter with streams of machine gun fire, Marshall closed in even as the German gunner in the back opened up. "I was too busy to notice," said Marshall of the bullets streaming past his cockpit. "I saw hits on his wing roots right away and he started to burn." The pilot was unable to escape, spiraling into the ground and exploding on impact. "That was all," said Marshall, meaning the job was done. Marshall would later become an ace.[511]

Lieutenant Joe Conklin spotted a FW-190 as he flew over the Vernouillet Airfield in Dreux, France, 50 miles southwest of Paris. The photo-reconnaissance pilot was in a P-51 armed with six .50-caliber machine guns. He yanked his plane around, maneuvered into position, and poured a burst into the Focke-Wulf. It went down.[512]

Fighter ace Colonel Hubert Zemke pounced on a FW-190 and forced the pilot to crash into the ground after a turning chase. He saw a second German and yanked to get behind, but a P-51 flashed across his own windshield and shot it down. "The Focke-Wulf immediately burst into flames and the pilot bailed out," remembered Zemke. "I could see his clothes were afire and flames were licking around his head. Fixing the descending pilot in my sight I opened fire to end his pain and misery."[513]

Altogether, American air forces claimed thirty-three German aircraft destroyed, at least a dozen chased off before combat, and fourteen damaged.[514]

Air operations at military airbases are usually known only by the forces that occupy that base. Rare would it be for an American to observe Luftwaffe operations or for Germans to witness those of the Americans. D-Day, though, afforded just such a view.

Henry Woodrum was in a B-26 when it was shot down during a raid against a bridge over the Seine River near Paris on June 2. He escaped capture and was taken in by the Resistance, which moved him to an apartment on the top floor of a building that had a line-of-sight view of the German airbase at Villacoublay. From here he would witness the airwar. "At first there was only moderate activity, but on D-Day things really picked up," he wrote later. "It was seven o'clock in the morning when I heard the sound of so many engines [that] I pulled a chair over to the window and waited for something to happen. The revving of the engines continued and suddenly a red nosed Me-109 with red wing tips leaped up in a very steep angle, starting a left climbing turn." Woodrum was watching the standard departure pattern used by the Luftwaffe as a defensive maneuver to minimize their vulnerability as they took off. "Others followed immediately and with each new launch the stack grew higher and higher forming one great, ever enlarging corkscrew-shaped spiral. When the last airplane was airborne there must have been at least 50 fighters involved."[515]

As the planes disappeared over the horizon, Woodrum left the window no wiser to the goings on than anyone else in Paris. He lost track of time, but later, when he heard the planes again, he went back to the window. The Messerschmitts were returning, using a steep dive to get down on the ground quickly. Clearly they had been engaged in combat. "About two hours later I heard several aircraft coming in from the west and looked out the living room window. The red-nosed Messerschmitt slanted hurriedly in, knifing down for a landing. Before he touched down, out of sight behind the trees ringing the field, others flew in from the same direction. Several trailed smoke, one badly. Then another group came in, milling about over the field as they set up a landing priority. Some were Focke-Wulf FW-190s. There must have been nearly a hundred fighters altogether. I remember counting more than sixty and I missed several flights."

That Woodrum knew he was watching the results of D-Day was thanks to a woman on a nearby balcony who riddled the mystery. She had heard the news on the radio. "*Le débarquement! Le débarquement!*" she cried.[516]

By midafternoon, the Allied forces were on the beaches. By nightfall, the leading element was inland. Behind them, shells still thumped down on the sand, while at sea the ships worked at a feverish pace to move supplies ashore. From the sky, the ocean seemed to be a quilted mosaic of black and gray, dark vessels and churning water littering the horizon as far as the eye could see.

As Cornelius Ryan would later say, it had indeed been the longest day. But it was not yet over.

The first indication of a new air attack was the distant sound of engines that suddenly swelled into a roar as a cluster of Ju-88 twin-engine bombers crested the beachhead and streaked over the ocean. In an instant they had arrived, but no sooner were they above the ships than they were in the clutches of ship-based searchlights that seemed to hold them motionless in the sky. Thousands of rounds of shells streamed upward etching lines of tracers so intense that the bullets themselves illuminated the bombers in a cone of light that was in fact the intersection of hundreds of shells. The bombers blew apart in a grisly brew of shredded metal, hunks of flesh, and burning fuel. "The barrage was magnificent, thunderous, terrifying," remembered an airman stationed as a flight controller on one of the ships offshore. "The Ju-88 burst into flames from wingtip to wingtip."[517] The twenty-one bombers were from Luftwaffe KG54, hurried down from German airbases in Juvincourt, France, and Soesterberg, Netherlands.

So rushed was their arrival that they flew in the camouflage paint from the Italian campaign.[518] One of the Ju-88s crashed behind the beachhead. Some days later, three American soldiers were photographed as they examined what little was left of its wings, nose, and tail. Fifteen of the bombers were shot down, but six narrowly escaped.[519]

The elaborate deception the Americans undertook to hide the true landing site was a complete success. But far from resting on their laurels, the deception plan continued on D-Day. Juan Pujol Garcia ran a spy network in England for the German intelligence service Abwehr. He had some twenty-four agents in Great Britain, who, with unnerving regularity, provided the German intelligence service with accurate data about convoy movements and pending operations, including a British plan to invade Norway. At 0300 hours on June 6, Pujol attempted to reach his handlers by radio to alert them to the D-Day invasion, but he failed to make any contact whatsoever. It wasn't until 0800 that he finally got through to report that an invasion was taking place and that the location was Normandy and that it was happening right now. The Germans could scarcely believe their good fortune and no doubt congratulated themselves on having such fine spies. On his part, Pujol's reputation was now unimaginably enhanced, and his reports gained top-level credibility.

The story, though, was far from over. On June 9, Pujol sent another message, this one puzzling to some, but not to Hitler. Pujol's message was a warning not to believe that the landings on the Normandy beaches were the real thing. He said that an entire Allied army with twenty-five divisions had been held in reserve for the real thing, and that the real invasion would take place in the Pas-de-Calais area. Hitler thought as much and was pleased to have direct confirmation from his trusted agent.

On July 29, 1944, a grateful German nation used the radio to inform Juan Pujol Garcia that he had been secretly awarded Germany's Iron Cross First Class. Interestingly, he was also awarded England's Most Excellent Order of the British Empire. There would, of course, be no invasion at Pas-de-Calais. Pujol was a double agent, and his "intelligence" was common knowledge in England, but because of time shifting and confusion, his information seemed fresh and accurate, at least in the eyes of the Germans. In fact, Pujol's message was nothing more than the continuation of the deception plan. It confused Hitler enough to keep German forces pinned down a hundred miles away when they were desperately needed to battle the landings.[520]

Fischer spent a quiet afternoon in the sun. From the side of the pool, he watched Allied fighters in the air—Spitfires or Mustangs, he wasn't sure which—as they cut lazy circles 20,000 feet above him. His respite, though, was interrupted late that afternoon by orders to take off on a new mission. Fischer was to join up with a group of fighters that had just landed at Senlis and would fly under the command of Group Commander Hauptmann Herbert Huppertz.

Huppertz had been in the air twice already on D-Day and had downed three Allied planes over Caen. He was to lead a group of eight pilots to intercept gliders that were inbound with more Allied soldiers. The new sortie was organized. They took off, but en route to their target came upon a battle between some American fighter pilots and a German convoy. The convoy was on the receiving end of repeated dive-bombing. "We sighted a dozen Mustangs strafing a convoy of German military vehicles heading towards the invasion front," wrote Fischer. "All thoughts of the gliders were abandoned. Our first duty lay in helping our comrades on the ground here and now." The Mustangs were intently focused on their attacks and were oblivious to the arrival of the Germans, who immediately winged over and came down on their exposed backsides. Fischer found a plane and banked onto the tail of a P-51 and squeezed off a short burst, killing the pilot. The rest of the German planes split up and the dogfight traced spiraling paths over the ground. In the end, Fischer's group claimed eight kills, although American records show that only four Mustangs were shot down. Either way, it was a stunning German success. They landed at Senlis as the last rays of daylight drained from the sky. It was 2130 hours on June 6.[521]

Though Fischer's group had claimed a great victory, it was a small feat overall. American fighters from the Eighth Air Force pounced on bridges, marshaling yards, railway junctions, road intersections, convoys, and even a tunnel. Locomotives were blown up, and more than two hundred trucks were turned into heaps of twisted metal. Bullets found German soldiers, staff cars, and trains all moving toward the front.[522] One group of P-47s exemplified the attacks. While flying interdiction, they spotted a convoy of trucks loaded with German soldiers. Pulling deep breaths through their oxygen masks, they wheeled around and came in. Pilot John Driscoll remembered the attack: "I saw four trucks with about twenty soldiers each and a staff car, so I went down and strafed them all, and I killed them. When you strafe with eight .50-caliber machine guns and hit a truck, all you see is a pile of dust. But all it took for a truck was a *brrr*! because you're firing thirty-two hundred rounds a minute. Each gun, eight of them, is firing four hundred rounds and we had about thirty-two hundred rounds in our wings. But all it took for a truck was a brrr! One burst and there it was." Driscoll considered coming around to see the results of the strafing but decided against it. "I thought, if I go back and see men twisting and turning on the ground, I'll never be able to do it again. So I didn't go back."[523]

Isolating the battlefield through interdiction had unfolded according to a plan so perfectly designed that it seemed to have been directed by a higher authority. Said one German soldier in exasperation,

"They bomb and shoot at anything that moves, even single vehicles and persons … the feeling of being powerless against enemy aircraft … has a paralyzing effect."[524]

The most puzzling German attack came at night near the end of the day. A ground crewman named Claude Allen had worked all day on D-Day and was preparing to bed down in his Belly Box apartment on the hardstand near his fighter when a German attacked his base. "I had been to the mess hall and then to the squadron area to pick up mail and some extra blankets because some of us in 'A' flight usually slept on the [flight] line near the ships. I was driving the bomb service truck and a Sergeant Van Tiny was riding in the back." Allen remembered that they stopped at the radio shack where they were told that a red alert was on, but they thought it was all clear for now. They were wrong. "I pulled back on the perimeter and headed towards 'A' flight area. Suddenly we heard this loud drone overhead, which sounded like an aircraft making a sharp turn, coming in from the direction of [the village of] Leiston and lights started flashing from the aircraft's guns." Allen and his partner jumped into a ditch.[525]

Joe DeShay, another mechanic, picked up the story from there. "I was out on the flight line working on an aircraft at that hour of the night. I heard the burst of gunfire, and it seemed as though flares lit up the area. I knelt down on one knee near a hard spot with my Thompson submachine gun across my other knee. The enemy aircraft zoomed over me from my blind [back] side, and I looked upward and could see the flame from his exhaust stacks of his engine, and he was mighty low." The German's cannon fire found the base's mess hall and blew a hole in it. The men inside hit the deck, yelling for the cooks to shut off the lights. A report filed the next day indicates that it was an Me-109 and that it was shot down by a British Spitfire.[526]

This would be the last recorded attack by a German fighter on D-Day.

Every airman had his own war experiences, and they often differed greatly even from the same mission. Some of the things they remembered were ordinary; others were unusual and stuck in their minds for decades. First Lieutenant Howard F. Johnson heard Eisenhower's speech announcing the landings on Normandy, although he was not at the airbase at the time. "I will always remember that on the way back our radio operator, Roger Rafford handed me earphones to listen to General Dwight Eisenhower announcing the Normandy landings to an excited world. But our day was not over. On return and some rest, we took off for a second mission, the group's third of the day."[527]

John Hedenberg, a fighter pilot, remembered the soldiers as he wrote in his diary: "Weather terrible, flying in the rain most of the time. I'll bet the poor infantry is cussing the weather."[528]

One corporal reflected on duty. "Everyone knew that the ensuing days would determine whether or not all the months of steady hammering had been in vain, whether or not a buddy in some parachute battalion or a brother in some tank corps or a cousin in some artillery unit would live or die as a result of the air protection we would provide. If we had been extremely important before D-Day we were certainly indispensable now."[529]

Many of the airmen took the occasion to write extra notes to their loved ones. One bomber pilot addressed a letter to his parents. Like many of the aviators, he saw the shells hitting the beaches, the men huddling in their landing craft, the ships burning, and some sinking with all hands on board. He had the presence of mind to recognize his own good fortune. "Guess those poor boys on the ground are really catching it so I'm not kicking about losing a little sleep and not eating regularly. We fly, come back and go to bed and fly again—yeah we get to eat every now and then but we don't have any certain hours to go to the 'Gobble Shop.'" The pilot had to close his letter because the chatter in his hut welled up. "Well," he wrote, "a big invasion bull session is going on so I'll sign off and write tomorrow night."[530]

The last missions came back in the same bad weather that the first mission took off in. The storms had covered western France and England all day, a typical summer front. The last planes came down in the dark, crosswinds buffeting the airfields, the runways slickened by the rains. It was near midnight, and the weather took its final toll. One P-38 came down through the dark and landed short of its runway, skidding through a field, and losing a propeller that broke off like a loose flywheel. A pair of B-17s came back and landed long. The first bomber skidded off the runway and nosed over in the soft grass. The second landed long, too, and slammed into the first. A B-24 had no better luck. It hit the runway in a tricky crosswind, and the right landing gear simply collapsed as the bomber ground looped to a stop.[531] "All of East Anglia was a mess," remembered John Taylor, a fighter pilot who flew more than seven hours on two missions during D-Day. "Several fields were shooting flares and it was difficult to identify your own." Taylor's formation dropped down through the clouds and lined up to land. They were possibly the last American planes to touch down on June 6, 1944. "We were down at 23:53," remembered Taylor. "Home free."[532]

As the clock ticked past midnight and the day came to an end, one P-51 pilot reflected on what it had all meant. "Our war was over, the exclusive war of the Eighth and Ninth Air Forces by day and the RAF by night," he said. "We'd be trucking bombs over, more of them, more often, but it wasn't our private show anymore. The boys who take it the slow way had the bright lights on them now."[533]

The soldiers were ashore. D-Day was done. And with that, the airmen claimed an hour of sleep and prepared to fly another day.

CHAPTER 23

D + 1

A thin layer of smoke hung over the invasion beaches. The stains of combat blotted the sand. The skies were darkened by storm clouds, and visibility remained poor. After the blizzard of steel that marked the previous day, June 7, 1944, by all rights should have been a day of rest. But it was not. It was D-Day plus 1.

The advance that began as soon as the soldiers broke out from the beaches was in some places now as far inland as 10 miles. The Allied Expeditionary Air Force's command center held its first post-D-Day conference and issued new field orders. The heavies would once again target chokepoints such as bridges, rail centers, and fortified positions; the fighters would be split between air cover, dive-bombing, and sweeps.[534]

The Germans activated Threatening Danger West, but it was, of course, too late. An invasion has to be repelled on the beach. By the time the Luftwaffe was in any position to counterattack, the Allied invasion already had a firm toehold inland with reinforcements flowing ashore like water through a pipe.

Forward of the infantry, the aviators though were back at work. The mediums of the Ninth Air Force delivered their bombs with unrelenting precision, while the dive-bombers continued to prick one target after the other like darts in a dartboard. Germans were found, their positions were passed from one pilot to the next, and a P-47 would roll over to deliver a wing-mounted bomb or a burst of .50-caliber machine gun fire. Said one German, it "was a nightmare of ditching the car, running for cover, being machine-gunned, resuming the journey, and having the same events repeated every few miles."[535]

The statistics rolled in as the airmen were debriefed. Seven troop carriers, forty one trucks, seven locomotives, and fifteen flatcars heavy with German trucks were hit and destroyed. One group claimed forty-five freight and ammunition cars; another group came down to strafe some one thousand Germans who were advancing toward the beaches and showered them with .50-caliber lead.

The ground interdiction campaign was every bit a part of the D-Day airplan, and it made the German advance "slower than that of a typical American Civil War march of some eighty years earlier," as one historian wrote, but it wasn't as simple as that.[536] American fatalities on D-Day totaled 2,499 men killed, while the battle for Normandy, which would rage for weeks, would account for 425,000 casualties on both sides.[537]

The weather on D+1 scarcely cooperated, yet the B-17s and B-24s were undaunted, mounting missions against rail yards, tunnels, bridges, and airfields, although a number of missions were aborted or canceled. "We prayed for a return trip bad weather or not," a copilot wrote in his diary. "We feel terrible that we are unable to give more support to our invasion troops." A similar entry was made on June 8 after the bomber crews tried to help the soldiers but in the end were grounded yet again. An airman made an entry in his diary that seemed to sum it all up: "Took off at 5:00 AM again for the invasion area. Weather still terrible. Target was just ahead of our invasion troops.

Clouds were so thick we dared not drop our bombs for fear of killing allied soldiers. Back at our base we stood by all day for a return run. At 4:00 PM we boarded our ships and waited for 'start engines.' Trip was scrubbed again. Our inability to help our invasion forces with at least two missions a day is very demoralizing. We could help save so many of our men if the weather would allow us to do what we do best."[538] Four hundred bombers failed to find success on June 8, but 735 found holes in the clouds large enough to hit their targets and thus eke out a measure of support for the soldiers fighting on the ground.[539]

On D+1, the German Luftwaffe was better organized, and they put some 150 fighters into the sky, engaging the perimeter defenses in effective dogfights. Cannon shells and .50-cal bullets swept from one plane to the next. The Eighth would take its share of casualties on this day; twenty-five of their fighters were shot down defending the beachhead.[540]

By June 8, D+2, seven German fighter groups were now in Normandy engaging the Americans, but the airplan held them off. The Eighth again walled off the beaches, with good results.[541] So bloodied were the Germans by the combat that by June 16 the Luftwaffe withdrew five of its groups for repairs.[542]

For fourteen consecutive days after D-Day, the bombers, fighters, and reconnaissance planes flew at maximum effort. Every available aircraft and every available aircrew flew on days when flying was possible. It was only on June 20 that Doolittle dropped the maximum-effort requirement to 60 percent of crews and planes. The aircrews were as worn down as the soldiers on the ground.

Ninth Air Force engineering battalions landed on D-Day and fought across the sand through the hail of bullets to make their way to the top of the ridge just above Omaha Beach. They scraped off the topsoil behind the bluffs and laid out an emergency airstrip, which was sufficiently prepared to land planes that very night. Better airfields quickly followed. An improved airfield with a runway 5,000 feet long opened on June 11, thus beginning the movement of American airplanes from Britain to bases in France. Within ten days of D-Day, four airfields were ready for use, allowing American aircraft to be based in France for the first time ever since the start of World War II.

Some of the first planes to land were the P-38s. As they came down, they taxied to the side of the runway, and before they were left for the night, a canvas cover was pulled over the cockpit canopies. Near them a windsock snapped in the wind.[543]

With the construction of airfields and the advance of American soldiers, it was no longer true that bailing out over Europe meant a near-certain trip to a POW camp.[544] Remembered one of the pilots to occupy the first airfield, the conditions were crude, but at least it was in France: "D+1 we were in France … we were on a dirt airfield. You had to wait until the guy ahead of you took off, until the dust and junk could clear, before you could take off."[545] They were on French soil for the first time since the Battle of Britain, for the first time since Pearl Harbor, for the first time since the landings in North Africa. One Ninth Air Force pilot was moved to Advanced Landing Strip A01, located behind the beaches at St. Pierre-du-Mont. His squadron lived in five-man tents and they ate K rations and reconstituted beef. They flew in support of the infantry using their .50-caliber machine guns to help the soldiers advance against the Germans.

The new airfields were surrounded by American 90-mm antiaircraft guns to protect them from attack. One airman complained that the shrapnel falling from the bursting shells of the American flak was a far greater hazard than the nighttime raids by the German Air Force. He may have well noted, too, that for the first time since the Schweinfurt raid, the Germans were now on the receiving end of the sort of flak that had killed so many of his own friends.[546]

General Ira Eaker, of the Fifteenth Air Force, was in Moscow with the U.S. ambassador to Russia, Averell Harriman, when he heard the news about D-Day. The invasion held particular significance to the Russians, who had waited an eternity for the Allies to open a second front before their own soldiers collapsed against the German onslaught in the East. "Moscow was awash with a boozy good feeling," Harriman wrote. One of his assistants was in a Moscow restaurant when the news broke. "[He] found himself being toasted and embraced all night long by Russians he had never met." Harriman went to the Kremlin on June 10 to give Stalin an update on the progress in Normandy. The strain from years of war seemed to have vanished. Stalin seemed to be a new man. "Stalin at last acknowledged the tremendous achievement of Allied arms successfully crossing the Channel. He said, 'The history of war has never witnessed such a grandiose operation.'"[547]

Perhaps understandably, the mood in Washington, D.C., was quite different from that of Moscow. American involvement in the war was now in its third year. The war had already cost so many families so much; the invasion only meant more death and injury to the men overseas. While in Moscow, the invasion was seen as the beginning of the end of the terrible deaths, in Washington it was seen as the beginning of more. "D-Day in Washington was more a day of prayer than elation," said Katherine Marshall, George Marshall's wife. "The churches were crowded. There was no celebration such as there had been on the night of the African landings. Our hospitals by now were filled with wounded."[548]

General Pete Quesada won the eternal gratitude of the ground commanders for his remarkable fighting spirit and his pioneering work in close air support. His fighter pilots roamed the skies above their fellow soldiers and swooped down to help as often as they could, many times at the cost of their own lives. The night before Quesada was to rotate back to the United States, a packed room said their goodbyes. Eisenhower, Bradley, and George Patton were among those sending him off. "I have never seen so much affection between air and ground officers as I saw last night when General Quesada left us," said one airman.[549]

Sometime after the war, Ike asked Omar Bradley to rank the thirty most important generals in the order of the importance they played in the defeat of Germany. Eisenhower's own chief of staff General Walter Bedell Smith ranked first, followed by Tooey Spaatz, then the great ground general Courtney Hicks Hodges. George Patton was sixth, and the well-known Doolittle was seventeenth. But Sir Elwood R. "Pete" Quesada, knighted by the King, came in at number four.[550] "I realize that their work may not catch the headlines any more than does the work of some of our foot soldiers," said Bradley of Quesada's ground pounding pilots, "but I am sure that I express the feelings of every ground-force commander from squad leaders to myself as Army Commander when I extend my congratulations on their very fine work."[551]

Quesada retired in 1951 and had a successful career in private industry as well as in public service. Among his accomplishments, newly elected President Dwight D. Eisenhower made him the first director of the new Federal Aviation Administration.

Tooey Spaatz's resolve to win air supremacy before D-Day was a gamble that paid off handsomely. The British, who had successfully fought off the Germans in the skies over England in 1940, had wanted to fight them off in the skies over the Normandy beaches, but Spaatz had argued otherwise. Spaatz didn't want the Luftwaffe in Normandy at all. His application of all-in airpower, which had succeeded in North Africa, was the catalyst that animated the airwar against Germany. He reduced their forces in Western Europe to a few hundred fighters. His 130-mile wall blocked the Nazis' forward movement. His airfield plan created the chaos he wanted and slowed the Luftwaffe from marshaling a meaningful attack on D-Day. Spaatz ushered in the era of airpower and wrote his precepts across the skies over Europe.

Spaatz left Europe after the German surrender to take over the American bombing against Japan. One of the earliest of all military aviators, Spaatz would oversee the first use of the atomic bomb. In 1947, Spaatz became the first chief of staff for the newly independent United States Air Force.

The divide between British and American senior air officers was not resolved by the success of Pointblank or by the airwar victory of D-Day. RAF Air Marshal Arthur Travers Harris' insistence on bombing German cities by night versus the far more effective American strategy of bombing military targets by day created friction that only deepened as the war went on. Spaatz later commented on it in one of his rare postwar assessments. "We always attacked only legitimate military targets with one exception—the capital of a hostile nation," said Spaatz, speaking about American daylight bombing versus the British raids that targeted cities. "Berlin was the administrative and communication center of Germany and thus became a military target … Our stand was that we would bomb only strategic areas—not areas. I believed we could win the war more quickly that way. It was not for religious or moral reasons that I did not go along with urban area bombing."[552]

Faulty British intelligence did little to mitigate the friction between the Americans and their British counterparts. British estimates of German air strength stretched American manufacturing resources thin and often forced Hap Arnold to use his advocacy to increase production of bombers and fighters when it was entirely unnecessary. Arnold had tens of thousands of freshly graduated airmen ready to come to England, and a like number of airplanes, all at considerable and, as it turned out, unnecessary expense. The sudden success in the air blindsided Arnold and forced him to cancel hard-earned programs back home and send his well-trained aviators to the other branches. This only added to the resentment he'd harbored against the British throughout most of the war. Arnold spoke to his diary on D+6 and vented some of his frustrations: "What have RAF done to defeat GAF since Battle of Britain? Have they tried to increase range of their fighters? Did they give us any encouragement when we said that we were going to force the GAF to fight us and we were going to defeat and destroy them? Did they keep the belly tanks on the P-51s we gave them? No. Have they used any to penetrate into the heart of Germany? No. Could they put additional gas in their Spitfires? No. We did and raised the range to 1,300 miles. It took us but 2 months, and yet they tell the world the strength of the GAF and we accept their figures."[553]

Hap Arnold had more than Germany on his plate. As the overall commanding general of the Army Air Forces, he had two theaters to concern himself with. Even before VE Day, May 8, 1945, Arnold had turned his attention to the airwar against Japan. He overhauled his command in the Pacific, installing Spaatz and General Curtis LeMay to direct operations from Guam. Arnold's vision, which resulted in the long-range B-29, proved providential. The Superfortress was the only bomber that could reach Japan from forward bases in Guam, and it helped end the war without a single American soldier setting foot on the island nation.

During World War II, Arnold suffered multiple heart attacks, but he never retired and he was never replaced. Upon the end of hostilities against Japan, he finally stepped down and retired to his ranch in Sonoma, California. In 1949, Congress recognized his enormous achievement and promoted him to the permanent rank of General of the Air Force. When he died in 1950, Arnold was given a state funeral.

The D-Day air offensive was staggering and truly multinational in scale. In addition to the RAF and USAAF, there were twenty-eight air squadrons from Canada, fourteen squadrons from Poland, seven from Australia, six from France, five from New Zealand, and two squadrons each from Czechoslovakia, Belgium, Holland, and Norway.[554]

The B-17s and B-24s flew 2,362 sorties that day using 1,729 different Forts and Liberators with the loss of just three aircraft, two due to a midair collision and one to flak. The Ninth Air Force launched 4,371 sorties, losing twenty-two aircraft, including two F-6 reconnaissance aircraft, the modified P-51, nine fighter-bombers, and eleven mediums.[555]

The Eighth's fighters flew 1,949 sorties with twenty-five lost and four heavily shot up.[556] The Ninth shot down five Germans, two by the mediums and three by the reconnaissance pilots.[557]

Reconnaissance pilots flew 168 sorties on D-Day, one third of them in unarmed P-38s. On the night of June 6–7, their photography labs developed some 10,000 prints, which photo interpreters swarmed over to glean the latest intelligence and prepare the next days' target lists.[558]

The GAF flew 309 sorties of all types, the overwhelming majority of which failed to reach the beaches. Thirty-three fighters were shot down.[559]

Pointblank succeeded, but at an enormous price. Between January 1 and June 31, 1944, a total of 22,946 U.S. airmen were casualties of the air campaign, all but 2,723 of whom were killed or taken prisoner. The Eighth and Ninth lost 1,523 fighters, and the Eighth and Fifteenth lost 1,935 B-17s and B-24s in combat. The Ninth lost another 116 light and medium bombers.[560]

The Normandy invasion involved 6,939 Allied ships and landing craft. The British, Canadians, and Americans put 156,000 men ashore on D-Day. A total of 11,590 RAF and USAAF aircraft were available to support the landings.[561]

The Eighth Air Force remained in England, but in liberated France, airfields were now available to the aircrews, and what a difference it made. A damaged bomber with wounded men on board could now get down quickly, without having to hobble across the English Channel and hope for the best. Between D-Day and the end of 1944, 517 shot-up aircraft landed in France and were salvaged. On June 10, 1944, Pete Quesada wired London to announce that he had formally relocated his command; it was now on European soil, a milestone of great significance to those who feared the landings would be pushed back into the sea. "Headquarters IX Tactical Air Command established on the continent," it said, and that was enough.[562] Headquarters for the VIII Fighter Command, the fighter arm of the Eighth Air Force, was established in Belgium on February 1, 1945.[563]

Aerial reconnaissance had helped unravel the riddle of the German aircraft industry. Eighty-three factories had been bombed at least twice, and more than thirty had been hit four times, but new airplanes kept rolling off the lines as if nothing had happened.[564]

When Hitler came to power, just a handful of companies were building aircraft, including Focke-Wulf, Messerschmitt, Heinkel, and Junkers. Hitler's ambitions went well beyond what could come out of a few unimportant aircraft plants building passenger liners for civilian use, so he ordered up new engineering for an all new generation of advanced military fighters and bombers. In short order, the German aircraft industry was nationalized, competition was set aside, and patents and engineering were shared under a new Air Ministry plan that made it easy to play musical chairs with production facilities. For components such as wings, tails, landing gear, and cockpit canopies, multiple subcontractors were given identical contracts to manufacture identical parts. If one subcontractor was bombed out, another simply took its place.

This unusual redundancy helped explain some of the recuperative powers of the German aircraft industry—but not all of it. In addition to shared patents and engineering, German factories operated on a single shift but typically used two buildings and two production lines for most steps in the manufacture process. If one building were destroyed, the other production line would pick up the slack by adding a second shift and thus maintaining the overall output as if nothing had happened. As soon as the damaged production line was returned to normal, back went the workers to a single shift. The genius of it all was in its simplicity.[565]

The attacks by the Forts halted a good deal of the overall fighter production—some 18,492 airplanes that would otherwise have been produced were not, according to one estimate—but plenty more planes continued to be manufactured.[566]

The final answer was revealed in the tiniest increments of unexpected artifacts in the photographs brought back by the recon pilots. New rail spurs and roadways appeared in photos, but they seemed to be going nowhere. Rows of Messerschmitts and Junkers were spotted in places where they ought not to be, in clusters along the edges of forest or next to an autobahn. The facts started to come together, and it became evident that the Germans had moved underground. Indeed, when Germany was finally overrun it was discovered that Daimler-Benz had moved some of its production into a gypsum mine near Heidelberg and some other production into a granite quarry near Budapest. BMW had moved manufacturing into a railroad tunnel near Strasbourg, while Junkers chose a road tunnel for their planes. Messerschmitt moved part of the Me-262 jet into an underground mine, and Heinkel began to produce its Ju-88 in a subway tunnel on the outskirts of Berlin.[567]

It was a far cry from the proud start of the German aircraft industry. Like Saddam Hussein many decades later, some of the proudest names in German industry and some of the most talented engineers in Hitler's Third Reich were now operating out of a hole in the ground.

Air superiority changed life for the Allied airmen. Getting home was no longer entirely fraught with worry. One fighter pilot particularly relished the combination of flying such a fine aircraft as his Mustang without concern that he'd be bounced by a Messerschmitt: "On our return flight, we frequently broke off into flights of four, and by the time we were over territory held by the Allies, we would be down to a low altitude, often as low as 100 feet as we came across France or Belgium. I would remove my oxygen mask and thoroughly enjoy my first cigarette in some hours. The formation would loosen up, and I would enjoy watching the countryside roll by, smoking, maybe eating a candy bar."[568]

The men themselves experienced a wide range of reactions to their airwar. "Guess you're hearing how rough it was over on the French coast a couple of days ago," wrote a pilot to his parents on June 8. "The Jerries are getting a taste of their own medicine now and will be from now on. That is one day I was glad I was flying."[569]

Said Martin Garren, a pilot who flew a B-17 during the war: "It was a matter of honor, duty, family. I was defending my mother, my sister, from invasion. I never felt I was a hero."[570]

A B-17 navigator paraphrased Winston Churchill as he talked about the men he had served with and how they had overcome fear. "Brave men are not necessarily fearless," he said, "but rather they are men that can perform their duties despite their fear."[571]

Others tried to balance it all. Said one gunner after it was over, "I wouldn't take a million dollars for the experience and I wouldn't take a million dollars to go through it again."[572]

Of course, in victory there are plenty of accolades to go around, and as the airmen considered everything that had happened, the traditional rivalries between fighter pilots and bomber crews were set aside. "Fighter pilots get a lot of attention," remembered P-51 fighter pilot Joe Bennett. "But my hat is off to the bomber crews. It takes grit and guts to crawl in a bomber day after day after you saw the hits they took."[573]

But a bomber pilot disagreed. "If it weren't for them, we wouldn't have won the war," he said of the fighter boys.[574]

Better still was the good fortune that B-17 pilot Robert Copp's crew enjoyed: "It was unbelievable to me that my crew went through this ordeal without as much as a scratch."[575] For some things there were simply no explanations.

The airwar was won by men and materiel, but it was won by commanders, too. There is no doubt that America's ability to manufacture planes played a role—B-17s and P-51s were in plentiful supply and the training bases stamped out highly qualified pilots and crewmen as if they, too, were on a production line.

But there was something more to the D-Day victory than that, and it had to do with the make-up of George Marshall, who selected Hap Arnold, and the make-up of Hap Arnold, who replaced Ira Eaker with Tooey Spaatz and Pete Quesada, who in turn outthought and outbattled the German Air Force.

Harry Hopkins, President Roosevelt's close advisor and one of the only American civilians to attend all but one of FDR's summits with Churchill and Stalin during the war, gave thought to the "X" factor of America's commanders. Robert E. Sherwood, Hopkins' biographer, spoke to Hopkins in the final months of his life. "There was one miracle he could not explain," wrote Sherwood. "How did it happen that the United States, an unwarlike and unprepared country if there ever was one, was suddenly able to produce so large and so brilliant a group of military leaders, competent to deal with situations that had never before existed in the history of the world? Where did they come from?"

Sherwood wrote that Hopkins offered no answer. But the question he framed was profound. Where indeed?[576]

Pointblank paved the way to D-Day, which clearly paved the way to the surrender of Germany and the end of World War II. Said Eisenhower after the battles were over, "The brilliant preparatory work of the air forces, a belief in the effectiveness of which was the very cornerstone of the original invasion conception, began months ago and reached its highest intensity at the very moment of landing. It is my conviction that except for this aerial preparation, including as a special mission a prolonged campaign against the transportation systems of northwest Europe, the venture could not have logically been undertaken."[577]

Said Albert Speer of the impact of Pointblank: "The real importance of the airwar consisted in the fact that it opened a second front long before the invasion of Europe. That front was the skies over Germany."[578]

German Field Marshal Albert Kesselring was less circumspect: "Allied air power was the greatest single reason for the German defeat." Hermann Goering echoed Kesselring's perspective: "The Allies must thank the American Air Force for winning the war. If it were not for the American Air Force the invasion would not have succeeded."[579]

Wrote historian Stephen Ambrose of the pilots and their crews, "They had isolated the battlefield from much of the French railway system, they had made it difficult if not impossible for German trucks and tanks to move by day, they had driven the Luftwaffe out of the skies of France."[580]

In late June 1944, Spaatz revealed his own thoughts in a letter to one of his commanders: "The concentrated attacks on Luftwaffe production and product paid the dividends that we always envisioned, the dividend beyond expectation. During the entire first day of the invasion enemy opposition in the air, either fighter or bomber, was next to nil."[581]

As the front line moved inland, church bells rang in the belfries of liberated villages and towns across France, Holland, and Belgium.

Arnold and Marshall met Ike for a dinner at Buckingham Palace with Prime Minister Churchill and King George VI. What a change since the early days of the war when things were so bleak. Wrote Arnold: "It has been three years since I was at Buckingham Palace. I arrived there then just after a heavy GAF bombardment in which some considerable damage was done. The King and Queen narrowly escaped injury, the windows in the Palace were broken, the drafts through the halls made it a most cheerless place. The King was looking for a ray of sunshine. How different now when there is no German threat from land, sea or air. It is a very welcome change, one that is commented on by all, the results of air supremacy and air power."[582]

A week after the landings, Hap Arnold visited Omar Bradley, and together they went to the Normandy beaches. World War II was far from over, but one had to take one's moments when one could. As they walked the very sands that had for months been the focus of their lives, the two generals allowed themselves a small smile and placed a congratulatory arm on each other's shoulders. A photographer captured this unguarded moment, which seemed to honor the thousands of men who had died to liberate this small piece of Western Europe.

And what a journey it had been. The transformation of American factories that ramped up production to make tens of thousands of bombers and fighters. The hard-fought aerial combat. The missions to Regensburg and Schweinfurt and Münster. The airplan, the interdiction plan, the deception, and the secrecy. Yes, the boys were ashore, and they would never turn back as they marched through bitter combat toward final victory. But today, for this brief moment forever memorialized on film, D-Day was behind them. The invasion had succeeded. This sand was now their sand. This beach was now their beach. This walk was a well-earned reward for a job well done.

Tomorrow would come soon enough.

NOTES

1   Applebaum, Cpl. Melvin. *Within the Parenthesis*. Unpublished manuscript, The Mighty Eighth Air Force Museum, Collections. Courtesy of the Mighty Eighth Air Force Museum, Pooler, GA, 2006.0360A.0131. Mighty Eighth Air Force Museum referred to hereafter as MEAFM.

Preface

2   Ethell, Jeffrey L., and Dr. Alfred Price. *Target Berlin: Mission 250: 6 March 1944*. London: Greenhill Books, 2002, pp. 113–114.

3   *Ibid*.

4   Astor, Gerald. *The Mighty Eighth*. New York: Dell Publishing, 1998, pp. 233–234.

Chapter 1

5   Nail, N. Kenneth, Ed. *Mississippians in the Mighty Eighth*. Tupelo, MS: Mississippi Chapter—Eighth Air Force Historical Society, 1999, p. 29.

6   Clements, James, Ed. *Silent Heroes Among Us: Final Flights of the Mighty Eighth*. Far Hills, NJ: New Horizons Publishing Company, 1996, p. 191.

7   Hawkins, Ian. *B-17s over Berlin*. Dulles, VA: Potomac Books, 1990, p. 95.

8   Hawkins, *B-17s over Berlin*, p. 264.

9   Hawkins, *B-17s over Berlin*, p. 121.

10   Ethell and Price, *Target Berlin*, p. 38.

11   Lindsley, George A., and Margaret E. Lindsley, et al. *Always Out Front: The Bradley Story*. Retrieved June 6, 2012, from http://www.ibiblio.org/hyperwar/AAF/Bradley/index.html.

12   Bowman, Martin. W. *Great American Air Battles of World War II*. Shrewsbury, UK: Airlife, 1994, p. 104.

13   Boiten, Theo and Martin Bowman. *Battles with the Luftwaffe: The Bomber Campaign Against Germany 1942–1945*. New York: HarperCollins, 2001, p. 136.

14   Griggs, Alan L., Ed. *Flying Flak Alley: Personal Accounts of World War II Bomber Crew Combat*. Jefferson, NC: McFarland & Company, 2008, p. 192.

15   Hawkins, *B-17s over Berlin*, p. 19.

16   Griggs, *Flying Flak Alley*, p. 55.

17   Astor, *The Mighty Eighth*, p. 262.

18   Boiten and Bowman, *Battles with the Luftwaffe*, pp. 49, 66, 110, 138, 165, 204, 209.

19   Hawkins, *B-17s over Berlin*, p. 103.

20   Ethell and Price, *Target Berlin*, pp. 63, 133; "Hitler …": Roberts, Andrew. *The Storm of War: A New History of World War II*. New York, Harper Perennial, 2011, p. 435.

21   Hawkins, *B-17s over Berlin*, pp. 162, 205.

22   Griggs, *Flying Flak Alley*, p. 94.

23   Dickfeld, Adolf. Translated by David Johnston. *Footsteps of the Hunter*. Winnipeg, Canada: J. J. Fedorowicz Publishing, 1993, p. 168.

24   Hawkins, *B-17s over Berlin*, p. 189.

25   Griggs, *Flying Flak Alley*, p. 102.

26   Robert Copp. Oral History, 392nd Bomb Group Memorial Collection, MEAFM, 2005.0020.0543.

27   Griggs, *Flying Flak Alley*, p. 34.

28   Astor, *The Mighty Eighth*, p. 505.

29   Astor, *The Mighty Eighth*, p. 200.

30   Norris, Joe. L., Captain. *The Combined Bomber Offensive 1 January to 6 June 1944*. Washington, DC: AAF Historical Offices, p. 10.

31   Galland, Adolf. *The First and the Last*. New York: Henry Holt, p. 148.

32   *Ibid.*

33   Craven, Wesley Frank and James Lea Cate. *The Army Air Forces in World War II*, 7 vols. Chicago: University of Chicago Press, Table 35.

34   Applebaum, *Within the Parenthesis*, 2006.0360A.0131.

35   Ambrose, Stephen. *D-Day June 6, 1944*. New York: Touchstone, 1995, p. 239n*.

Chapter 2

36   Fischer, Wolfgang, *Luftwaffe Fighter Pilot: Defending the Reich Against the RAF and the USAAF*, Edited and translated by John Weal. London: Grub Street, 2010, p. 126, "lights like water fleas," Galland, p. 132; average kills in 1943: Caldwell, Donald. *The JG 26 War Diary: Volume Two 1943–1945*. London: Grub Street, 1996, p. 169; Dickfeld, *Footsteps of the Hunter*, p. 165.

37   Luftwaffe strength, see: http://www.feldgrau.com/stats.html, last accessed February 2012.

38   Dickfeld, *Footsteps of the Hunter*, p. 153.

39   Milch quoted in Eric Hammel, *The Road to Big Week: The Struggle for Daylight Air Supremacy over Western Europe*. Pacifica, CA: Pacifica Press, 2009, p. 267.

40   Koppel, Erwin. Wisconsin Veterans Museum Research Center, 2003, p. 14.

41   Griggs, *Flying Flak Alley*, p. 48.

42   Tracy, Edward H. *The War Years: The Memoirs of Edward H. Tracy*. Unpublished manuscript, December 1999, p. 23, MEAFM, 2003.1617.0001

43   Koppel, Erwin. Wisconsin Veterans Museum Research Center, 2003, p. 5.

44   Griggs, *Flying Flak Alley*, p. 187.

45   Stout, Jay A. *The Men Who Killed the Luftwaffe: The U.S. Army Air Forces Against Germany in World War II*. Mechanicsburg, PA: Stackpole Books, 2010, p. 225.

46   Boiten and Bowman, *Battles with the Luftwaffe*, p. 21.

47   Astor, *The Mighty Eighth*, p. 291.

48   Bill Kamemitsa. Oral History, MEAFM, 2005.0020.0538.

49   Toothman, M. Lee. *My War Years*. Unpublished manuscript. MEAFM, 2003.0051.0001.

50 Ethell, *Target Berlin*, pp. 41–42.

51 Quoted in Hansen, *Fire and Fury*, p. 158.

52 Donald, David, Ed. *American Warplanes of World War II*. London: Aerospace Publishing, 1995, p. 17.

53 Boiten and Bowman, *Battles with the Luftwaffe*, p. 15.

54 Bekker, Cajus. *The Luftwaffe War Diaries*. Translated and edited by Frank Ziegler. New York: Ballantine Books, 1975, p. 490.

55 Dickfeld, *Footsteps of the Hunter*, p. 165.

56 Boiten and Bowman, *Battles with the Luftwaffe*, p. 21.

57 *Ibid.*

58 Dickfeld, *Footsteps of the Hunter*, p. 165.

59 Buchner, *Stormbird*, p. 192.

60 Galland, *The First and the Last*, p. 179.

61 Galland, *The First and the Last*, p. 155.

62 *Ibid.*

63 Holmes, Tony, Ed. *Dogfight: The Greatest Aerial Duels of World War II*. Oxford, UK: Osprey Publishing, 2011, p. 137.

64 Caldwell, Donald L. *JG 26, Top Guns of the Luftwaffe*. New York: Ivy Books, 1993, p. 189.

65 Ethell, Jeffrey. *Bomber Command*. Osceola, WI: Motorbooks, 1994, p. 139.

66 Ethell, Jeffrey. *Target Berlin*, p. 69.

67 Astor, *The Mighty Eighth*, p. 217.

68 Cowley, Robert, Ed. *No End Save Victory, Perspectives on World War II*. New York: Berkley Trade, 2002, p. 275.

69 Caldwell, *The JG 26 War Diary: Volume Two 1943–1945*, p. 254.

70 Astor, *The Mighty Eighth*, p. 230.

71 Cowley, *No End Save Victory*, p. 264.

72 Astor, *The Mighty Eighth*, p. 291.

73 Craven and Cate, *The Army Air Forces in World War II*, pp. 331–333.

74 Robert Copp. Oral History, 392nd Bomb Group Memorial Collection, MEAFM, 2005.0020.0543.

75 Cowley, *No End Save Victory*, pp. 269–270.

76 Perret, Geoffrey. *Winged Victory: The Army Air Forces in World War II*. New York: Random House, 1997, p. 275.

77 Hawkins, *B-17s over Berlin*, p. 65.

78 Cowley, *No End Save Victory*, p. 270.

79 Perret, *Winged Victory*, p. 276.

80   Roy Kennett. Oral History, 392nd Bomb Group Memorial
      Collection, MEAFM, 2005.0020.0544.
81   Ethell, *Target Berlin*, p. 91.
82   Nail, *Mississippians in the Mighty Eighth*, p. 112.
83   Astor, *The Mighty Eighth*, pp. 147–148.
84   Hawkins, *B-17s over Berlin*, p. 70.
85   Caldwell, *JG26*, p. 164.
86   Astor, *The Mighty Eighth*, p. 238; Münster data from Caldwell,
      JG26, p. 188.
87   Cowley, *No End Save Victory*, p. 271.
88   Nail, *Mississippians in the Mighty Eighth*, p. 188.
89   Münster attack casualties: Hansen, *Fire and Fury*, p. 138;
      Luftwaffe statistics: Caldwell, *JG26*, pp. 188–189; Miller, Donald
      L. *Masters of the Air: America's Bomber Boys Who Fought the Air
      War Against Nazi Germany*. New York: Simon & Schuster, 2006,
      p. 208.
90   Cowley, *No End Save Victory*, pp. 269–270.
91   Hawkins, *B-17s over Berlin*, p. 60.

Chapter 3

92   Hansen, *Fire and Fury*, p. 279.
93   Norris, *The Combined Bomber Offensive 1 January to 6 June 1944*,
      p. 26.
94   Harrison, Gordan A. *Cross Channel Attack*. Washington, DC:
      Center of Military History, U.S. Army, 1993, p. 68.
95   Norris, *The Combined Bomber Offensive 1 January to 6 June 1944*,
      p. 25.
96   Hall, R. Cargill. *Case Studies in Strategic Bombardment*.
      Washington, DC: Air Force History and Museum Program, p.
      192. Several dates exist for Pointblank, but its issuance was dated
      June 10, 1943.
97   Craven and Cate, *The Army Air Forces in World War II, 1942–
      1943*, p. 670.
98   Miller, John "Jack" R. Wisconsin Veterans Museum Research
      Center, 1994, p. 12.
99   Keeney, L. Douglas, Ed., *The War Against the Luftwaffe: 1943–
      1944*. Campbell, CA: FastPencil, 2012, p. 92.
100   McFarland, Stephen and Wesley Phillips Newton. *To Command*

the Sky: The Battle for Air Superiority over Germany, 1942–1944.
Washington, DC: Smithsonian Institution Press, 2006, p. 136.

101   Norris, *The Combined Bomber Offensive 1 January to 6 June 1944*,
       p. 10.
102   Koppel, Erwin. Wisconsin Veterans Museum Research Center,
       2003, pp. 15–16.
103   Nail, *Mississippians in the Mighty Eighth*, p. 29.
104   Perret, *Winged Victory*, p. 277.
105   Koppel, Erwin, Wisconsin Veterans Museum Research Center,
       2003, p. 13.
106   Miller, John "Jack" R. Wisconsin Veterans Museum Research
       Center, 1994, p. 15.
107   Hawkins, *B-17s over Berlin*, p. 124.
108   Photos retrieved November 11, 2011, from http://www.
       thirdreichruins.com/schweinfurt.htm.
109   Statistics: USAAF.
110   Craven and Cate, *The Army Air Forces in World War II, 1942–
       1943*, p. 719.

Chapter 4

111   Letters of William J. Moore, pilot 85th BG, MEAFM,
       2008.0242.0118.
112   Freeman, Roger A. *Airfields of the Eighth Then and Now*. London:
       Battle of Britain Prints International, 1978, p. 7.
113   Van Ellis, Mark, Interviewer. Transcript of an Oral History with
       Kermit E. Bliss, Eighth Air Force Photo-Reconnaissance Pilot,
       European Theater, WWII, p. 6.
114   Astor, *The Mighty Eighth*, p. 206.
115   Nail, *Mississippians in the Mighty Eighth*, p. 47.
116   Boiten and Bowman, *Battles with the Luftwaffe*, p. 30.
117   Koppel, Erwin. Wisconsin Veterans Museum Research Center,
       2003, p. 12.
118   Bill Kamemitsa. Oral History, MEAFM, 2005.0020.0538.
119   *Ibid.*
120   Baldridge, Lt. Arlen. *Welcome to the 368th*. Unpublished
       manuscript, MEAFM, 2010.0092.0001.
121   Robert Copp, Oral History, 392nd Bomb Group Memorial
       Collection, MEAFM, 2005.0020.0543.

122   Mackay, Ron. *First in the Field: The 1st Air Division over Europe in World War II*, Atglen, PA, Schiffer Publishing Ltd., 2007, p. 151.

123   Lundy, Will. "Guard Duty." MEAFM, 2005.0804.0593.

124   Ankeny, Harry R. *Sorties and Combat Flying Time of Capt. Harry R. Ankeny, 22 August 1944*, MEAFM, 2006.0360A.0036.

Chapter 5

125   Havers, Robin. *The Second World War: Europe, 1939–1943, Volume 4*. Abingdon, Oxford, UK: Routledge, 2003, p. 69.

126   McFarland, *To Command the Sky*, p. 135.

127   Craven and Cate, *The Army Air Forces in World War II, Vol. 3*, pp. 328, 338.

128   Craven and Cate, *The Army Air Forces in World War II, Vol. 3*, pp. 322, 338; Carter, Kit C. and Robert Mueller. *The Army Air Forces in World War II: Combat Chronology, 1941–1945*. Washington, DC: Center for Air Force History, p. 173. Hereafter referred to as *Combat Chronology*.

129   McFarland, *To Command the Sky*, p. 113.

130   *Ibid.*

131   Mets, David R. *Master of Airpower: General Carl A. Spaatz*. Novato, CA: Presidio Press, 1997, p. 36.

132   Davis, Richard G. *Carl A. Spaatz and the Air War in Europe*, Appendix 9. Washington, DC: Center for Air Force History.

133   Galland, *The First and the Last*, p. 144.

134   Hughes, Thomas Alexander. *Over Lord: General Pete Quesada and the Triumph of Tactical Air Power in World War II*. New York: The Free Press, 2002, p. 96.

135   Mets, Donald R., *Master of Airpower*, p. 156.

136   Galland, *The First and the Last*, p. 144.

137   Davis, *Carl A. Spaatz and the Air War in Europe*, p. 140.

138   Davis, *Carl A. Spaatz and the Air War in Europe*, p. 287.

139   Davis, *Carl A. Spaatz and the Air War in Europe*, p. 300.

140   "Concede fact:" McFarland, *To Command the Sky*, p. 307; Doolittle quoted in Davis, *Carl A. Spaatz and the Air War in Europe*, p. 359.

141   Hammel, *The Road to Big Week*, p. 302.

Chapter 6

142   Mets, *Master of Airpower*, p. 183.
143   Davis, *Carl A. Spaatz and the Air War in Europe*, Appendix 8. This
      includes aircraft assigned to the Ninth over which Spaatz had
      administrative control and no small measure of influence, as well
      as aircraft in Italy.
144   Mets, *Master of Airpower*, p. 191.
145   Davis, *Carl A. Spaatz and the Air War in Europe* p. 358.
146   Hawkins, *B-17s over Berlin*, p. 213.
147   Davis, *Carl A. Spaatz and the Air War in Europe*, p. 360.
148   Davis, *Carl A. Spaatz and the Air War in Europe*, p. 301.

Chapter 7

149   It would later be moved to June.
150   Cooling, Benjamin Franklin, Ed. *Case Studies in Achievement of
      Air Superiority*. Washington, DC: Air Force History and Museum
      Program, p. 285.
151   Buchner, *Stormbird*, p. 208.
152   Fischer, *Luftwaffe Fighter Pilot*, p. 130.
153   Norris, *The Combined Bomber Offensive, 1 January to 6 June 1944*,
      pp. 102–106.
154   Boiten and Bowman, *Battles with the Luftwaffe*, p. 143.
155   Mombeek, Eric. *Luftwaffe: A Pictorial History*. Wiltshire, UK:
      Crowood Press Ltd., 1997, p. 126.
156   Miller, *Masters of the Air*, p. 71.
157   Miller, *Masters of the Air*, p. 247.
158   Hall, *Case Studies in Strategic Bombardment*, p. 214.
159   McFarland, *To Command the Sky*, p. 202.
160   Hall, *Case Studies in Strategic Bombardment*, p. 216; "bait them
      and kill them:" Hansen, *Fire and Fury*, p. 172; "Your job," Hall,
      Case Studies in Strategic Bombardment, p. 213; Norris, *The
      Combined Bomber Offensive, 1 January to 6 June 1944*, p. 101.

Chapter 8

161   Koppel, Erwin. Wisconsin Veterans Museum Research Center,
      2003, p. 9.

NOTES

162   Toothman, *My War Years*, 2003.0051.0001.
163   Oral History, Robert Copp, 392nd Bomb Group Memorial
       Collection, MEAFM, 2005.0020.0543.
164   Howland, John W. *D-Day Raid on Gold Beach June 6, 1944*.
       Unpublished manuscript. Savannah, GA: The Eighth Air Force
       Historical Society, 2000. 2007.0086.0002, p. 9.
165   Miller, John "Jack" R. Wisconsin Veterans Museum Research
       Center, 1994, p. 18.
166   Howland, John W. *D-Day Attack By The 8th Air Force*. Savannah,
       GA: The Eighth Air Force Historical Society, 2000.
       2007.0086.0002, p. 9.
167   Toothman, *My War Years*, 2003.0051.0001.
168   Ward, Geoffrey C., and Ken Burns. *The War: An Intimate History,
       1941–1945*. New York: Alfred A. Knopf, 2007, p. 120.
169   Craven and Crate, *The Army Air Forces in World War II. Volume II*,
       p. 271.
170   Norris, *The Combined Bomber Offensive 1 January to 6 June 1944*,
       pp. 70–72.
171   Hall, *Case Studies in Strategic Bombardment*, p. 241n3.
172   Wood, Richard A. *War Stories of the O&W A History of the 486th
       Bomb Group (Heavy)*. RSB Publications, 1996, p. 87.
173   Sullivan, John J. *Overlord's Eagles: Operations of the United States
       Army Air Forces in the Invasion of Normandy in World War II*.
       Jefferson, NC: McFarland & Company, 2005, p. 107.

Chapter 9

174   Taylor, Glenn E. *Sitting One Out*. Unpublished manuscript,
       MEAFM, 2003.1674.0001.
175   Davis, *Carl A. Spaatz and the Air War in Europe*, p. 323.
176   Retrieved March 2, 2012, from http://www.taphilo.com/
       history/8thaf/8aflosses.shtml.
177   Hansen, *Fire and Fury*, p. 172.
178   Hammel, *The Road to Big Week*, p. 339.
179   Hammel, *The Road to Big Week*, p. 338.
180   Ethell, *Target Berlin*, p. 32.
181   Hammel, *The Road to Big Week*, p. 345; see also: http://www.taphilo.
       com/history/8thaf/8aflosses.shtml, last accessed March 12, 2012.

182   Hammel, *The Road to Big Week*, p. 348.
183   McFarland, *To Command the Sky*, p. 180.
184   McFarland, *To Command the Sky*, p. 188.
185   Hammel, *The Road to Big Week*, p. 353; see also http://www.taphilo. com/history/8thaf/8aflosses.shtml, last accessed March 12, 2012.
186   Davis, *Carl A. Spaatz and the Air War in Europe*, p. 323.
187   Davis, *Carl A. Spaatz and the Air War in Europe*, p. 326.
188   McFarland, *To Command the Sky*, p. 354.
189   Davis, *Carl A. Spaatz and the Air War in Europe*, p. 323.
190   Hammel, *The Road to Big Week*, p. 344.

Chapter 10

191   Quesada was second in command but operated under the ineffective leadership of General Lewis Brereton.
192   Groups varied. A reconnaissance group may have had as few as thirty airplanes, but the typical fighter group had 110 or more. See: Hughes, *Over Lord*, pp. 112, 124.
193   Norris, *The Combined Bomber Offensive 1 January to 6 June 1944*, pp. 183–184; Hughes, *Over Lord*, p. 127.
194   Hughes, *Over Lord*, pp. 128–129.
195   Rust, Kenn C. *The Ninth Air Force in World War II*. Fallbrook, CA: Aero, 1990, p. 64.
196   Davis, *Carl A. Spaatz and the Air War in Europe*, p. 409; Hughes, *Over Lord*, p. 136.
197   Fairfield, Terry A., *The 479th Fighter Group in World War II in Action over Europe in the P-38 and P-51*. Atglen, PA: Schiffer Publishing, 2004, p. 61.
198   *Ibid.*
199   Ethell, *Fighter Command*, p. 149.
200   Astor, *The Mighty Eighth*, pp. 184, 206.
201   Ethell, *Fighter Command*, p. 164.
202   Ethell, *Fighter Command*, p. 131.
203   *Ibid.*
204   "bait them and kill them:" Hansen, *Fire and Fury*, p. 172; "Your job:" Hall, *Case Studies in Strategic Bombardment*, p. 213.
205   McFarland, *To Command the Sky*, p. 284n22.
206   McFarland, *To Command the Sky*, p. 270n22.
207   Craven and Cate, *The Army Air Forces in World War II*, Table 128.

Chapter 11

208   Miller, John "Jack" R. Wisconsin Veterans Museum Research
       Center, 1994, p. 15.
209   Crowley, *No End Save Victory*, p. 265.
210   _____. *German Air Forces in Air Defense Operations*.
       AFHRA, Maxwell AFB, 1956, AFD-090519-039, pp. 590, 600.
211   See Roberts, *The Storm of War*; McFarland, *To Command the Sky*,
       p. 121; "8th Air Force of the Army Air Force, World War II,"
       retrieved June 6, 2012, from http://www.taphilo.com/
       history/8thaf/index.shtml.
212   Otten, *Battles with the Luftwaffe*, p. 131.
213   Muller, Werner. *The Heavy Flak Guns, 1933–1945*. Translated by
       Dr. Edward Force. West Chester, PA: Schiffer Publishing, 1990,
       pp. 21, 110, 131, 139.
214   Tilman, Barrett. *Brassey's D-Day Encyclopedia*. Dulles, VA:
       Potomac Books, 2004, p. 30.
215   Davis, *Carl A. Spaatz and the Air War in Europe*, p. 375 (caption);
       Muller, *The Heavy Flak Guns*, p. 139.
216   Muller, *The Heavy Flak Guns*, p. 88.
217   Cowley, *No End Save Victory*, p. 503.
218   Tracy, *The War Years*, p. 41.
219   Cowley, *No End Save Victory*, p. 503; "German Air Defenses:
       Flak," retrieved June 6, 2012, from http://histclo.com/essay/war/
       ww2/air/eur/sbc/gd/flak.html.
220   Ethell, *Target Berlin*, p. 98.
221   O'Neil, Brian D. *Half a Wing, Three Engines, and a Prayer*. New
       York: McGraw-Hill, 1999, p. 215.
222   Boiten and Bowman, *Battles with the Luftwaffe*, p. 131.
223   Ethell, *Target Berlin*, p. 96.
224   Hogg, Ian V. *Barrage: The Guns in Action*. London: MacDonald &
       Co., 1971.
225   Astor, *The Mighty Eighth*, pp. 181–182.
226   Tracy, *The War Years*, p. 47.
227   _____. *German Air Forces in Air Defense Operations*, p. 600.

Chapter 12

228 Craven and Cate, *The Army Air Forces in World War II, Vol. 3*, p. 139.

229 Craven and Cate, *The Army Air Forces in World War II, Vol. 3*, pp. 150–181.

230 Davis, *Carl A. Spaatz and the Air War in Europe*, p. 306.

231 Craven and Cate, *The Army Air Forces in World War II, Vol. 3*, pp. 150–181.

232 Ethell, *Target Berlin*, p. 20.

233 Ethell, *Target Berlin*, pp. 3–4.

234 Hawkins, *B-17s over Berlin*, p. 67.

235 Hall, *Case Studies in Strategic Bombardment*, p. 217.

236 Hall, *Case Studies in Strategic Bombardment*, p. 218.

237 Ethell, *Target Berlin*, p. 29; Davis, *Carl A. Spaatz and the Air War in Europe*, p. 373.

238 Hall, *Case Studies in Strategic Bombardment*, p. 218.

239 Ethell, *Target Berlin*, pp. 29–30; Perret, *Winged Victory*, pp. 290–291.

240 Ankeny, *Sorties and Combat Flying Time of Capt. Harry R. Ankeny, 22 August 1944,* 2006.0360A.0036.

241 Davis, *Carl A. Spaatz and the Air War in Europe*, p. 373.

242 McFarland, *To Command the Sky*, pp. 214–215.

243 See "Eighth Air Force Combat Losses: Eighth Air Force Combat Losses in World War II." Retrieved June 6, 2012, from http://www.taphilo.com/history/8thaf/8aflosses.shtml.

244 Perret, *Winged Victory*, p. 292.

245 Hawkins, *B-17s over Berlin*, p. 150.

Chapter 13

246 Craven and Cate, *The Army Air Forces in World War II*, Vol. 3, Table 159.

247 Johnson, Charles R. *The History of the Hell Hawks*. Anaheim, CA: Southcoast Typesetting, 1975, p. 64.

248 Keeney, *The War Against the Luftwaffe*, p. 156.

249 Pressentin, Donald "DC." Oral History, Wisconsin Veterans Museum Research Center, 1997, p. 17; Ethell, *Fighter Command*, p.17.

250   Ethell, *Fighter Command*, p. 158.

251   Baldridge, *Welcome to the 368th*, p. 96.

252   *Ibid.*

253   Caldwell, *The JG 26 War Diary*, Volume 2, p. 239.

254   Astor, *The Mighty Eighth*, p. 442.

255   Dickfeld, *Footsteps of the Hunter*, p. 18.

256   Boiten and Bowman, *Battles with the Luftwaffe*, p. 83 (caption).

257   Keeney, *The War Against the Luftwaffe*, p. 153.

258   Carter and Mueller, *Combat Chronology*, p 355.

259   Norris, Joe L. *The Combined Bomber Offensive, 1 January to 6 June 1944*, pp. 114–119.

260   Joiner, O. W., Ed. *The History of the 364th Fighter Group.* Marceline, MO. Walsworth Publishing Company, 1991, p. 108.

261   Bowers, Clifford W. Wisconsin Veterans Museum Research Center, 1994, p. 9.

262   Woodrum, Henry C. *Dogfight over Paris: Aero Album.* Fallbrook, CA: Aero Publishers, 1968. Via MEAFM, 2006.0360A.0103.

263   *Ibid.*

264   George, Lt. Col. Robert H. *Ninth Air Force April to November 1944*. Washington, DC: Army Air Forces Historical Offices, pp. 38–40.

265   Norris, *The Combined Bomber Offensive, 1 January to 6 June 1944*, pp. 162–165; Davis, *Carl A. Spaatz and the Air War in Europe*, p. 410.

266   Craven and Cate, *The Army Air Forces in World War II, Vol. 3*, p. 167.

267   *Ibid.*

268   Craven and Cate, *The Army Air Forces in World War II, Vol. 3*, p. 168.

269   Craven and Cate, *The Army Air Forces in World War II, Vol. 3*, p. 169.

270   Baldridge, *Welcome to the 368th*, p. 101.

271   Buchner, *Stormbird*, p. 230.

272   Buchner, *Stormbird*, p. 242.

273   Craven and Cate, *The United States Army Air Forces in World War II*, Table 118. Retrieved June 6, 2012, from http://www.usaaf.net/digest/t118.htm.

274   Koppel, Erwin. Wisconsin Veterans Museum Research Center, 2003, p. 9.

Chapter 14

275   Harrison, *Cross Channel Attack*, p. 76.
276   Harrison, *Cross Channel Attack*, p. 60.
277   Harrison, *Cross Channel Attack*, p. 77.
278   Harrison, *Cross Channel Attack*, p. 55.
279   Harrison, *Cross Channel Attack*, pp. 56–57.
280   *Ibid.*
281   Ruppenthal, Roland C. *Logistical Support of the Armies, Vol. 1, May 1941–September 1944*. Washington, DC: Center of Military History, United States Army, p. 178.
282   Hennessy, Juliette. *Tactical Operations of the Eighth Air Force 6 June 1944 to 8 May 1945*. Maxwell Air Force Base, AL: USAF Historical Division, p. 19.

Chapter 15

283   Lindsley and Lindsley, *Always Out Front: The Bradley Story.* Retrieved June 6, 2012, from http://www.ibiblio.org/hyperwar/AAF/Bradley/index.html.
284   Letter to Joe DeShay from Pete Peterson. April 30, 1996. MEAFM, 2006.0360A.0095.
285   Hawkins, *B-17s over Berlin*, p. 262.
286   Astor, Gerald, *The Mighty Eighth*, p. 496.
287   Baldridge, *Welcome to the 368th*, p. 95.
288   Galland, *The First and the Last*, pp. 252, 255.
289   Galland, *The First and the Last*, p. 254.
290   Galland, *The First and the Last*, p. 255.
291   Galland, *The First and the Last*, p. 259.
292   Davis, *Carl A. Spaatz and the Air War in Europe*, p. 513.
293   Pressentin, Donald "DC" p. 17.
294   Coenan, Clayton "Clyde" J. Wisconsin Veterans Museum Research Center, 2000, p. 10.
295   Buchner, *Stormbird*, p. 222.
296   Cowley, *No End Save Victory*, p. 504.
297   Huston, Major General John W., Ed. *American Airpower Comes of Age: General Henry H. "Hap" Arnold's World War II Diaries*, 2 vols. Honolulu, HI: University Press of the Pacific, 2004, p. 158.
298   Gruen, Adam L. *Preemptive Defense: Allied Air Power Against Hitler's V-Weapons, 1943–1945*. Washington, DC: Air Force

History and Museum Program, p. 16.

299 Cowley, *No End Save Victory*, pp. 505–506.

300 Norris, *The Combined Bomber Offensive, 1 January to 6 June 1944*, p. 94.

301 _____. *German Air Forces in Air Defense Operations*, p. 600.

Chapter 16

302 Craven and Cate, *The Army Air Forces in World War II, Vol. 3*, p. 185. Figures for operations based on 96 medium bombers per bomb group, 111 fighters per fighter group, adjusted for in-service rates. Squadron strength varied, although more formally there were twenty-five fighters and between seven and nine bombers in a squadron: Craven and Cate, *The Army Air Forces in World War II, Vol. VI*, p. 58.

303 Hennessy, *Tactical Operations of the Eighth Air Force 6 June 1944 to 8 May 1945*, p. 18.

304 George, *Ninth Air Force April to November 1944*. Washington, DC: Army Air Forces Historical Offices, pp. 19, 69.

305 George, *Ninth Air Force April to November 1944*, pp. 19, 21; Hennessy, *Tactical Operations of the Eighth Air Force 6 June 1944 to 8 May 1945*, p. 21.

306 Hennessy, *Tactical Operations of the Eighth Air Force 6 June 1944 to 8 May 1945*, p. 22.

307 Hennessy, *Tactical Operations of the Eighth Air Force 6 June 1944 to 8 May 1945*, pp. 9–10.

308 Hennessy, *Tactical Operations of the Eighth Air Force 6 June 1944 to 8 May 1945*, pp. 11, 16, 20–21.

309 Hennessy, *Tactical Operations of the Eighth Air Force 6 June 1944 to 8 May 1945*, p. 23.

Chapter 17

310 Mets, *Master of Airpower*, p. 205.

311 Davis, *Carl A. Spaatz and the Air War in Europe*, pp. 313, 413.

312 Griggs, *Flying Flak Alley*, pp. 56, 57, 69.

313 Griggs, *Flying Flak Alley*, p. 69.

314 Buchner, *Stormbird*, p. 113.

315   Hansen, *Fire and Fury*, p. 134; "the morale of the pilots …:"
       quoted in Bekker, *The Luftwaffe War Diaries*, p. 471.
316   Baldridge, *Welcome to the 368th*, p. 83.
317   George E. Graham, Jr. Oral History, 392nd Bomb Group
       Memorial Collection, MEAFM, 2005.0020.0540.
318   Galland, *The First and the Last*, p. 195.
319   Ethell, *Target Berlin*, p. 69.
320   Hall, *Case Studies in Strategic Bombardment*, p. 195.
321   Holmes, *Dogfight: The Greatest Aerial Duels of World War II*, p. 137.
322   Hall, *Case Studies in Strategic Bombardment*, p. 237.
323   Ethell, *Target Berlin*, p. 106.
324   Ankeny, *Sorties and Combat Flying Time of Capt. Harry R. Ankeny,
       22 August 1944*. MEAFM, 2006.0360A.0036, p. 8.
325   Cornelius, Rupert G. Oral History, Wisconsin Veterans Museum
       Research Center, p. 20.
326   Ethell, *Target Berlin*, p. 49.
327   Boiten and Bowman, *Battles with the Luftwaffe*, p. 42.
328   Griggs, *Flying Flak Alley*, p. 115.
329   Bowers, Clifford W. Oral History, Wisconsin Veterans Museum
       Research Center, 1994, p. 8.
330   Driscoll, John K., Interviewer. Transcript of an Oral History
       Interview with Harold C. Brown Pilot, U.S. Army Air Corps, World
       War II, 2004, Wisconsin Veterans Museum Research Center, p. 6.
331   Mets, *Masters of Airpower*, p. 206.
332   Craven and Cate, *The Army Air Forces in World War II, Vol. II*, p. 151.
333   Craven and Cate, *The Army Air Forces in World War II, Vol. III*, p. 154.

Chapter 18

334   Ethell, *Fighter Command*, p. 165.
335   Van Ellis, Mark, Interviewer. Transcript of an Oral History
       Interview with Kermit E. Bliss 8th Photo-Reconnaissance Pilot,
       European Theater, WWII, 1995, p. 12.
336   Harlick, Joseph I. *Photographic Career: My Beginning*.
       Unpublished manuscript. MEAFM, 2008.0499.001, p. 6.
337   *Ibid*; Stanley, Col. Roy M. *World War II Photo Intelligence: The First
       Complete History of the Aerial Photo Reconnaissance and Photo
       Interpretation Operations of the Allied and Axis Nations*. New York:
       Scribner, 1981, p. 94.

338 Ethell, *Fighter Command*, p. 167.

339 Ethell, *Fighter Command*, p. 165.

340 Kermit Bliss. Oral History, Wisconsin Veterans Museum Research Center, p. 7.

341 Van Ellis, Mark, Interviewer. Transcript of an Oral History Interview with Kermit E. Bliss 8th Photo-Reconnaissance Pilot, European Theater, WWII, 1995, p. 7.

342 Ethell, *Fighter Command*, p. 169.

343 Van Ellis, Mark, Interviewer. Transcript of an Oral History Interview with Kermit E. Bliss 8th Photo-Reconnaissance Pilot, European Theater, WWII, 1995, p. 11; Stanley, *World War II Photo Intelligence*, pp. 204, 249–250.

344 George, *Ninth Air Force April to November 1944*, pp. 47–48.

345 Van Ellis, Mark, Interviewer. Transcript of an Oral History Interview with Kermit E. Bliss 8th Photo Reconnaissance Pilot, European Theater, WWII, 1995, p. 17.

346 Kermit E. Bliss. Oral History, Wisconsin Veterans Museum, p. 17.

347 34th RPS Association. *Ding the Beaches*. Retrieved June 6, 2012, from http://www.34thprs.org/html/operations/dicing.html; Stanley, *World War II Photo Intelligence*, p. 248.

348 George, *Ninth Air Force April to November 1944*, p. 48.

349 Coles, Harry L. *The Army Air Force in Amphibious Landings in World War II*. Maxwell Air Force Base, AL: USAF Historical Division, 1953, p. 103.

350 George, *Ninth Air Force April to November 1944*, p. 48.

351 34th RPS Association, *Ding the Beaches*.

352 *Ibid.*

353 Lanterman, Raymond E. *D-Day: The Best Laid Plans of Mice and Men...* Retrieved June 6, 2012, from http://www.34thprs.org/html/rlanterman/main.html.

354 Ethell, *Fighter Command*, p. 169.

Chapter 19

355 Ankeny, *Sorties and Combat Flying Time of Capt. Harry R. Ankeny, 22 August 1944*, p. 20.

356 Astor, *The Mighty Eighth*, p. 303.

357 Hall, *Case Studies in Strategic Bombardment*, p. 257.

358 George, *Ninth Air Force April to November 1944*, p. 36; Norris, *The Combined Bomber Offensive, 1 January to 6 June 1944*, p. 166.

359 George, *Ninth Air Force April to November 1944*, pp. 40–44.

360 Carter and Mueller, *Combat Chronology*; see also: *Aircraft Division Industry Report, Second Edition, January 1947*. Retrieved June 6, 2012, from http://www.sturmvogel.orbat.com/airrep.html#Ch2; Craven and Cate, *The Army Air Forces in World War II*, Table 118.

361 George, *Ninth Air Force April to November 1944*, p. 33.

362 Hall, *Case Studies in Strategic Bombardment*, p. 262.

363 Johnson, *The History of the Hell Hawks*, pp. 67–68.

364 Hughes, *Over Lord*, p. 122; Davis, *Carl A. Spaatz and the Air War in Europe*, p. 411; see also Hennessy, *Tactical Operations of the Eighth Air Force 6 June 1944 to 8 May 1945*, p. 180.

365 Buchner, *Stormbird*, p. 196.

366 Boiten and Bowman, *Battles with the Luftwaffe*, p. 41.

367 Norris, *The Combined Bomber Offensive 1 January to 6 June 1944*, p. 196.

368 Ethell, *Target Berlin*, p. 27.

369 Boiten and Bowman, *Battles with the Luftwaffe*, p. 133.

370 Carter and Mueller, *Combat Chronology*; see also: *Aircraft Division Industry Report, Second Edition, January 1947*. Retrieved June 6, 2012, from http://www.sturmvogel.orbat.com/airrep.html#Ch2.

371 Lindsley and Lindsley, *Always Out Front: The Bradley Story*. Retrieved June 6, 2012, from http://www.ibiblio.org/hyperwar/AAF/Bradley/index.html.

372 Davis, *Carl A. Spaatz and the Air War in Europe*, p. 409.

373 Perret, *Winged Victory*, p. 294.

374 Hughes, *Over Lord*, pp. 127, 130–131.

375 Hughes, *Over Lord*, p. 154.

376 Davis, *Carl A. Spaatz and the Air War in Europe*, p. 410; Hughes, *Over Lord*, pp. 130–131.

377 Caldwell, *The JG26 War Diary*, p. 264.

378 McFarland, *To Command the Sky*, p. 233.

379 Caldwell, *The JG26 War Diary*, p. 264; Davis, *Carl A. Spaatz and the Air War in Europe*, Appendix 26.

380 Davis, *Carl A. Spaatz and the Air War in Europe*, p. 409; Hughes, *Over Lord*, p. 135.

381 *Ibid.*

382   Davis, *Carl A. Spaatz and the Air War in Europe*, p. 409; Hughes, *Over Lord*, p. 136.
383   Hughes, *Over Lord*, p. 138.
384   Hall, Anthony. *D-Day: Operation Overlord Day by Day*. Minneapolis, MN: Zenith Press, 2003, pp. 61–62; Kershaw, Robert J. *Piercing the Atlantic Wall*. Sittingbourne, England: Ian Allan, 1993, pp. 33–34; Hughes, *Over Lord*, pp. 134–135. For information about St. Paul's school, see: http://www.lbhf.gov.uk/Directory/News/D_Day_landings_commemorated.asp, last accessed November 7, 2011.
385   Bernard Nelson, Jr. Questionnaire, MEAFM, 2011.0146.001.

Chapter 20

386   Ambrose, *D-Day*, p. 82.
387   Donovan, Lt. Col. Michael J. *Strategic Deception: Operation Fortitude*. Carlisle Barracks, Carlisle, PA: U.S. Army War College, 2002, p. 1.
388   Tavares, Jr., Major Ernest S. *Operation Fortitude: The Closed Loop D-Day Deception Plan*. Research Paper. Maxwell AFB, AL, 2001, p. 14.
389   Craven and Cate, *The Army Air Forces in World War II, Vol. III*, p. 168.
390   Craven and Cate, *The Army Air Forces in World War II, Vol. III*, p. 171.
391   Craven and Cate, *The Army Air Forces in World War II, Vol. III*, p. 180.
392   Hesketh, Roger. *Fortitude: The D-Day Deception Campaign*. London: St. Ermin's Press, 1999, p. 388.
393   Craven and Cate, *The Army Air Forces in World War II, Vol. III*, p. 148.
394   Hesketh, *Fortitude*, p. 121.
395   Craven and Cate, *The Army Air Forces in World War II, Vol. III*, p. 144.
396   Cowley, *No End Save Victory*, pp. 387–388, 399.

Chapter 21

397   Carter and Mueller, *Combat Chronology*; Lindsley and Lindsley, *Always Out Front: The Bradley Story*. Retrieved June 6, 2012, from http://www.ibiblio.org/hyperwar/AAF/Bradley/index.html.

398   Harlan, Ross E. *Strikes: 323rd Bomb Group in World War II*. Oklahoma City, OK: Oklahoma Cavanal Publishers, 2005 p. 62.

399   Keen, Patricia Fussell. *Eyes of the Eighth: A Story of the 7th Photo Reconnaissance Group 1942–1945*. Sun City, AZ: CAVU Publishers, 1996, p. 123.

400   Keen, *Eyes of the Eighth*, p. 122.

401   Davis, *Carl A. Spaatz and the Air War in Europe*, pp. 410–413, 416.

402   Ethell, *Target Berlin*, p. 108

403   Fairfield, *The 479th Fighter Group in World War II in Action over Europe with the P-38 and P-51*, p. 57.

404   Ryan, Cornelius. *The Longest Day*. New York: Simon & Schuster, 1994, pp. 19–21.

405   Fairfield, *The 479th Fighter Group in World War II in Action over Europe with the P-38 and P-51*, p. 57.

406   Lindsley and Lindsley, *Always Out Front: The Bradley Story*. Retrieved June 6, 2012, from http://www.ibiblio.org/hyperwar/AAF/Bradley/index.html.

407   Todd, Webb C. *History of the 68th Bomb Squadron 44th Bomb Group: The Flying Eightballs*. Nashville, TN: Turner Publishing, 1997, p. 174.

408   Driscoll, John K., Interviewer. Transcript of an Oral History Interview with Harold C. Brown Pilot, U.S. Army Air Corps, World War II, 2004, Wisconsin Veterans Museum Research Center, p. 8.

409   Beevor, Antony. *D-Day: The Battle for Normandy*. New York: Penguin, 2010, p. 49.

410   Roberts, *The Storm of War*, p. 469.

411   Applebaum, *Within the Parenthesis*, 2006.0360A.0131.

412   *Ibid.*

413   Fischer, *Luftwaffe Fighter Pilot*, pp. 143–153; see also Cooling, *Case Studies in Air Superiority*, p. 304. Cooling makes the case that rotating fighters not only confused mission planners but resulted in exceptionally low battle losses to the frontline fighter aircraft

largely because they were usually gone by the time a base was attacked or they got off the ground before the attack.

414   Ryan, *The Longest Day*, pp. 80–81.

415   Ryan, *The Longest Day*, p. 85; Priller's squadrons consisted of FW-190s, see Tilman, *Brassey's D-Day Encyclopedia*, pp. 21, 194.

416   Ryan, *The Longest Day*, p. 85.

417   Boiten and Bowman, *Battles with the Luftwaffe*, p. 146. The second group, deployed to Mont de Marsan-Biarritz was deployed to Régime, according to Ryan, in *The Longest Day*, pp. 85–86.

418   Ryan, *The Longest Day*, pp. 85–86.

Chapter 22

419   Ambrose, *D-Day*, p. 241.

420   Davis, *Carl A. Spaatz and the Air War in Europe*, p. 413.

421   Perret, *Winged Victory*, p. 304.

422   Jablonski, A1C Dave. "Young, Old Celebrate 55th Past," *Air Pulse*. Offut AFB, NE, 2005.0804.0133.

423   Applebaum, *Within the Parenthesis*, 2006.0360A.0131.

424   Griggs, *Flying Flak Alley*, p. 70.

425   Caldwell, *The JG 26 War Diary, Vol. Two, 1943–1945*, p. 269.

426   Hughes, *Over Lord*, p. 3; For D-Day statistics, see: http://www.ddaymuseum.co.uk/ faq.htm#casualities, last accessed February 22, 2012.

427   Ambrose, *D-Day*, p. 241.

428   Hughes, *Over Lord*, p. 4.

429   "Marshall received telex:" Perry, Mark. *Partners in Command: George Marshall and Dwight Eisenhower in War and Peace.* New York: Penguin, 2008, p. 298; "at home:" Arnold, H. H. *Global Mission.* Tab Books, 1989, p. 503; Eisenhower quoted in Huston, *American Airpower Comes of Age*, p. 144; stats via Davis, *Carl A. Spaatz and the Air War in Europe*, p. 413.

430   Astor, *The Mighty Eighth*, p. 302.

431   Astor, *The Mighty Eighth*, p. 308.

432   Todd, *History of the 68th Bomb Squadron 44th Bomb Group: The Flying Eightballs*, p. 175.

433   Paynter, Harry. "An Account of One Pilot's Thoughts and Experiences on D-Day, 1944," *War Stories of the O&W: A History*

of the 486th Bomb Group (Heavy). Richard A. Wood, Ed. Columbus, OH: RSB Publications, 1996, p. 92.

434   Author. *The Wartime Diary of John W. Howland*. MEAFM, 2007.0086.0002.

435   Boiten and Bowman, *Battles with the Luftwaffe*, p. 151.

436   Miller, Kent. *The 365th Fighter Squadron in World War II in Action over Europe with the P-47*. Atglen, PA: Schiffer, 2006, p. 23.

437   Ambrose, *D-Day*, p. 249.

438   Hughes, *Over Lord*, p. 140.

439   Tilman, *Brassey's D-Day Encyclopedia*, p. 192.

440   Driscoll, John K., Interviewer. Transcript of an Oral History Interview with Harold C. Brown Pilot, U.S. Army Air Corps, World War II, 2004, Wisconsin Veterans Museum Research Center, p. 9.

441   Jablonski, "Young, Old Celebrate 55th Past," *Air Pulse*, 2005.0804.0133.

442   Paynter, "An Account of One Pilot's Thoughts and Experiences on D-Day, 1944," *War Stories of the O&W*, p. 92.

443   Lindsley and Lindsley, *Always Out Front: The Bradley Story.* Retrieved June 6, 2012, from http://www.ibiblio.org/hyperwar/AAF/Bradley/index.html; Ambrose, *D-Day*, p. 250.

444   Glenn E. Taylor. Oral History, Eighth Air Force Museum, 2005.0061.0001.

445   George, *Ninth Air Force April to November 1944*, pp. 13–14, 82; Davis, *Carl A. Spaatz and the Air War in Europe*, p. 414.

446   Driscoll, John K., Interviewer. Transcript of an Oral History Interview with Harold C. Brown Pilot, U.S. Army Air Corps, World War II, 2004, Wisconsin Veterans Museum Research Center, p. 8.

447   Todd, *History of the 68th Bomb Squadron 44th Bomb Group: The Flying Eightballs*, pp. 175–176.

448   Hennessy, *Tactical Operations of the Eighth Air Force 6 June 1944 to 8 May 1945*, pp. 23–27.

449   Hennessy, *Tactical Operations of the Eighth Air Force 6 June 1944 to 8 May 1945*, p. 25.

450   Ambrose, *D-Day*, p. 245.

451   Doolittle, General James H. "Jimmy," with Carroll V. Glines. *I Could Never Be So Lucky Again*. New York: Bantam Books, 2001, p. 402.

452   Hennessy, *Tactical Operations of the Eighth Air Force 6 June 1944 to 8 May 1945*, p. 25.

453   *Ibid.*

454   Driscoll, John K., Interviewer. Transcript of an Oral History Interview with Harold C. Brown Pilot, U.S. Army Air Corps, World War II, 2004, Wisconsin Veterans Museum Research Center, p. 9.

455   Fairfield, *The 479th Fighter Group in World War II in Action over Europe in the P-38 and P-51*, p. 57.

456   Bishop, Stanley D., and John A. Hey. *Losses of the U.S. 8th and 9th Air Forces*. Bishop Book Productions, 2004, p. 548.

457   Ambrose, *D-Day*, pp. 242–243.

458   Ambrose, *D-Day*, p. 244.

459   Ambrose, *D-Day*, pp. 245–246.

460   *Ibid.*

461   Ambrose, *D-Day*, p. 239.

462   George, *Ninth Air Force April to November 1944*, p. 76; Hughes, *Over Lord*, p. 5.

463   Bishop and Hey, *Losses of the U.S. 8th and 9th Air Forces*, p. 29; Ambrose, *D-Day*, pp. 245–248.

464   Bishop and Hey, *Losses of the U.S. 8th and 9th Air Forces*, pp. 330–336, 554–565.

465   Rust, *The Ninth Air Force in World War II*, p. 83.

466   *Ibid.*

467   *Ibid.*

468   Hennessy, *Tactical Operations of the Eighth Air Force 6 June 1944 to 8 May 1945*, p. 29.

469   Dickfeld, *Footsteps of the Hunter*, p. 158.

470   Dickfeld, *Footsteps of the Hunter*, p. 188.

471   Craven and Cate, *The Army Air Forces in World War II, Vol. III*, p. 160.

472   Keen, *Eyes of the Eighth*, p. 127.

473   George, *Ninth Air Force April to November 1944*, pp. 76, 79.

474   Keen, *Eyes of the Eighth*, p. 127.

475   Hennessy, *Tactical Operations of the Eighth Air Force 6 June 1944 to 8 May 1945*, p. 28.

476   *Ibid.*

477   *Ibid.*

478   Miller, *The 365th Fighter Squadron in World War II in Action over Europe with the P-47*, p. 24.

479   Applebaum, *Within the Parenthesis*, 2006.0360A.0131.

480 Todd, *History of the 68th Bomb Squadron 44th Bomb Group: The Flying Eightballs*, p. 175.

481 Tilman, *Brassey's D-Day Encyclopedia*, p. 8.

482 Doolittle, *I Could Never Be So Lucky Again*, p. 403.

483 Chapman, James H. Diary and Oral History, MEAFM, 2008.0096.0056.

484 Fairfield, *The 479th Fighter Group in World War II in Action over Europe with the P-38 and P-51*, p. 61.

485 Levitt, Sgt. Saul. "High-Low. D-Day Bombing," *Yank Magazine*. June 18, 1944; reprint, MEAFM, 2005.0804.0491.

486 Levitt, "High-Low. D-Day Bombing," 2005.0804.0491.

487 Fairfield, *The 479th Fighter Group in World War II in Action over Europe with the P-38 and P-51*, p. 59.

488 Galland, *The First and the Last*, p. 212.

489 Ryan, *The Longest Day*, pp. 245–248.

490 Fischer, *Luftwaffe Fighter Pilot*, p. 133.

491 Boiten, *Battles with the Luftwaffe*, p. 146.

492 Galland, *The First and the Last*, p. 214.

493 Mombeek, *Luftwaffe: A Pictorial History*, p. 125.

494 Movement of units per Luftwaffe Order of Battle: see http://www.feldgrau.com/luftair.html, last accessed February 21, 2012.

495 Hennessy, *Tactical Operations of the Eighth Air Force 6 June 1944 to 8 May 1945*, pp. 181–182.

496 Galland, *The First and the Last*, pp. 213–215. Most accounts place the number of available aircraft at 319. Galland states this as well but applies faulty math. According to his memoirs, on June 5 the Luftwaffe had "481 aircraft, 64 of them reconnaissance and 100 of them fighter aircraft." This adds up to 317 aircraft, not the more widely reported 319.

497 Miller, *Masters of the Air*, p. 292.

498 Galland, *The First and the Last*, p. 211.

499 Tilman, *Brassey's D-Day Encyclopedia*, p. 99; Ryan, *The Longest Day*, p. 85n.

500 Miller, *Masters of the Air*, p. 259.

501 Ryan, *The Longest Day*, pp. 245–248.

502 Tilman, *Brassey's D-Day Encyclopedia*, p. 194.

503 Ryan, *The Longest Day*, pp. 245–248.

504 Ryan, *The Longest Day*, p. 247.

505 Caldwell, *The JG26 War Diary*, p. 266; Ryan, *The Longest Day*, pp. 247–248.

506 Fischer, *Luftwaffe Fighter Pilot*, pp. 133 134; this account is clarified here: http://falkeeins.blogspot.com/2010/03/lt-wolfgang-fischer-ijg2.html, last accessed November 18, 2011.

507 Fischer, *Luftwaffe Fighter Pilot*, pp. 136–138.

508 *Ibid.*

509 *Ibid.*

510 Fischer, *Luftwaffe Fighter Pilot*, p. 139.

511 Various news accounts filed in 2005.0804.0169 via MEAFM.

512 Perret, *Winged Victory*, p. 306; Tilman, *Brassey's D-Day Encyclopedia*, p. 201.

513 Perret, *Winged Victory*, p. 306.

514 Hennessy, *Tactical Operations of the Eighth Air Force 6 June 1944 to 8 May 1945*, p. 28; Ramsey, John F. *Ninth Air Force in the ETO [European Theater of Operations], 16 October 1943 to 16 April 1944.* Washington, DC: Army Air Forces Historical Offices, 1945, p. 76.

515 Woodrum, *Dogfight over Paris*, 2006.0360A.0103.

516 *Ibid.*

517 Ambrose, *D-Day*, pp. 242–243; Mombeek, *Luftwaffe: A Pictorial History*, p. 125c.

518 Hennessy, *Tactical Operations of the Eighth Air Force 6 June 1944 to 8 May 1945*, p. 28.

519 Mombeek, *Luftwaffe: A Pictorial History*, p. 125.

520 Isby, David C. "World War II: Double Agent's D-Day Victory," *World War II Magazine.* Retrieved June 6, 2012, from http://www.historynet.com/world-war-ii-double-agents-d-day-victory.htm.

521 Fischer, *Luftwaffe Fighter Pilot*, pp. 140–141. See also: http://falkeeins.blogspot.com/2010/03/lt-wolfgang-fischer-ijg2.html, last accessed November 18, 2011.

522 Hennessy, *Tactical Operations of the Eighth Air Force 6 June 1944 to 8 May 1945*, p. 28.

523 Driscoll, John K., Interviewer. Transcript of an Oral History Interview with Harold C. Brown Pilot, U.S. Army Air Corps, World War II, 2004, Wisconsin Veterans Museum Research Center, p. 9.

524 Hansen, *Fire and Fury*, p. 188.

525 Olmsted, Merle. *The Luftwaffe Attack on Leiston Airfield.* Unpublished account, August 2002. MEAFM, 2006.0360.0011.

526   *Ibid.*

527   Martin, Robert J., Ed. *Second Air Division, 8th Air Force, USAAF.* Nashville, TN, Turner Publishing Company, 1994, p. 106.

528   Fairfield, *The 479th Fighter Group in World War II in Action over Europe with the P-38 and P-51*, p. 61.

529   Applebaum, *Within the Parenthesis*, 2006.0360A.0131.

530   Letters of William J. Moore, pilot 85th Bomb Group, MEAFM, 2008.0242.0118.

531   Bishop and Hey, *Losses of the U.S. 8th and 9th Air Forces*, p. 337.

532   Joiner, *The History of the 364th Fighter Group*, p. 94.

533   Miller, *Masters of the Air*, p. 294.

Chapter 23

534   Hennessy, *Tactical Operations of the Eighth Air Force 6 June 1944 to 8 May 1945*, p. 33.

535   Hughes, *Over Lord*, pp. 142–153.

536   *Ibid.*

537   Portsmouth Museum and Records quoting the D-Day Museum, see: http://www.ddaymuseum.co.uk/faq.htm#casualities, last accessed April 2, 2012.

538   War diary of Lt. Ronald A. Cadoret. MEAFM, 2009.0063.0001.

539   Carter and Mueller, *Combat Chronology*, p. 406.

540   Hennessy, *Tactical Operations of the Eighth Air Force 6 June 1944 to 8 May 1945*, p. 33.

541   Hennessy, *Tactical Operations of the Eighth Air Force 6 June 1944 to 8 May 1945*, pp. 31–33.

542   Davis, *Carl A. Spaatz and the Air War in Europe*, pp. 425–426.

543   George, *Ninth Air Force April to November 1944*, p. 99. The first field was called a strip; later all continental airfields were called Advanced Landing Grounds. In most cases, the ALGs were not officially opened until several days after these dates.

544   George, *Ninth Air Force April to November 1944*, pp. 76, 79; Hughes, *Over Lord*, p. 154.

545   Pressentin, Donald "DC." Wisconsin Veterans Museum Research Center, 1997, p. 17.

546   Ward and Burns, *The War*, p. 224.

547   Parton, James. *"Air Force Spoken Here:" General Ira Eaker and the Command of the Air*. Bethesda, MD: Adler & Adler, 1986, pp. 6–7.

548   Marshall, Katherine Tupper. *Together: Annals of an Army Wife.*
New York: Tupper and Love, 1947, p. 197.

549   Hughes, *Over Lord*, p. 155.

550   Hughes, *Over Lord*, p. 302.

551   Hughes, *Over Lord*, p. 155.

552   Mets, *Master of Airpower*, p. 182.

553   Huston, *American Airpower Comes of Age*, p. 150.

554   Beevor, *D-Day*, p. 79.

555   Tilman, *Brassey's D-Day Encyclopedia*, pp. 249–250; Coles, Harry
L. *The Army Air Force in Amphibious Landings in World War II.*
Maxwell Air Force Base, AL: USAF Historical Division, pp. 105,
107; Boiten and Bowman, *Battles with the Luftwaffe*, pp. 81, 107;
Carter and Mueller, *Combat Chronology*, p. 404; Coles, *The Army
Air Forces in Amphibious Operations in World War II*, p. 107;
George, *Ninth Air Force April to November 1944*, p. 81. An
additional 127 gliders and troop carriers were lost during the
invasion: Carter and Mueller, *Combat Chronology*, p. 404.

556   Hennessy, *Tactical Operations of the Eighth Air Force 6 June 1944
to 8 May 1945*, p. 29.

557   George, *Ninth Air Force April to November 1944*, p. 76.

558   Stanley, *World War II Photo Intelligence*, p. 61.

559   Roberts, *The Storm of War*, p. 468.

560   Davis, *Carl A. Spaatz and the Air War in Europe*, Appendixes 4, 5,
11, and 23.

561   *Ibid.*

562   Hughes, *Over Lord*, p. 154.

563   Hennessy, *Tactical Operations of the Eighth Air Force 6 June 1944
to 8 May 1945*, pp. 6–7.

564   U.S. Strategic Bombing Survey, Aviation Division Industry
Report, Second Edition, January 1947, p. 70. Retrieved
November 11, 2011, from http://www.sturmvogel.orbat.com/
airrep.html#Ch2.

565   *Ibid.*

566   *Ibid.*

567   *Ibid.*

568   Baldridge, *Welcome to the 368th*, p. 90.

569   Letters of William J. Moore, pilot, 85th Bomb Group. MEAFM,
2008.0242.0118.

570   Astor, *The Mighty Eighth*, p. 493.

571   Hall, *Case Studies in Strategic Bombardment*, p. 224; "brave men
       are not…:" Hawkins, *B-17s over Berlin*, p. 77.

572   VanBlair, Dale. *Looking Back: A Tail Gunner's View of WWII*.
       Lexington, KY: 1stBooks Library, 2003, p. 304.

573   Astor, *The Mighty Eighth*, p. 494.

574   Cornelius, Rupert G. Wisconsin Veterans Museum Research
       Center, p. 13.

575   Robert Copp. Oral History, 392nd Bomb Group Memorial
       Collection, Eighth Air Force Museum, 2005.0020.0543.

576   Sherwood, Robert E. *Roosevelt and Hopkins: An Intimate History*.
       New York: Harper & Brothers, 1948, p. 807.

577   Eisenhower, Dwight. D. *Report of the Supreme Commander to the
       Combined Chiefs of Staff on the Operations in Europe of the Allied
       Expeditionary Force 6 June 1944 to 8 May 1945*. Washington, DC:
       Government Printing Office, p. 51.

578   Parton, *"Air Force Spoken Here,"* p. 309.

579   Hughes, *Over Lord*, p. 300.

580   Ambrose, *D-Day*, p. 251.

581   Davis, *Carl A. Spaatz and the Air War in Europe*, p. 414.

582   Arnold, *Global Mission*, p. 157.

SELECT BIBLIOGRAPHY

_____. "Target Recon Data Occupied Europe—Luftwaffe Airfields." Retrieved May 21, 2012, from http://members.shaw.ca/rfortier/BoB/deurope.PDF.

_____. *United States Strategic Bombing Survey, Aircraft Division Industry Report*, second edition. January 1947. Retrieved May 22, 2012, from http://www.sturmvogel.orbat.com/airrep.html#Ch2.

Ambrose, Stephen E. *D-Day: June 6, 1944*. New York: Touchstone, 1994.

Ambrose, Stephen. *Citizen Soldiers: The U.S. Army from the Normandy Beaches to the Bulge to the Surrender of Germany*. New York: Simon & Schuster, 1997.

Ambrose, Stephen. *The Wild Blue: The Men and Boys Who Flew the B-24s Over Germany 1944–1945*. New York: Touchstone, 2001.

Arnold, H. H. *Global Mission*. New York: Harper & Row, 1949.

Astor, Gerald. *The Mighty Eighth*. New York: Dell Publishing, 1997.

Atkinson, Rick. *An Army at Dawn: The War in North Africa, 1942–1943*. New York: Henry Holt, 2002.

Bekker, Cajus. *The Luftwaffe Diaries*. Translated and edited by Frank Ziegler. New York: Ballantine Books, 1969.

Bishop, Stan D., and John A. Hey. *Losses of the US 8th and 9th Air Forces, Vol. II*. Suffolk, United Kingdom: Bishop Book Productions, 2009.

Boiten, Theo and Martin Bowman. *Battles with the Luftwaffe: The Bomber Campaign Against Germany 1942–1945*. New York: HarperCollins, 2001.

Bowman, Martin W. *Great American Air Battles of World War II*. Shrewsbury, United Kingdom: Airlife, 1994.

Bowman, Martin W. *B-24 Combat Missions: First Hand Accounts of Liberator Operations over Nazi Germany*. New York: Fall River Press, 2009.

Boyne, Walter J. *Clash of Wings*. New York: Simon & Schuster, 1994.

Boyne, Walter J. *Beyond the Wild Blue: A History of the United States Air Force 1947–1997*. New York: Thomas Dunne Books, 1997.

Buchner, Hermann. *Stormbird: One of the Luftwaffe's Highest Scoring Me262 Aces*. Crowborough, United Kingdom: Hikoki Publications, 2000.

Caldwell, Donald. *JG 26: Top Guns of the Luftwaffe*. New York: Ivy Books, 1991.

Caldwell, Donald. *JG 26: Photographic History of the Luftwaffe's Top Guns*. Osceola, WI: Motorbooks, 1994.

Caldwell, Donald. *The JG 26 War Diary: Volume Two, 1943–1945*. London: Grub Street, 1998.

Carter, Kit C., and Robert Mueller. *The Army Air Forces in World War II: Combat Chronology, 1941–1945*. Washington, DC: Center for Air Force History, 1991.

Cate, James L. *Origins of the Eighth Air Force: Plans, Organization, Doctrines*. Washington, DC: Army Air Forces Historical Offices, 1944.

Chamberlain, C. N., and Charles Freudenthal, Eds. *Second Air Division*. Nashville, TN: Turner Publishing, 1994.

Clements, James, Ed. *Silent Heroes Among Us: Final Flights of the Mighty Eighth*. Pearland, TX: New Horizons Publishing, 1996.

Coles, Harry C. *Ninth Air Force in the Western Desert Campaign to 23 January 1943*. Washington, DC: Army Air Forces Historical Offices, 1945.

Coles, Harry L. *The Army Air Forces in Amphibious Landings in World War II*. Maxwell Air Force Base, AL: USAF Historical Division, 1953.

Cooling, Benjamin Franklin, Ed. *Case Studies in the Achievement of Air Superiority*. Washington, DC: Air Force History and Museums Program, 1994.

Cornford, Stan. *Meterology and D-Day, 6 June 1944*. Washington, DC: Weather Risk Management Association, nd. Retrieved May 22, 2012, from www.wrma.org/2009_euro.../MeteorologyandD-Day6June1944.pdf.

Craven, Wesley Frank and James Lea Crate. *The Army Air Forces in World War II*, 7 vols. Chicago: University of Chicago Press, 1948.

Crosby, Harry H. *A Wing and a Prayer: The "Bloody 100th" Group of the U.S. Eighth Air Force in Action over Europe in World War II*. New York: HarperCollins, 1993.

Davis, Richard G. *Carl A. Spaatz and the Air War in Europe*. Washington, DC: Center for Air Force History, 1993.

Dickfeld, Adolf. *Footsteps of the Hunter*. Translated by David Johnston. Winnipeg, Canada: J. J. Fedorowicz Publishing, 1993.

Donald, David, Ed. *American Warplanes of World War II*. London: Aerospace Publishing, 1995.

Doolittle, General James H. "Jimmy" with Carroll V. Glines. *I Could Never Be So Lucky Again*. New York. Bantam Books, 1991.

Eighth Air Force. "Tactical Operations in Support of the Allied Landings in Normandy, 2 June–17 June 1944." Abilene, KS. Dwight D Eisenhower Library, nd.

Ethell, Jeffrey L. *Bomber Command*. Osceola, WI: Motorbooks, 1994.

Ethell, Jeffrey L., and Dr. Alfred Price. *Target Berlin: Mission 250: 6 March 1944*. London: Greenhill Books, 1981.

Ethell, Jeffery L., and Robert T. Sand. *Fighter Command*. Osceola, WI: Motorbooks, 1991.

Fairfield, Terry A. *The 479th Fighter Group in World War II*. Atglen, PA: Schiffer Publishing, 2004.

Ferguson, Arthur B. *The Early Operations of the Eighth Air Force and the Origins of the Combined Bomber Offensive, 17 August 1942 to 10 June 1943*. Washington, DC: Army Air Forces Historical Offices, 1946.

Fischer, Wolfgang. *Luftwaffe Fighter Pilot: Defending the Reich Against the RAF and the USAAF*. Edited and translated by John Weal. London: Grub Street, 2010.

Foedrowitz, Michael. *The Flak Towers in Berlin, Hamburg and Vienna 1940–1950*. Atglen, PA: Schiffer Publishing, 1998.

Freeman, Roger A. *Airfields of the Eighth Then and Now*. London: Battle of Britain Prints International, 1978.

Galland, Adolf. *The First and the Last*. New York: Henry Holt, 1954.

Galland, A., K. Ries, and R. Ahnert. David Mondey, Ed. *The Luftwaffe at War: 1939–1945*. Dorheim, Germany: Podzon-Verlag, 1972.

George, Robert H. *Ninth Air Force, April to November 1944*. Washington, DC: Army Air Forces Historical Offices, 1944.

Grabmann, Walter. *German Air Force Air Defense Operations*. Washington, DC: Army Air Forces Historical Offices, 1956.

Griggs, Alan L., Ed. *Flying Flak Alley: Personal Accounts of World War II Bomber Crew Combat*. Jefferson, NC: McFarland & Company, 2008.

Hall, R. Cargill. *Case Studies in Strategic Bombardment*. Washington, DC: Air Force History and Museums Program, 1994.

Hallion, Richard P. *D-Day 1944: Air Power over the Normandy Beaches and Beyond*. Washington, DC: Air Force History and Museums Program, 1994.

Hammel, Eric. *The Road to Big Week: The Struggle for Daylight Air Supremacy over Western Europe*. Pacifica, CA: Pacifica Press, 2009.

Hansen, Randall. *Fire and Fury: The Allied Bombing of Germany 1942–1945*. New York: NAL Caliber, 2008.

Harlan, Ross E. *Strikes: 323rd Bomb Group in World War II*. Oklahoma City, OK: Oklahoma Cavanal Publishers, 2005.

Harrison, Gordon A. *Cross Channel Attack*. Washington, DC: Center of Military History, United States Army, 1993.

Hawkins, Ian L., Ed. *B-17s over Berlin: Personal Stories from the 95th Bomb Group (H)*. Dilles, VA: Potomac Books, 1990.

Hennessy, Juliette. *Tactical Operations of the Eighth Air Force, 6 June 1944–8 May 1945*. Maxwell Air Force Base, AL: USAF Historical Division, 1952.

Holmes, Tony, Ed. *Dogfight: The Greatest Air Duels of World War II*. Oxford, United Kingdom: Osprey Publishing, 2011.

Holmes, Tony. *Vintage Aircraft Recognition Guide*. New York: Collins, 2005.

Hughes, Thomas Alexander. *Over Lord: General Pete Quesada and the Triumph of Tactical Air Power in World War II*. New York: The Free Press, 1995.

Huston, Major General John W., Ed. *American Airpower Comes of Age: General Henry H. "Hap" Arnold's World War II Diaries*, 2 vols. Honolulu, HI: University Press of the Pacific, 2004.

Ivie, Tom. *Aerial Reconnaissance: The 10th Photo Recon Group in World War II*. Fallbrook, CA: Aero Publishers, 1981.

Johnson, Charles R. *The History of the Hell Hawks*. Anaheim, CA: Southcoast Typesetting, 1975.

Johnson, Lt. David C. *U.S. Army Air Forces Continental Airfields (ETO) D-Day to VE Day*. Maxwell Air Force Base, AL: 1988.

Joiner, O. W., Ed. *The History of the 364th Fighter Group*. Marceline, MO: Walsworth Publishing, 1991.

SELECT BIBLIOGRAPHY

Keen, Patricia Fussell. *"Eyes of the Eighth:" A Story of the 7th Photo Reconnaissance Group 1942–1945*. Sun City, AZ: CAVU Publishers, 1996.

Keeney, L. Douglas, Ed. *The War Against the Luftwaffe: 1943–1944*. Campbell, CA: FastPencil, 2011.

Lanterman, Raymond E. "D-Day: The Best Laid Plans of Mice and Men…," Retrieved May 22, 2012, from www.34thprs.org/html/rlanterman/main.html.

Levitt, Sgt. Saul. "High-Low. D-Day Bombing," *Yank* Magazine. Object ID: 2005.0804.0491. Mighty Eighth Air Force Museum, June 18, 1944, reprint.

Mackay, Ron. *First in the Field: The 1st Air Division over Europe in World War II*. Atglen, PA: Schiffer Publishing, 2007.

Mackay, Ron. *Third In Time: The 3rd Air Division Over Europe in World War II*. Atglen, PA: Schiffer Publishing, 2009.

McFarland, Stephen L. and Wesley Philips Newton *To Command the Sky: The Battle for Air Superiority over Germany, 1942–1944*. Washington, DC: Smithsonian Institution Press, 1991.

Mets, David R. *Master of Airpower: General Carl A. Spaatz*. Novato, CA: Presidio Press, 1988.

The Mighty Eighth Air Force Museum. Collections, Courtesy of the Mighty Eighth Air Force Museum, Pooler, GA.

> Cpl. Melvin Applebaum. *Within the Parenthesis*. Unpublished manuscript. Object ID: 2006.0360A.0131.

> Arlen Baldridge. *Welcome to the 368th*. Unpublished manuscript. Object ID: 2010.0092.001.

> John D. Beeson. "A Chronology…" Object ID: 2008.0502.001.

> Ronald A. Cadoret. Excerpts from Diary. Object ID: 2009.0063.0001, 1989.

> Robert Coop. 392nd Bomb Group Association Collection. Object ID: 2005.020.544.

> Letter to Joe DeShay from Pete Peterson, April 30, 1996. Object ID: 2006.0360A.0095.

> William R. Dunlap, M.D. *D-Day Raid Gold Beach June 6, 1944*, unpublished manuscript. Object ID: 2006.0360A.0148.

> George E. Graham, Jr. 392nd Bomb Group Association Collection. Object ID: 0020.0540.

> Joseph I. Harlick. *My Beginning*, unpublished manuscript. Object ID: 2008.0499.0001.

John W. Howland. *D-Day Attack by the 8th Air Force*, unpublished manuscript. Object ID: 2007.0086.0002.

John W. Howland. The wartime diary of. Object ID: 2007.0086.0001.

Bill Kamemitsa. 392nd Bomb Group Association Collection. Object ID: 2005.0020.0538.

Will Lundy. *Guard Duty*, unpublished manuscript. Object ID: 2005.0804.0593.

Bernard Nelson. Object ID: 2011.0146.0001.

Merle Olmsted. *The Luftwaffe Attack on Leiston Airfield*, unpublished account. August 2002. Object ID: 2006.0360.0011

Glenn E. Taylor. Object ID: 2003.1674.001 through 004.

M. Lee Toothman. *My War Years*, unpublished manuscript. Object ID: 2003.0051.0001.

Edward H. Tracy. *The War Years*, unpublished manuscript. Object ID: 2003.1617.0001, 1989.

Miller, Donald L. *Masters of the Air: America's Bomber Boys Who Fought the Air War Against Nazi Germany*. New York: Simon & Schuster, 2006.

Miller, Kent. *The 365th Fighter Squadron in World War II*. Atglen, PA: Schiffer Publishing, 2006.

Muller, Werner. *The Heavy Flak Guns 1933–1945*. Translated by Dr. Edward Force. West Chester, PA: Schiffer Publishing, 1990.

Nail, N. Kenneth, Ed. *Mississippians in the Mighty Eighth*. Tupelo, MS: Mississippi Chapter–Eighth Air Force Historical Society, 1999.

Norris, Joe L. *The Combined Bomber Offensive, 1 January to 6 June 1944*. Washington, DC: Army Air Forces Historical Offices, 1947.

Parton, James. *"Air Force Spoken Here:" General Ira Eaker and the Command of the Air*. Bethesda, MD: Adler & Adler, 1986.

Perret, Geoffrey. *Winged Victory: The Army Air Forces in World War II*. New York: Random House, 1993.

Peterson, Pete. Oral History, Conducted by Brian Shoemaker. Searsport, ME: The American Polar Society and the Byrd Polar Archival Program of the Ohio State University, 2000.

Philo, Tom. "Eighth Air Force Combat Losses in World War II." Beaverton, OR. Retrieved May 22, 2012, from http://www.taphilo.com/history/8thaf/8aflosses.shtml.

Ramsey, John F. *Ninth Air Force in the ETO [European Theater of Operations], 16 October 1943 to 16 April 1944*. Washington, DC: Army Air Forces Historical Offices, 1945.

Ruppenthal, Roland G. *Logistical Support of the Armies, Vol. I*. Washington, DC: Center of Military History, United States Army, 1995.

Rust, Kenn C. *The 9th Air Force in World War II*. Fallbrook, CA: Aero Publishers, 1967.

Schmid, Josef. *The German Air Force Versus the Allies in the West*. The German Air Defense, 1954.

Schmid, Josef and Walter Grabmann. *The German Air Force Versus the Allies in the West: The Air War in the West*. Washington, DC: Army Air Forces Historical Offices, 1954.

Spaatz, Lt. General Carl to General H. H. Arnold, Commanding General of the United States Army Air Corps. "Effects of Allied Air Power on First Month of OVERLORD Operations," 17 July 1944. Robert Arnold Collection.

Stanley, Col. Roy M. *World War II Photo Intelligence: The First Complete History of the Aerial Photo Reconnaissance and Photo Interpretation Operations of the Allied and Axis Nations*. New York: Scribner, 1981.

Stormont, John W. *The Combined Bomber Offensive, April Through December 1943*. Washington, DC: Army Air Forces Historical Offices, 1946.

Stout, Jay A. *The Men Who Killed the Luftwaffe: The U.S. Army Air Forces Against Germany in World War II*. Mechanicsburg, PA: Stackpole Books, 2010.

Sullivan, John J. *Overlord's Eagles: Operations of the United States Army Air Forces in the Invasion of Normandy in World War II*. Jefferson, NC: McFarland & Company, 1997.

Swanston, Alexander and Malcolm Swanston. *The Historical Atlas of World War II*. New York: Chartwell Books, 2008.

Tavares, Jr., Major Ernest S. *Operation Fortitude: The Closed Loop D-Day Deception Plan*. Maxwell Air Force Base, AL: Air University, 2001.

VanBlair, Dale. *Looking Back: A Tail Gunner's View of WWII*. Lexington, KY: 1st Books Library, 2003.

Webb, Todd C. *History of the 68th Bomb Squadron 44th Bomb Group: The Flying Eightballs*. Nashville, TN: Turner Publishing, 1997.

Wisconsin Veterans Museum Research Center Oral History Project. Madison, WI. Retrieved May 22, 2012, from http://www.wisvetsmuseum.com/collections/oral_history.

C. Joseph Antonie. Interviewed by Grady Brown, 2003.

Kermit E. Bliss. Interviewed by Mark Van Ells, 1995.

Harold C. Brown. Interviewed by John K. Driscoll, 2004.

Clayton "Clyde" J. Coenen. Interviewed by James McIntosh, 2000.

Rupert G. Cornelius. Interviewed by Mark Van Ells, 1994.

Thomas F. Diener. Interviewed by John K. Driscoll, 2005.

Erwin Koppel. Interviewed by John K. Driscoll, 2003.

Donald "DC" Pressentin. Interviewed by Mark Van Ells, 1997.

Williams, David P. *Day Fighters*. Bristol, United Kingdom: Cerberus Publishing, 2002.

Wilson, Paul and Ron MacKay. *The Sky Scorpions: The Story of the 389th Bombardment Group in World War II*. Atglen, PA: Schiffer Publishing, 2006.

Wolf, William. *U.S. Aerial Armament in World War II: The Ultimate Look*, Vol. 1. Atglen, PA: Schiffer Publishing, 2009.

Wood, Richard A. and Robert S. Bee, Eds. *War Stories of the O&W: A History of the 486th Bombardment Group (Heavy)*. Columbus, OH: RSB Publications, 1996.

Woodrum, Henry C. *Dogfight over Paris*. Aero Album, Mighty Eighth Air Force Museum, Object ID: 2006.0360A.0103. Fallbrook, CA: Aero Publishers, Summer 1968.

INDEX

INDEX